In the Shadow of the Clock

The History of the Square Statesville, North Carolina

1790–1990

Steve Hill

Copyright © 2022 Steve Hill

All rights reserved. This book or parts thereof may not be reproduced in any form, stored in any retrieval system, or transmitted in any form by any means—electronic, mechanical, photocopy, recording, or otherwise—without prior written permission of the publisher, except as provided by United States of America copyright law. For permission requests, write to the publisher, at "Attention: Permissions Coordinator," at the address below.

Redhawk Publications
The Catawba Valley Community College Press
2550 US Hwy 70 SE
Hickory NC 28602

ISBN: 978-1-952485-64-0

Library of Congress Number: 2022933563

Steve's collection of Statesville related memorabilia and stories has culminated into this fascinating book about our downtown square. I am a current occupant of one of the buildings "on the Square." Steve takes readers on a wonderful historical journey that gives new meaning to the term, "if these walls could talk." In the Shadow of the Clock is definitely a book you will want in your library for each of your children and grandchildren to read.

—Gloria Hager, Owner, GG's Art Frames Gifts

The square. A metaphor. An axis of intersection of North and South, East and West. Over the ages folks have crossed this intersection and contributed meaningfully and richly to the social, economic, and political fabric of life in Statesville. And my grandfather the Reverend J. H. Pressly, who came to progressive 1892 Statesville because Statesville had streetlights, crossed that axis thousands of times as he served his church for 54 years. Never learning to drive an automobile, he walked and rode his horse through that intersection as he served his congregation. We trust J. H. Pressly, by crossing that axis, made lives in Statesville richer, more meaningful, and a source of great faith to so many.

—David Pressly, Statesville Mayor, 1983-1985

This book is an important narrative on places and times in our history that some will remember, but many won't. It's the story of the trials and tribulations of a growing community around a common geographic core, its beloved town square. Sit back and enjoy the 200 years of interesting stories that make up the beautiful city of Statesville, North Carolina.

—Ralph Bentley, Statesville Mayor, 1985-1993

I have always been appreciative of community landmarks and am grateful that our town clock is still there. It reminds me of the past, announces the present, and holds promise for the future. It calls me home.

—John Marshall, Statesville Mayor, 1993-2005

Steve Hill combines his knowledge of our city with his beautiful writing style to show the reader why we love Statesville. Once you read In the Shadow of the Clock, you will share our great pride.

—Costi Kutteh, Statesville Mayor, 2005-present

Steve Hill has truly transcended time. Take a copy of this book on a walk in downtown Statesville and you can see what happened before you got there. This book is filled with well documented images and stories that allow us to experience multiple periods in history, from one source. You will meet all sorts of people engaging in all sorts of activities, quite a busy place for just a four block area. Steve invites you to look over their shoulder and marvel.

—Richard Eller, Historian-in-Residence, Catawba Valley Community College

Table of Contents

Table of Contents...i

Acknowledgements..iii

Foreword..v

Photo Credits...vii

Chapter 1: Introduction..1

Chapter 2: The Early Years..7

Chapter 3: Flag Poles and Scales.......................................15

Chapter 4: Let's Settle this Like Real Men.......................19

Chapter 5: The Town Clock...25

Chapter 6: Everybody's Day...37

Chapter 7: 1900s-1940s...47

Chapter 8: 1950s-1980s...79

Chapter 9: The Circus...99

Chapter 10: Characters Found Loitering Around the Square...................105

Chapter 11: Public Transportation Serving the Square........................115

Chapter 12: The Square Egg..123

Chapter 13: Christmas on the Square..............................129

Chapter 14: "Casey" Jones—Keeper of Law & Order on the Square...........135

Chapter 15: Sammy the Fire Dog......................................143

Chapter 16: No Left Turns..147

Chapter 17: Parallel or Diagonal? That is the Question....................155

Chapter 18: Mystery of the Misaligned Buildings..........................161

Chapter 19: Cruising..167

Chapter 20: The Northeast Corner..................................173

Chapter 21: The Southeast Corner..................................189

Chapter 22: The Southwest Corner.................................227

Chapter 23: The Northwest Corner.................................247

Chapter 24: Conclusion...263

Appendix: Footprint Views...269

Acknowledgements

I suppose everyone believes that the town in which they grew up is "the best." I sure do. Statesville was and is a wonderful place to grow up, work, play, raise a family, and retire. No matter where I've traveled over the past nearly 70 years, I can't wait to get back to Statesville.

I am fortunate to have had parents and grandparents who took time to tell me about "the old days." They were proud of their childhood neighborhoods in Davie and Iredell Counties, and they instilled in me a love for mine. They were fond of telling tales about long passed family members, neighbors, friends, foes, scallywags, and ghosts from their adolescence, the same way legends transcend generations through songs. Their stories told of the rigors of the Great Depression, life on the farm, school friendships, lost loves, the perils and rewards of war, etc.

I am also appreciative of the outstanding teachers I had as an introverted, undistinguished student at Monticello, Wayside, Troutman, and South and North Iredell High Schools. Somehow, they inspired me to love history and writing (but math and science, not so much). Fortunately, back then teachers had the flexibility to weave healthy doses of local history into their lessons, something that today is strictly forbidden by the state standard course of study "police."

After high school, it was the instructors at Mitchell Community College who really got me excited about the field of history. Louis Brown, Steve Herman, and Oscar Stradley became my friends and mentors as I pursued a degree in history at Appalachian State University. They are the ones who taught me the importance of local history in the whole scheme of civilization and how, without the smaller pieces, the big puzzle can never be complete. They taught me that all history is important, and that global history is an amalgamation of local histories.

At ASU I was fortunate to study under some of the country's most noted scholars, including Drs. Roy Carroll, Winston Kinsey, Eugene Drozdowski, and Raymond Pulley. As an undergraduate student in the History Department, they kindled within me a love for American history and provided me with time-proven research skills I utilize even today.

As for my love for collecting, I have no idea who to acknowledge for that. I've been a collector all my life (no, it ain't hording if it's cool stuff). I suppose some credit would have to go to Pat Gainey, my U. S. History and Civics teacher at North High. His classroom walls were like a museum. They were covered with photos, clippings, and all sorts of historical memorabilia. Students in need of an extra point on a test grade could bring in an artifact to add to the wall of history. I recall on one occasion that I cashed in on the extra point offer by donating a facsimile set of wanted posters featuring gangsters Al Capone and John Dillinger. I had ordered them through the mail by writing to the FBI office in D. C., thus far my only interaction with the FBI.

As a young adult, I developed memorable friendships with some of the older residents of the city who would kindly share their stories about early life in Statesville. Caroline Avery, Ralph Sloan, Betty Boyd, Mary Merritt, and others would sit and chat with me for hours. I will always value those special times, and I strive to honor them by keeping their stories alive for posterity.

I met W. N. "Red" Watt, author of "Statesville—My Home Town," after he retired and moved back home in the 1980s. He became a good friend who taught me the importance of accuracy when doing research. Red paid attention to the smallest details. He would spend days deciphering a 1700s deed, letter by letter, but when he was finished, his product was gospel.

The person who has had the most profound influence on my appreciation for Statesville and Iredell history was the dean himself, Homer Keever. As a youngster, I had the opportunity to enjoy short conversations with Mr. Keever. When I would uncover an interesting photograph or document at a flea market or auction, I would drag it to his doorstep like a little puppy looking for a pat on the head. By that time, he was long retired and had been relegated to a little desk and typewriter in the newsroom of the *Statesville Record & Landmark* office where he spent his days sifting through microfilm for his weekly column and special features. I was in such awe of his vast knowledge. Admittedly, I was also a little intimidated by his reputed brusque nature, but each time he would patiently school me on the minute details of the bone I had dug up for him and then politely thank me and encourage me to keep digging. And I have.

And then there are my more contemporary friends with whom I've enjoyed working. Their passion for local history has been invaluable to our community and to me. They include Mildred Miller, O. C. Stonestreet, Joel Reese, Jimmy Allie, John Clark, Graham Neilson, David Pope, Norman Hope, Harry Watt, Sam Hall, Gene Krider, Mac Lackey, John Schneider, and Ken Adams.

Ray Starrette and Jeff Howard have been especially influential in my historical research journey. The three of us have spent many days exploring cemeteries, mills, creeks, back roads, and rail tracks striving to solve age old mysteries and better understand our county's fascinating past.

I am especially appreciative for the friendship of Dr. Tom Poston. Thankfully, he has been by my side almost daily for 10 years and, through him, I have relived a hundred years of history.

For nearly the past half century Bill Moose, now retired Mitchell Community College professor, has dedicated his life to teaching world, American, state, and local history. He has been my coach and mentor when I hit a dead-end or need to understand how a minor local historical event fits into the larger picture. Since 1979 Bill has scoured hundreds of miles of microfilm researching his popular weekly *R&L* column, "Out of Our Past." Professor Moose is a friend and colleague I converse with almost daily as we try to outdo each other in our never-ending search for the most obscure, frivolous piece of Iredell County history trivia (Bill always wins).

Oh, did I mention my wife? I am the luckiest man in the world to have had the love and support of two beautiful, smart, amazing women—Annette the first 20 years of marriage and Penny the past 20. They were/are saints for putting up with me and my obsessive avocation. And thanks to my children who were always good sports when the family vacation turned into a historical scavenger hunt. And even the grandkids are learning to play along with my corny (but accurate) lessons on how most everything in life is in some way connected to Statesville, North Carolina.

And, thanks to the many others who in their own unique ways have contributed to this project.

Foreword

Steve Hill has been studying Statesville and Iredell County history since before he got his driver's license. It started with collecting a few Statesville items. A Statesville business calendar. A Statesville Coca Cola bottle. Steve is always on the lookout for those physical artifacts. That is why the size and scope of collection today is so impressive today. You have to see it to believe it. And remember that you can't even see it all.

Steve has always understood that the objects have so much more meaning if you know the stories that go with them. And, in the words of Oscar Stradley, being a "good schoolman" when he had the objects and the stories, he had to share them. School presentations, civic club meetings, church groups, ghost tours, Steve has done them all. The best way share in this Statesville-palooza is to visit the museum and then sit around the table and talk.

The book you hold today is about a particular part of Steve's work. Statesville's greatest artifacts aren't found in flea markets, yard sales or even on E-bay. They are her buildings, especially those around The Square. He knows who occupied those buildings. Where was the first movie theater? Ask Steve. The building is still here. Steve isn't content to know just the downtown we see around us today. He wants to know the buildings that preceded them and their stories. How have fires shaped Statesville? How did the first courthouse shape Statesville?

I love the old saying about the relationship of geography and history. Geography is the stage upon which history is enacted. If that is true, then The Square is certainly the stage upon which a significant part of Statesville's history has been enacted.

Thanks, Steve. For first collecting it and now compiling it. It will go on the shelf next to Homer. Keever, that is.

Bill Moose

Photo Credits

Statesville is fortunate to have enjoyed the services of more than a half dozen outstanding professional photographers over the years. The city's most productive local photographers were W. Jasper Stimson (1860-1929), Ben Stimson (1893-1969), Tobias W. Ellis (1866-1916), Elbert Ammon (1885-1975), Van Ammon (1921-1986), Max Tharpe (1920-2010), and Bob Plyler (1926-). These men were pioneers in their field, and miraculously the majority of the work they created has been preserved in either the Iredell County Public Library or the Statesville Historical Collection.

The photos used within these pages are displayed or archived at the Statesville Historical Collection, either in original or digital form. Every attempt has been made to properly credit each photographer for his valuable work. The name of the photographer is posted under each photograph. When the identity of the photographer is uncertain, the photo is tagged "SHC" (Statesville Historical Collection).

Legend

American — The *Statesville American* newspaper began as the *Iredell Express* in 1858. Owner E. B. Drake became a Republican after the Civil War and changed the name from *Express* to *American*. It was Statesville's sole paper until 1874 when the *Landmark* came onto the scene.

Ammon — Elbert Ammon was a military photographer during WWI and operated a successful photography service in town after the war through the 1940s. Elbert's son, Van Ammon, continued the family photography business through the 1960s. The father and son team maintained a studio over Holmes Drug on the square. They specialized in portrait, aerial, institutional, and corporate photography.

Beck — Ray "Pete" Beck lived on Boulevard in south Statesville, drove a bus for Statesville Motor Coach and worked at the Carnation plant on West Front Street. He was an avid photographer, and his work was donated to the Statesville Historical Collection by his daughter Dianna Beck King and Mickey Holton.

Brady — Company photos from the Brady Printing Company were donated to the Statesville Historical Collection by Jean Brady.

Daily Record — The *Statesville Record* was started in 1931 by Ben Scronce and was sold to Chester Middlesworth in 1938. The name was changed to *Statesville Daily Record* in 1941. The *Record* was merged with the *Landmark* in 1951 to become the *Statesville Record & Landmark*.

DSDC — Several hundred photo files from the Downtown Statesville Development Corporation were donated to the Statesville Historical Collection.

Evening Mascot — The *Evening Mascot*, Statesville's first daily newspaper, was founded by O. E. Crowson in 1893. James Hartness purchased the business in 1897, and in 1909 the name was changed to the *Sentinel*. Hartness closed the paper and sold the printing equipment to Ben Scronce who started the *Statesville Record* in 1931.

Express — See *Iredell Express*.

Gaither — An album with photos from the Gaither family was purchased on eBay by the Statesville Historical Collection in 2017.

hdi.uky.edu — University of Kentucky Human Development Institute website.

Hill – Steve Hill is the keeper of the Statesville Historical Collection.

Iredell County Public Library — The Iredell County Public Library has the largest collection of local photographs of any community in the state. Local historian Joel Reese has been the driving force behind archiving thousands of Stimson and Tharpe photographic images.

Iredell Express — The *Express* was founded in 1857 by Whig Party loyalist Eugene B. Drake and his son William. It continued through the Civil War and ceased operation when its office was burned by General Stoneman's Union troops in April 1865. A few months later Drake established the *Statesville American*, a voice of the Conservative Party.

Lackey — Lentz McSherry "Mac" Lackey, Jr. was a local historian and weekly columnist for the *Charlotte Observer's Iredell Neighbors* edition during the 1980s and 90s.

Landmark — The *Landmark*, a Democrat-leaning paper, commenced publication June 19, 1874. Founding owner and editor John B. Hussey sold the paper to J. S. Ramsey in 1877 and then it was bought by its most successful editor, J. P. Caldwell in 1880. Rufus R. Clarke became the owner and editor in 1906 and sold the company to Pegram Bryant in 1918. Bryant began the *Statesville Daily* in 1920 but kept the *Landmark* as a semi-weekly paper, primarily using copy from the *Daily*.

Love — Betty Love donated photos of Superior Dairies from her father, Frank Redmond, founder and manager of the company.

Newspapers.com — Many of the newspaper clippings used in this publication were located using the Newspapers.com search engine.

Newton — Teddy Newton, SHS graduate and amateur photographer donated his archives to the Statesville Historical Collection.

Ramsey — Images from aviator and photographer Ed Ramsey were donated to the Statesville Historical Collection by his daughter, Clayton Ramsey. The Ramsey family ran the Ramsey-Bowles Department Store.

Record & Landmark — The *Statesville Record* was started in 1931 by Ben Scronce and was sold to Chester Middlesworth in 1938. Middlesworth changed the name to *Statesville Daily Record* in 1941. Pegram Bryant sold the *Daily* and the *Landmark* to a New York firm that was secretly representing Middlesworth and the *Daily Record*. In 1954 the *Daily Record* and the *Landmark* became the *Statesville Record & Landmark*.

Sams — Bill Sams who, along with his father Fuller Sams, owned over a dozen movie theaters across the state, including the Playhouse, State, Crescent, Villa Heights, and I-77 theaters in Statesville, donated the theater files to the Statesville Historical Collection.

Sentinel — The *Statesville Sentinel* began as the *Evening Mascot*, founded by James Hartness. In 1909 the name was changed to *Sentinel*. When Hartness became the NC Secretary of State, he closed the paper and sold the equipment to Ben Scronce who started the *Statesville Record*.

SHC — Archived and/or displayed at the Statesville Historical Collection in downtown Statesville.

Stimson — (W. J. and Ben) William Jasper Stimson was the town's most prominent photographer, opening his downtown studio in 1890 and continuing through the 1920s. His most widely celebrated work was the five-photo series of the Bostian Bridge train wreck in 1891. When Jasper retired, his son Ben followed his father in the family business. The Stimson's did it all, portraits, aerials, schools, churches, government, corporate, and special events of all types. Their corporate studio was located over Brady Printing on West Broad and their portrait studio was over the Polk Gray and Holmes drug stores on the square. The bulk of the Stimson's negatives were purchased by Jimmy Alley in the 1990s and are now archived at the Iredell County Public Library. I am especially appreciative of Richard Boyd, grandson of Ben and great grandson of Jasper, who over the years preserved additional important volumes of his grandfathers' works and shared them with the Statesville Historical Collection for the community to enjoy.

Tharpe — Max Tharpe was the town's most prolific local photographer in the 1930s-1960s. His body of work is preserved in the Iredell County Public Library and the Statesville Historical Collection. Like his colleagues, Tharpe did a variety of photography work. He worked for the local newspapers and his work won state and national awards and found its way onto the covers of dozens of state and national magazines. He was especially skilled at capturing compelling action shots of everyday people, especially children at play and compelling faces.

unc.music.edu — The University of North Carolina Music Department website.

Watt — William Neri "Red" Watt (1910-1998) was a Statesville native and was known as one of the most talented athletes to graduate from Statesville High School. He spent most of his adult life working for the U. S. Soil Conservation Service in Georgia and after retirement in 1971, moved back to NC where he spent the next quarter century researching Alexander and Iredell County history. He authored several history books including "Statesville—My Home Town, 1789-1920." As an historian, Watt was especially proficient in researching early land deeds.

Front Cover Photos — Both the town clock photo, circa 1905, and the N. B. Mills building photo, circa 1910, were taken by William Jasper Stimson.

Back Cover Photo — The square, circa 1948, is from the Van Ammon files in the Statesville Historical Collection.

Chapter 1
Introduction

In the Shadow of the Clock: The History of "the Square"
Statesville, North Carolina
1790-1990

Introduction

Brady

Whether you call it "the town square," "the city square" or just "the square," everybody around Statesville, North Carolina knows the place you're referring to. It's the heart of our city. It's the crossroads of our county. And to many natives like me, it's the center of the universe.

An out-of-town driver passing through Statesville in 1940 complained that "the size of a town can be determined by how long its traffic light on the square stays red, and with that being said, Statesville is a really small town" (actually 11,428 citizens strong at the time). Drivers have complained about that traffic light and congestion at the square for 150 years. But a crowded town square is a problem that most towns would love to have. It's a sign of prosperity. Instead of complaining, the visitor should have appreciated the chance to pause a few extra seconds to enjoy the place known across the state at the time as "the Best Town in North Carolina."

So, what exactly is a "town square?" Nebraska urban planner Stephanie Rouse studied town squares from ancient Greece to Times Square. She describes a town's square as a central hub of activity, a place for gathering to celebrate, for receiving information, for conducting business, or for simply sitting—"more like a piece of art than a fully functioning space."

One thing that is obvious when traveling across this country, town squares are pretty common. It seems that almost every crossroads of substantial size has one. Some are plain and cold, often a drab sea of concrete with strategically placed non-descript buildings. Others are showplaces you can't resist stopping to explore. Some were obviously designed by linear-thinking bureaucrats sitting in windowless offices, and others by intuitive dreamers lounging in gardens. Each is unique and each helps establish "the feel" or the atmosphere of the town.

Rouse suggests that three characteristics can be attributed to the success of a "town square." First, it must provide physical features that create a place the public can enjoy visiting. Whether it is artwork, a play area for kids, seating, or creative landscaping that enables it to look more like a park than an urban intersection, each town square must be inviting.

The second characteristic relates to its social functionality. It needs to be a venue that is adaptable to varying sizes of users to work, socialize, celebrate, etc. Movable seating and tables can be found on Statesville's square and there is enough room for portable seating and stages for street festivals and small concerts.

DSDC **Local violinists perform at Weekend in the Village, 1980s** *DSDC*

Local band performance for Pumpkinfest, 2019 *DSDC*

Statesville has a long history of organized celebrations on her square. Events such as Everybody's Day, Old Fashioned Bargain Days, Moonlight Madness, and Weekend in the Village have lured shoppers to the streets around the square for years. Antique car shows, street fairs, carnivals, political rallies, church services and even livestock shows have also graced the square.

More recently, the square is the rallying point for "Pumpkinfest," "Wine Walk," "Art Crawl," trick-or-treat, bicycle racing, tethered hot air ballooning, concerts, arts & crafts, and more…

SHC   **Antique car caravan, 1969**   *SHC*

...and parades, oh the parades. The square has always been the spot on the parade route where bands, dancers, drill teams, jugglers, bicyclists, clowns, and performers of all types pause to showcase their very best performances, and where beauty queens flash their biggest smiles. It's also where parading military units show off their spiffy uniforms and precision marching drills.

SHC   **High school bands...**   *SHC*

SHC   **...saving their best performances for the square**   *SHC*

And over the years, like all towns, Statesville has seen its share of politicians, preachers, protestors, snake oil salesmen, and even a few lunatics screaming at passers-by from a curb on the square. The square has hosted public auctions of homes, belongings, and farms. It has even witnessed the sale of hundreds of enslaved human beings. It has served as a central meeting place for everything from the celebrating of life through song or sermon, to the taking away of life by public execution. The square has watched it all, both the good and the not so good.

Finally, the most common characteristic of a successful town square is that it is surrounded by a diverse mixture of uses—housing, offices, shops, restaurants, bakeries, pharmacies, personal services, etc. Check, check, check. Statesville's square can mark all those boxes. It is a beautiful and inviting spot to visit, work or play, or to just sit and watch the world go by on its way.

The decision by the Statesville City Council in 2012 to widen the sidewalks, bury utilities, improve crosswalks, create unique outdoor seating and dining areas, and enhance the whole package with beautiful vegetation, transformed Statesville into a true showplace and tourist destination. Their decision, though controversial at the time, was an example of governmental intestinal fortitude in action. Today, out-of-town visitors to the downtown shopping district consistently comment on how beautiful the place is. And who could disagree?

The town clock wasn't around during the first century of the town's history, but for the past 130 years she has watched over this special place. I hope this narrative will motivate you to stroll the streets of downtown Statesville and experience "the square in the shadow of the clock."

The view from the town clock　　　　　*Hill*

Chapter 2
The Early Years

The Early Years

In 1744, the King of England granted Lord Granville a large part of the upper part of North Carolina. Granville was an heir of the eight Lord Proprietors who had been granted all of North Carolina, South Carolina, and Georgia by Charles II in 1665. So, the land where Statesville is located was a small tract in the Granville grant.

By 1750, settlers began moving into this area. Most were Scots-Irish Presbyterians who had come to America looking for cheap farmland and fewer challenges to their religious freedom. By then, most of the cheap fertile land near the port of Philadelphia where they arrived had been taken, so they were forced to either look west where the winters were long and the Indians were restless, or forge southward, down the Great Wagon Road through the Shenandoah Valley to these rich lands between the Yadkin and Catawba Rivers.

John Oliphant purchased the land that would become the town of Statesville on November 26, 1753 and sold his 640-acre tract to a fellow land speculator, Fergus Sloan, on March 15, 1755.

Fergus Sloan donated land for the Fourth Creek Church (First Presbyterian) and cemetery in the late 1750s. After the County of Iredell was established in 1788 and the town of Statesville in 1789, Sloan sold 50 acres of land to the commissioners for the purpose of building the new town. In 1790 leaders surveyed the parcel, divided it into lots, and sold the lots to the public. When the four most desirable lots were sold, the ones in the center, the town square was born.

The price Sloan got for the parcel was 30 pounds, or about $41.00. After a survey was conducted, however, the tract actually totaled 68¾ acres. So the commissioners got a bargain. Looking at the beautiful city of Statesville today, it is apparent they got a *really good* bargain.

Immediately after completing the survey, work began to build a courthouse and lay out the streets. It is believed that the location for the center of town, the square, was chosen because it was on a knoll, which allowed for ample drainage in all directions. This would help with the mud problem that was prevalent in the unpaved village streets of those days.

One early surveyor, however, said that the ultimate location of the center of the new town was chosen because it was unsuitable for farming or anything else productive. It was a thicket of briars, just a rocky ridge of chinquapin bushes, a hiding place for the wolves, bear and panthers. Yes there were black panthers in the area.

It's probably a mistake to suggest that this "high ground" was chosen in order to keep a close watch on threats from the area Indian tribes. Concern over Indian attacks may have lingered in the minds of the old-timers, but most of the problems with the Indians had been "resolved" by that time.

The first courthouse was made of logs and stood in the center of the square. The commissioners wisely designed the two main streets to be 100 feet wide, mainly in order to give passers-by room to maneuver around the courthouse. Some suggest that 100-feet is the minimum distance needed to make a u-turn with a horse and wagon without having to back up.

Scots-Irishmen were known to be frugal, apparently even with proper nouns. They chose utilitarian names for the town's two main streets, "Broad" and "Center." In later years, Center Street was also at times referred to as "Main Street," and Broad was intermittently called "College Street." The three other streets in the original layout had equally functional names: Meeting, which ran to the meeting house (church); Front, which ran in front of the courthouse; and Tradd, possibly a spelling variation of "trade." Those streets were only 66 feet wide.

Two hundred years later, local historian W. N. (Red) Watt conducted extensive research on the 124 original town lots. He created a map of the lots to accompany his 1996 book, *Statesville—My Home Town, 1789-1920*. The lots were approximately a half acre each.

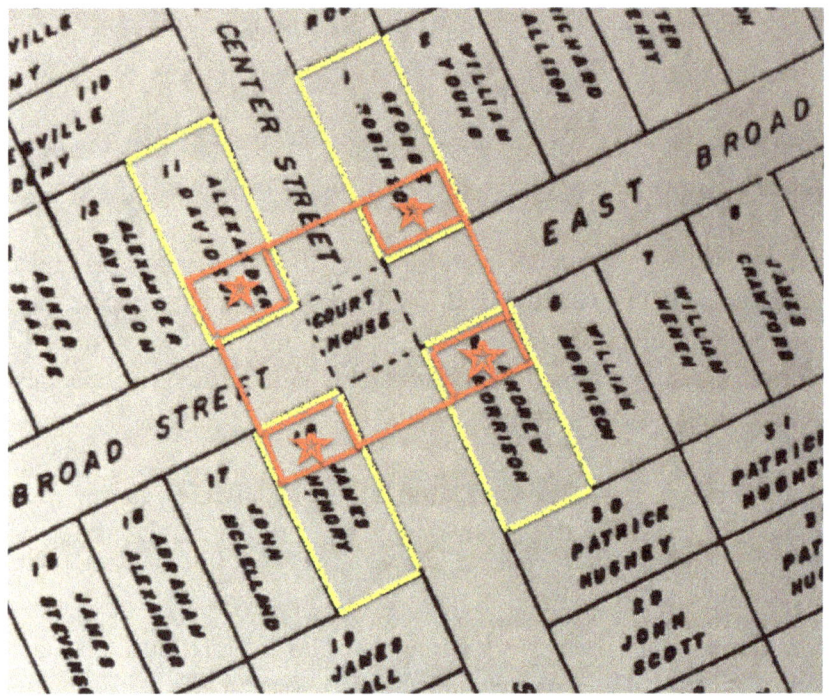

Layout of original lots by W. N. Watt, drawn by Grier Surveying
(The original lots outlined and the current square starred)

When the original lots for Statesville were sold off by the Iredell County Commissioners on August 13, 1790, the most desirable parcels were on the square, Lots 1, 5, 11 and 18. They were purchased by speculators who were willing to make considerable wagers on the success of the fledgling village. George Robinson bought Lot 1; Andrew Morrison, Lot 5; Alexander Davidson, Lot 11; and James Hendry, Lot 18.

Tracing ownership of the parcels for the first few years is not easy. Property changed hands quickly and often, an indication that most of the original buyers were speculators. For other owners, the slow initial growth of the village may have disincentivised them to stick it out. It was ten years before a building showed up on the lots.

Back in Colonial days, four tallow candles lit up the square, one on each corner. Soon, 25 kerosene lamps were scattered throughout town, and each night a bareback horse rider with a torch would light 'em up, and then come back around at 11:30 to snuff 'em out. Electric streetlights were installed in 1889, powered by the first municipally owned power plant in NC.

Granite stepping-stones spaced a few feet apart graced Broad and Center Streets so pedestrians could cross the streets without wading through mud and horse manure. At the time, the stones were heralded as the most useful state-of-the-art improvement in the town's history. They gave the little village a big city feel.

Old-timer Lessesne R. Allison remembered the stones as being randomly placed and unevenly aligned but forming an outline of the square. On rainy days, ladies would plan their shopping to avoid crossing the street. Not only did a lady risk slipping on the slick, flat stones and miring up ankle deep, but she also might have to raise her dress to a shocking height and risk revealing her ankles.

Cows, sheep, and swine wandered freely on the square attracting little attention.

The city's first and second courthouses stood right smack dab in the center of the square. The first one was made of logs and had a weather vane in the shape of a rooster on the roof. The second one was a more stoic two-story-brick structure. It lasted until the "Great Fire of 1854" that burned down about half the town.

That fire started at the northeast corner of North Meeting and West Broad. It burned every house and shop on the north side of West Broad, then burned down the courthouse, jumped to the south side of Broad, and burned everything down to Meeting Street as well as everything on the west side of South Center Street until it ran out of tinder at the town limits. Other than the courthouse, all of the buildings were built of wood.

A visitor passing through town two years later reported that Statesville looked like it "had a dark melancholy cloud hanging over it." "It is a dying village, with no rebuilding, no growth, no excitement, no spirit." But Statesville got its mojo back when it was announced in 1858 the Western North Carolina Railroad would be built through town, and it has been thriving ever since.

The first trial in the new courthouse on the square, the very first case to be tried, involved two "ladies" engaged in the world's oldest profession, which back then was called *fornication*, not a very flattering way for our devout Scots-Irish Presbyterian founding fathers to start their new town, was it?

Now these two ladies were Mary Poke (P-O-K-E) and Elizabeth Wales (W-A-L-E-S)—two prostitutes named Poke and Wales. Although that sounds like the beginning of a dirty joke—two prostitutes named Poke & Wales walk into a bar—it's true. And a jury of the county's most prominent men heard their cases and found Misses Poke & Wales... *NOT guilty*.

Without a doubt, the darkest days of any southern town were the days of slavery and Jim Crow laws, or essentially the first 175 years of Statesville's existence. It was on the front doorstep of the courthouse that the sheriff held regular auctions—selling off people's homes and farms. Prior to the Civil War, it was also on this exact spot that African American slaves were auctioned off to the highest bidders—sometimes individually — sometimes as entire families.

It's safe to say that the salt from many teardrops remains in the dirt beneath the town square sidewalk.

The town's first hanging took place in 1800 beside John Nesbit's store on the southeast corner of the square. A slave named Nichols was convicted of killing his master. Legend has it, that after the hanging, Nichols' head was cut off, stuck on a pole, and the pole was placed at the entrance to town over on Front Street as a warning to wayward slaves. It remained there so long that blue birds built nests in the eye sockets.

Eventually hangings were moved to either the outskirts of town or in later years behind the South Center Street courthouse where there was more standing room for gawkers.

From 1805 until 1873 the county jail was located next to the square at the current Cooper and Broad Street intersection. The most notorious occupant to be held there was Thomas Dula, more commonly known as Tom Dooley, who was incarcerated there for two years before his execution by hanging near the depot in 1868.

In the 1850s, the seedy side of town was the block bordering the square to the north. In a letter to the editor a half century later, an old-timer remembered it this way:

"On the north side of the courthouse was the rendezvous of the little cake and cider wagons, with booze in abundance; and capers, tantrums and cutting up like you never saw unless you have been to similar places on this side of pandemonium; cursing, swearing, quarreling, fighting, bragging and all sorts simply indescribable and inimitable antics that could only be found in a den where alcohol in all its forms is being dispensed and imbibed."

"There was a great deal of drunkenness, for whiskey was made and sold by anyone who wished to follow the nefarious business. Men made it and bought it and sold it and drank it...and drank it...and the wives and children enjoyed the destitution and deprivation, and starvation, and abuse, and all the discomforts of a drunkard's home."

No doubt, North Center Street was not an inviting place to visit.

During the Civil War, Confederate Army representatives set up their recruiting station on the square where hundreds of Iredell County men pledged their allegiance to the South before marching off to war. And after the War, for as long as they were physically able, these same men solemnly marched from the courthouse to the square and then over to the cemetery each May to honor their fallen comrades on Confederate Veterans Day.

Near the end of the war, federal troops, after torching supply warehouses and exploding ammo magazines in Salisbury, marched into Statesville. Initially, they exchanged shots with a small band of local furloughing troops on the square. But by the time the advance unit arrived on the evening of April 13, 1865, townspeople had scattered, and the place was dark, empty, and occupied mostly by women, children, and elderly men. Earlier, local scouts had ridden through the streets Paul Revere style sounding the alarm of the approaching U. S. Army headed up the Salisbury Road. The few men of fighting age who were still around had retreated to the forests to hide out, and valuables and food had been gathered up and hidden.

Soldiers under the command of Colonel Smith quickly took charge. The first shot fired was at C. L. Summers as he escaped to his home. He was wounded and taken prisoner.

From his horse on the square, a soldier fired a shot down Center Street toward the depot, an ominous statement that the Union had taken control of the town. The bullet lodged in the lintel of the door of the old Sharpe house which stood where the Vance Hotel now stands.

He fired another round and that shot lodged in a tree in front of Walker's Hotel at 211 South Center, where the City Center is located today. Then the night became eerily quiet. Pickets were placed around town arresting anybody trying to pass. By midnight the main body of 5,000 troops began arriving, including General Stoneman.

That night and the next day, before heading west towards Taylorsville, soldiers "paid their respects" to all the good citizens of Statesville. Colonel Smith had made assurances that property would be protected, but every house, smokehouse and barn was visited, and food and provisions were taken freely. To their credit, the Yankees did not treat the women badly, and for every horse they took, they left a worn out one in its place. But they made sure every store window and display case was broken by their rifle butts.

The troops billeted overnight on the campus of the college and built campfires with the picket fence that surrounded the campus. The next morning, they set fire to the Iredell Express newspaper office that stood a few doors west of the square, about where the Bank of America building is. They also burned the railroad depot buildings and some adjoining warehouses.

Another force of 2,000 troops under the direction of General Palmer made its way through the streets before the town was able to breathe a sigh of relief and begin recovery.

After the War, Statesville's emotional and economic recovery was slow. Much wealth and many lives had been wiped out. An old-timer reported that as late as the 1870s, cows grazed on the weeds growing on the square. Yet the federal government had enough confidence in the town to make it the western N. C. office for the Internal Revenue Service. Recovery would come soon.

An interesting item from the 1883 paper mentioned that county leaders had built a bonfire on the square to burn blank and cancelled county bonds to prevent them from getting into the hands of forgers.

On Saturday afternoons in 1889 Amos Moore, known around town as "the shoemaker," set up a preaching stand on the square using a wooden shipping crate. He was said to have entertained his audiences in his shirt sleeves and to have refused to take up a collection.

In those days, some town squares had fountains, others had statues, but at some point, a decorative marble base was installed at the intersection of Broad and Center in Statesville. It included an urn that held a palm plant. It lasted until 1889 when a buggy wheel hooked it and toppled it. The spot remained empty until a directional sign was placed there years later.

After the Opera Hall on the southwest corner of the square burned down in 1892, the lot on the southwest corner of the square remained vacant for eight years. During that time, it served as a community gathering spot. But local historian Ralph Sloan also remembered it as an eyesore, a pile of rubble with remnants of the former basement, overgrown with weeds and copal bushes.

Sloan recalled that a merry-go-round or tent show could frequently be found there. And there was a parade of patent medicine men performing music, dancing, or telling jokes to pump up their audience before delivering their well-oiled sales pitches. One medicine man wore a fancy cut-away coat with buttons made of $20 gold pieces.

Another snake oil salesman by the name of Dr. Drake had an interesting experience on the square. After a few hours of hawking his cure-all tonic, the doctor was bombarded by eggs thrown from an anonymous assailant. Drake quickly packed up his goods and headed out of town, but not before getting a refund on the peddler's license that he had been required to purchase. Mayor Harrill gladly reimbursed him as a peace-offering for his unpleasant welcome to Statesville. But that wasn't the end of the story.

A couple of weeks later, Dr. Drake had moved his operation to the streets of Winston. There he told the story of how while in Statesville he had found that the tonic business was slow and he wasn't going to be able to sell enough product to cover his license fee. So he devised a plan. He paid a young fellow a dollar to throw some eggs at him while he was standing on his box telling spectators about the attributes of his medicine. He said his plan had worked and he was able to get his $25 fee back.

When the *Winston Sentinel* published his tale, and it was picked up by the *Landmark*, Mayor Harrill quickly called Drake's hand. The mayor said, first of all, his license fee was $1.00 for one day and not $25.00. Secondly he said the eggs weren't launched by a man he had paid, but by some local rebel rousers. If previous acts of civic minded mischief are any indication, the egging was most likely the work of the "Hoe-down Club," a group of young men who used creative pranks as a method of improving their community—like a rogue Welcome Wagon.

After the devastating Opera Hall fire in 1892, it would be 1900 before the construction of the palatial N. B. Mills building would re-transform the square into a place of beauty for nearly the first half of the twentieth century.

Chapter 3
Flag Poles & Scales

Flag Poles and Scales

Like all freedom-loving nineteenth century towns, Statesville proudly displayed the American flag, and at times even hoisted other patriotic flags and banners, over her square. In a letter to the *Landmark* in 1900, Capt. H. A. Chambers recalled the town as he remembered it as a boy in the early 1850s. He recalled the town's flagpole standing in the middle of Center Street, just outside the front door of the courthouse. He remembered the pole having a cross beam halfway up, held by ropes, looking much like the mast of a ship. One day he watched P. C. Carlton, one of the town's most patriotic citizens, stand on the beam at a dizzying height and attach a large political flag featuring the words "Scott, Graham and the Union." Winfield Scott and William Graham were running for president and vice-president on the Whig ticket in 1852.

Prior to the 1884 presidential election, the county Democratic Party raised money to return a flagpole to the square (purportedly 131-feet high or 10-12 stories high!) to fly their 13 x 27-foot colors inscribed, "Cleveland, Scales, Henderson and Reform." That night the younger Democrats gathered around the pole and listened to patriotic speeches by W. D. Turner and C. H. Armfield. The boys then paraded through the streets with torches and transparencies until 10:30.

In 1888 when President Grover Cleveland was running for reelection, a huge banner touting his campaign was stretched diagonally across the square from the southwest corner to the northeast corner. When Cleveland ran again in 1892, his supporters planted another flagpole on the square, this one only 111 feet tall. That year, one staunch Democrat suggested that an arc light with a globe inscribed with Cleveland and Stevenson be run up the pole at night so that "those groping in the darkness might see the light shining, forsake the error of their way, and follow the pure light of democracy." Statesville men were serious about their politics.

Not to be shortchanged, in 1896 the local Republicans raised their own flagpole and it remained in place for a year.

In the 1880s a different kind of flagpole system stood on the "burn't corner," the southeast corner of the square. It was the town's 60-foot-tall weather pole. In an agrarian town, accurate weather forecasting was crucial. Weather dictated the farmer's day-to-day schedule. It determined whether he made a profit or suffered a loss, and whether or not he could pay his mortgage and feed his family.

Flags would be run up the pole each morning to forecast the day's weather. A white flag meant clear weather, blue meant rain or snow, a white flag with a square signaled a cold snap, etc. Forecasts were telegraphed from Raleigh. The flags were changed by some unlucky policeman who would be unmercifully ridiculed if the previous day's prediction had been wrong.

The weather pole was chopped down when the bank building was built in 1889 and wasn't replaced, forcing farmers to return to their own daily prognostication methods of watching the disposition of the farm animals and the flight paths of the birds, while consulting their Farmer's Almanacs and crystal balls. The policemen passed the hat to buy a new pole but came up short.

By the early 1880s Statesville had become a fledging cotton market. In any business where the price of the product is determined by its weight, such as agricultural goods, an accurate measurement system was a necessity. When farmers came to town to sell their products, they also spent some of their receipts with local businesses, so aldermen were always looking for ways to lure them into town. They voted to provide farmers and other businessmen a convenient and accurate set of scales to weigh their products.

The scales were a good way to keep buyers and sellers honest, which in turn, cut down on arguments, fights, and acts of violence during transactions. And the result was an improved quality of life for all. Users paid a small fee, so the service also provided the city with some additional income

The town scales and accompanying cotton platform were moved to the northeast corner of the square in 1882, beside the current Groucho's, making it easily accessible and open to public inspection. It was built up on a slight mound so water could drain out. A two-foot deep, 12x15-foot hole was dug so the floor of the platform could float on the scale mechanism. An arm ran up to a box that held the indicator. Some said the top of the scale looked like a tombstone.

In the beginning, the official weigh master was sort of a political plum appointed by the aldermen, but later the operation was relegated to a policeman who carried the key to the scale. He received a small cut from the fee and was responsible for pulling the wagon on and off the scale and then printing the tender ticket for the customer. After unloading, the driver came back across the scale to have his empty weight subtracted from the ticket.

The city eventually did away with the cut to the policeman after they figured out it amounted to about $3.00 a month in lost revenue. In 1902 the town's two city fireman were given a $2.50 per month salary increase, but their duties were also expanded to include manning the scale.

Anything from a beef cow to a wagon load of corn could be weighed on the town scales. In the first ten months of 1886, 581 bales of cotton had come across. Cotton sellers faced a $50 fine if they sold products in the city limits and failed to have it weighed by the public official in charge. An ordinance even gave citizens the option to require the local coal delivery companies to weigh their loads prior to delivery.

One night in 1908, the scale platform became a rallying point for the local Democrats. The paper announced that a thousand torches had been delivered to the scale and were filled, trimmed and ready for use. They were distributed at 7:30 for the parade through the streets that ended at the courthouse where orators provided a boisterous program.

One day a visitor asked about the man who was buried on the square named Chicago Scalesco. When his story was investigated, it was found he had mistaken the town scales for a tombstone. The white rounded top of the equipment was inscribed as such.

The town scales were moved to Light Street, near the current Farm & Garden Store, in 1910.

Chapter 4
Let's Settle this Like Real Men

Let's Settle this Like Real Men

In the late 1800s, the square was where men, we're talking real men, met to sort out their differences. It was also where an embarrassing little episode took place in 1882. For many years afterwards, it was simply referred to as the infamous "Robbins-Mott affair."

Major William Robbins was a respected lawyer and decorated Confederate veteran. Marshal Mott was the 20-something year old son of Dr. J. J. Mott, a local physician who happened to also be chairman of the NC Republican Party. The two got into it one morning at Hoffman's store, located in the building that stood where the Statesville Jewelry & Loan building stands today. It ended up being a story that spread far and wide and was re-told for many years.

The story was printed in newspapers across the state and went this way. Major Robbins had made a partisan talk at the state Democratic Convention. In his talk he brought certain charges against Dr. Mott. Young Mott took offense at what he believed to be an insult to his father. Robbins was lighting a cigar and Mott slipped up from behind and hit him three blows with a weapon, most likely brass knuckles.

With Robbins clearly overmatched, a crowd began to intervene. Mott waved his pistol, warned them to stand back and made his exit. He then quickly saddled up and high-tailed it out of town.

That afternoon the town began to buzz with rumors. Solicitor J. S. Adams was in the same store making a purchase and talking to the clerk about that morning's affray, when T. A. Gill, a revenue agent, heard the conversation and took exception to Adams' comments. At the time, all revenuers were Republicans since they were federal government appointees and President Garfield's administration controlled who got the jobs. Gill and Adams began arguing, and revenuer W. H. Stockton walked in and joined the discussion. As the argument got more heated, Stockton struck Adams and Adams struck Stockton, driving Stockton to the door. Stockton then reached in his pocket and hit Adams with a weapon, staggering him and leaving him unable to fight back. But Stockton continued to hit Adams several more blows.

As word of that ruckus spread through town, men began choosing sides and a large crowd assembled on the square around dark. Before it was over, store clerk John Osborne had drawn his pistol and shot C. S. Cooper, one ball striking his chest and another his head.

The *Winston Leader* newspaper lede the next day was, "Thursday was a bloody day in Statesville, and the news of the racket at that place sounds more like a report from a border town than from a moral burg in a civilized community." The *Charlotte Observer* said that Statesville was the darndest town in the state for people fighting in the streets over politics.

By the time the Robbins/Mott incident made the pages of the *New York Times*, the story had been told so many times, and embellished so many times, that the paper ended up reporting that the two combatants had shot and killed each other. Apparently fake news has been around a long time.

It was near that same spot, on the northwest corner of the square, that another politically charged altercation took place 16 years later—the Gregory-Cowles feud on April 25, 1898. Known as "the duel on the square," it became another legendary story involving the dangerous mixture of pride and gunpowder that was retold for many years.

The following story/song tells how the events of that day transpired. The site of the duel is the last stop on the "Statesville After Dark, Chapter II" historic walking tour.

The Bullet Tree
Steve Hill
2009

"A hole in a tree 'bout the size of a dime, like a black widow's web luring hapless house flies"

Captain Bill Gregory and Colonel Hank Cowles had been friends since they were boys and had fought together in the Civil War. One was a rich cotton broker, the other, clerk of the federal court. But at high noon on April 25th, 1898, they weren't feelin' real brotherly anymore.

The two had roamed these same streets, and they had joined the same lodge. They drank the same whiskey and served the same God. But the biggest thing they had in common was—their pride—too much of it, that is. You see, pride's a lot like gunpowder. A little bit goes a long way, but a little too much can blow you away.

And both were staunchly patriotic in their defense—but when it came to politics, that's where the similarities end. Cowles was a rabid Republican, Gregory a dogged Democrat. And that's what started this whole ridiculous spat.

The previous day the two had engaged in a public cussin' match over by the church, where Bill called Hank a liar. So obviously Hank had to defend his reputation (right guys?), by rubbing Bill's face in the dirt. Well, there are a couple things you should never steal from a man, one's his reputation, and the other's his clean shirt. And a crowd of laughing spectators made a bad situation even that much worse.

Wi-ill you fight for your dignity
When that deep line is drawn in the sand
It's a sad and lonely quandary
That only a man can understand

Bill went home, cleaned his pistol, and bragged to his friends that Hank was gonna have'ta pay. Hank got wind of his threat (from those same friends, by the way) so he, too, was packing heat that next day. And at his usual lunch time, Hank crossed the square, and when he got right about there, Bill yells, "You are the man who attacked me!" Now, for you peace lovers, "them's fightin' words" — loosely translated to mean "somebody's fixin' to get hurt."

So, what does ole Hank do? He throws open his coat, bows out his chest, and yells, "I am that man!" Now you gotta remember, back then men were real men...not necessarily real smart men, but real men. And with that said, they both grab their guns, and the shooting begins.

Wi-ill you fight for your dignity
When that deep line is drawn in the sand
It's a sad and lonely quandary
That only a man can understand

Bill popped off three rounds and, dad-gum-it his pistol jammed, and he wuz forced to take cover behind a small elm tree that stood about where I am. Hank fires a couple rounds, bum-rushes Bill, knocks him to the ground, hits him with his gun, and they wrassle around in the horse manure until a cop joins in on the fun.

I'm happy to report that somehow this embarrassing public pissin' match ended without bloodshed; Luckily, it was only testosterone that flowed in the street that day¬—for neither one was a very good aim. One of Hank's bullets lodged in that tree, and Bill nicked a couple of bricks on the bank building across the street.

But news of what became known as "the duel on the square" spread like wildfire everywhere, including a rumor that Bill had cowered behind a tree in the heat of the fight. So, he was forced to line up eyewitnesses at the newspaper office the next mornin' to testify...to testify that he wudn't tryin' to hide. Heck, he was just tryin' to save his hide.

Wi-ill you fight for your dignity
When that deep line is drawn in the sand
It's a dark and lonely quandary
That only a man can understand

And, that pretty much ended that thorny affair
And life got back to normal for that ornery pair
But not so much for the young boys of the town I'm afraid
Who would become unwitting victims of the events of that day

Remember that bullet hole in the tree
That's the sad chapter of this onerous creed
For the next 30 years boys lined up right here on this spot
To poke their sweaty little fingers into that hallowed slot

It was fun at first just a way to pass time, but each time
Its stark warning became more steeped in their minds
A chilling reminder that the day would soon come
When they, too, would have to choose whether to fight or to run

A hole in a tree 'bout the size of a dime
Like a black widow's web luring hapless house flies
We'll never know now who's courage it coerced
Or how many young lives were cut short by its curse

Gregory was eventually fined $25 for assault. The brouhaha was covered in the papers from Baltimore to Wilmington and from Norfolk to Asheville, and the people of Statesville got a great story that they could talk about for years. The tree with the bullet hole became a local landmark. It was known as "the bullet tree." Over the years, it became slick, since every boy in town had to stick his finger in it every time he walked by. And as the legend grew, so did the hole, as boys used their pocketknives to cut out chunks of it for good luck souvenirs.

One afternoon four years later, Cowles' son Henry C. Cowles, Jr. was pointing out the hole to a friend when old Captain Gregory just happened to pass by. Gregory believed the boys were making fun of him, probably correctly so, so he went home and wrote a strongly worded letter to young Cowles.

Cowles flew hot, went looking for him, found him at J. C. Turner's store, on the northeast corner of the square where Groucho's is today, grabbed him by the throat, and punched the old man in the face a few times. Since Gregory was a "real man," he attempted to resist, but was unable to get close enough to his young opponent to land a blow. He refused to press charges and that episode brought closure to the legendary Gregory-Cowles unpleasantness.

Sure, there would be other fights on the Square, but none would rival the petty political battles of the 1880s and '90s, and it would be public lovemaking on the square, not war-making, that would get people riled up and taking sides in the 1950s. Stay tuned.

The Gregory-Cowles "Bullet Hole Tree" *Stimson*
(Broad Street looking west from the square)

Chapter 5
The Town Clock

The Town Clock

In 1889 as the finishing touches were being put on the First National Bank building, someone suggested that the tower atop the three-story structure would be a great place for a clock. Soon a plan was being kicked around to form a partnership between the city and county to pay for a town clock. This caused a huge uproar that lasted for quite a while. Opposition groups, made up mostly of farmers, quickly organized from the Wilkes and Yadkin County lines all the way down to the Mecklenburg County line, "and every nook and cranny in between." For months, a heated debate was carried out on the pages of the *Landmark* newspaper.

The initial protest proclamation which had been made by the Cool Spring delegation was echoed by farmers' alliances and over 30 sub-alliances from every Iredell County community. Iredell's Populists were adamant that $175 of their hard-earned county tax money would not be wasted to place a public clock on a private building, even if they had to recall or even tar and feather the entire board of commissioners. One editorial even suggested nailing the ears of politicians to the bank tower.

The plan was for the city and county to each pay a quarter of the cost and the rest would be raised from private subscriptions solicited by the town aldermen. Distractors argued that the clock would be of no use to the farmers in the county who would be footing the bill. And besides, if a town clock chimed on the half hour, every watchmaker and clock salesman in Statesville would be put out of business. The *Progressive Farmer* quipped that "those who can't pay $1.50 for a watch have no business knowing the time of day anyhow." "And winding a watch is good exercise."

Samples of Farmers' Alliance proclamations in the *Landmark*

Despite all the harping and bellyaching, in January 1890 a quit claim was signed by the bank and city and county officials for the clock to be installed. The bell was purchased from the McShane Bell Company in Baltimore and was embossed as such along with the date, 1890.

The Landmark reported on January 19, "The town clock is about to begin business. Squire White and his big black mare, along with Bill Munday and other assistants yanked it to the top of the bank building this week. The dials are being painted on the tower, the bell is being hung, and yesterday it's melodious notes were heard. The clock aforesaid will soon be indicating the time of day soon."

The paper further ascertained, "It has had the distinction of being discussed more than any time piece in the world, the famous Strasbourg clock excepted."

Local historian Homer Keever opined that never in the history of Iredell County has a board of commissioners felt the wrath of public indignation as those who proposed spending $175 on a clock.

The town Clock bell sat on the roof of the First National Bank building *Stimson*

It would eventually be dubbed the "Alliance Clock," which is humorous because it was the "alliance" guys who lost the battle. Who says, "to the victor go the spoils" and thus earns the right to name the sites of the battles?

For the next 50 years the open-air bell chimed from the rooftop of the bank building. Since it sat below the roofline and couldn't be seen from the street, only the city workers who climbed to the roof to maintain the timekeeping system were able to fully appreciate its beauty.

J. A. Houpe in the Cool Spring township reported that when there was dampness in the atmosphere the strokes could be heard on his farm 11½ miles away. He said the clock had become a "weather prophet" for him. R. A. Montgomery in the same area also reported using the tolls as a weather predictor.

W. H. Lackey, 13-miles away as the crow flies in Alexander County swore that he heard the clock strike at 6:00 one morning.

After just four years of rain and snow, the wooden frame holding the bell had rotted and had to be replaced. The hands stopped turning for the first time on Christmas Day, 1908 and had to be repaired.

During World War II, the heavy brass bell was lowered from its perch by John Gilbert's construction crane and sold for scrap to support the war effort. Some workers at the bank said "good riddance." They feared it was going to shake the building apart. The fire department was the benefactor of the mear $400 it brought.

When it was hoisted down, it was taken to the fire station and put on display. Citizens had grown accustomed to hearing the old gal for many years but few had ever laid eyes on her. The firemen weighed it and it came in at 1,030 pounds without the clapper, considerably less than the 1,200 pounds quoted by the maker. They also found that the bell had a large crack and would have soon been usless for anything other than scrap.

In those early years, the hourly chimming of the clock was an important part of our town's business and social life. It regulated shop hours. It set the pace for a hard day of work, and signaled time for rest. It was always there. It was like an old friend.

One morning in 1919 the clock's one ton weight that was encased inside the interior wall of the building came crashing down three stories to the ground level. The bank employees ran outside, fearing an earthquake and thinking the building was coming down.

When the clock face got its fresh coat of paint sporadically, people on the street were always amazed that the face was about the same height as the man painting it. The tower itself is 20-feet tall. Its minute hand, made of oak, travels 16 feet in it's sweep and has made over a million revolutions in its lifetime. The tower has been painted black, white, green and yellow at varying times over 130 years, and possibly other colors as well.

Stimson

DSDC

DSDC

She has shown her colors over the years

DSDC

In the 1920s and 30s policeman Charlie Rumple was in charge of winding the clock. Some may remember him as the Sheriff of Iredell County in the 1960s. In the 1950s city employee James Beckham was the timekeeper. The city staff has done an excellent job tenderly coaxing the tempermental giant along for many years.

But from time to time over the years, the bell mechanism on the clock would freeze up and the clapper would quit striking. This would usually lead to readers calling the newspaper office, and then miracously the bell would be ringing again. In 1935 the clock's custodian, Stintz Alexander, was confident he could climb into the works with a goose feather and a drop of kerosene to get it running again. It's unknown whether or not he was successful.

It's 12 o'clock somewhere (twice) *Tharpe*
9, 10, 12, 12

This photograph began circulating around town one afternoon in the 1950s and became quite a conversation piece. It shows the southeast face of the clock. Some eagle-eyed observer noticed that there were two 12s on the face. Since that side of the clock is the least visible from the ground without binoculars, it was difficult to see until someone, probably Max Tharpe, snapped a shot of a man adjusting the hands.

No one could determine when the mistake had been made. Was it a prank? It wouldn't have taken a lot of creativity to saw and paint a chair slat to make the extra "1," but it would have taken some aerial acrobatics to make the measurements and complete the caper. Was it the work of those pesky "Hoe-down" club boys from 50 years before? The clock got a sprucing up every 10 years or so. Surely it hadn't gone unnoticed for 60 years.

Thus, to this day, the extra "1" remains one of Statesville's unsolved mysteries.

In later years, city employee Jim Elliott and James Stewart were keepers of the clock. Elliott explained to his clock watching fans that the beast was operated by five 100-pound weights and needed a good winding with a crank once a week.

In May 1957 the clock entered the electronic age. Overnight the clock hands were attached to a 10-pound electronic heart. The system converted impulse movement from electrical energy to mechanical energy to rotate the hands on the four clock faces. A master control unit resembling a grandfather clock was installed on the second floor. Each minute it would send an impulse to the new unit in the tower. The impulse would in turn operate the hands in minute clicks. Not only did the new equipment eliminate the necessity to wind the clock once a week, it also ensured that the clock was in continuous operation. The master control was a pendulum clock that was spring driven but electronically wound. That system remained in place until 1972.

The mechanics of the clock are described as pretty simple as far as machinery goes. A system that includes a pendulum, gears, universal joints and cogs keeps the four faces showing the same time.

Inside the tower is a 2,000 pound set of works bearing the markings of its maker, E. Howard & Co., Boston, Mass. On the wall inside the tower is a framed set of yellowed, instructions that begins, "If it be a striking clock, and the time for striking has been passed when setting…"

In 1972, after years of silence, it took an 11 year old girl named Laura White to get the chime working again. Laura began a letter writing campaign and soon a new electric bell system was installed on the roof of the building, then known as the Statesville Drug store building.

At noon on a Saturday afternoon in September of 1973, local jeweler Eli Cook wound 'er up and she let out 12 dongs. The weekend noon hour was chosen for the unveiling so children and working people could be in town to enjoy the return of the chime. Cook was paid $350 for the parts, including a bell he found in Rutherfordton, and for the repair work necessary to get her back in working order. The city also agreed to pay him $50 a month to keep it operating, but they declared that they would not be responsible for any injuries he might incure while performing the upkeep. That system lasted for 20 years or so.

The old town clock on the square, that beautiful iconic landmark that everyone from outside our city visualizes when they think of "Statesville," has been an institution for over 130 years. But for the past 25 or 30 years or so, she's been silent. Her chime is broken. As best anyone can remember, the last time she uttered a sound was in the early 1990s.

Many downtown business persons believe it's time for the grand old lady on the square to sing again. They believe a tolling of the hour would add a classy finishing touch to the streetscape makeover. It would offer a cheerful and inviting welcome to downtown shoppers and visitors.

Recently, Preservation Statesville, a group of local history enthusiasts, began working on a plan to bring her back to life again. It will be an expensive but a rewarding project. After all, if the beautiful hollow tone of the town clock could once again fill the streets, what better way to say, "Welcome to Statesville! We're glad you're here."

A November 2, 1922 Statesville *Landmark* newspaper article summed the town clock up this way. The title of the piece was, "Part of Life's Drama: The Town Clock is Always on Stage, Unconscious of its Importance."

> *"The town clock strikes nine. The bank shades go up. Lawyer's shingles rattle, school girls run breathlessly up the schoolhouse steps.*
>
> *Nine o'clock. Men and women who are now far away from their old hometown, who've long since flown the nest, glance up from their watches and that familiar image of home appears before their eyes. The Polk-Gray drug store on the square; the old Presbyterian Church; the college.*
>
> *Into the drama of everyone's life within the reach of its penetrating, resonant voice it enters, an actor, unconscious of the magnitude of its role.*
>
> *Ten years, 20 years may have passed, but these lines are as if spoken yesterday.*
>
> *Eight o'clock--"Tom was born at 8 o'clock."*
>
> *Four o'clock--"Louise was married at 4 o'clock;"*
>
> *10 o'clock--father left this earth just as the town clock was striking 10.*
>
> *They all remember; the old clock won't let them forget; each day anew as it sounds out the hour, fraught with the incident of their dramas, insinuating itself, enbedding itself, fast in memory. An actor. And always on stage.*
>
> *11 o'clock--a returning soldier steps off the train into eager arms--the hour sounds, and never sounds again without quickening the beat of a heart.*
>
> *An early morning vigil--Bill has the croup--that hour never to be forgotten. If not a tug at the heart, always a mental picture.*
>
> *6 o'clock--shop doors begin to bang shut--men trudge homeward, burden-laden--the faint chime, compliments the forlorn sound of a train leaving the station."*

In 2010 when talking with a WWII vet, the old soldier shared with this writer that the most homesick he'd ever been was in Europe during the war. He said he would have given anything to hear the chime of the old town clock one more time. The following song laments the absence of that beautiful "beckoning" sound that had once been a symbol of hope for anxious families during the dark days of war. It closes out the "Statesville After Dark" Chapter 1 walking tour:

Beckoning
Steve Hill
2010

High, over the square
Above all the laughter, strife and despair
Seeming no worse for the wear
But 'er spirit is gone

High, up on the roof
They hoisted her there back in '92
And at her formal debut
She sang them a song

She was the grandest of dames
Flooding her kingdom with melodious tones
Like a conductor on stage
And beckoning into the night…for her boys to come home

But, now she sleeps
There's no serenading the chimney sweeps
And no more battles to keep
The pigeons at bay

For two lifetimes or more
Tolling her heart out in peace time and war
But a lion that loses its roar
Dies in its cave

She was the grandest of dames
Flooding her kingdom with melodious tones
Like a conductor on stage
And beckoning into the night…for her boys to come home

It's way past time
To break out the oil can and patch up her chimes
And rouse her again to unwind
Her voice up on high

She was the grandest of dames
Flooding her kingdom with melodious tones
Like a conductor on stage
And beckoning into the night, for her boys to come home…for her boys to come home…
for her boys to come home

SHC **The Gears** *SHC*

SHC **The works** *SHC*

SHC **The pendulum** **The grand entrance** *SHC*

The author's favorite shot was taken by Bob Plyler

Chapter 6
Everybody's Day

Everybody's Day

One of the Statesville's earliest and most successful street fairs was called "Everybody's Day," a Saturday filled with entertainment, contests, games, and of course—shopping.

The idea to have a celebration honoring "everybody" came in the early 1900s from Captain Tom Rowland, the conductor on the AT&O railroad that ran between Charlotte and Statesville. Rowland was the town's most fervent cheerleader and the man who coined and propagated the slogan "Statesville—Best Town in North Carolina!" That's how he announced the next stop as the train approached town. And the slogan stuck for several decades as the official, unofficial tag line. Across the state, Statesville was called "the best town," sometimes begrudgingly, sometimes sarcastically, but none-the-less, the *best*. (Similarly, when approaching Charlotte, Rowland yelled, "next stop, Charlotte—Second Best Town in North Carolina!"). People loved it.

The first Everybody's Day was held August 29, 1903. It was a fund-raiser to establish a public library. There were prizes for the best decorated wagons and horses, and for the winners of a wide array of contests that included: the wheelbarrow race, the fat men's race, the bag race, the watermelon eating tournament, as well as the fattest man, best banjo picker, largest family, oldest man, youngest married couple, oldest fiddler, and prettiest baby competition.

And there was the ever-popular greased pole contest. Two grease-coated poles were erected outside the bank building upon which young men, raced each other to reach the $10 bills nailed atop the poles. Other fun activities included bicycle races, baseball games and a play area for the kids. Cake and lemonade flowed freely. And if history is any indicator, illegal spirits were imbibed freely in the alleys as well. Bands from as far away as Hiddenite performed.

Another popular Everybody's Day contest was the hidden dollar game where a dollar bill was hidden in the pocket of an anonymous person who was then sent out to mingle through the crowd. When the town clock chimed at noon, everybody stopped what they were doing and asked those near them if they were holding the hidden dollar. The person who asked the question to the actual secret bill-holder won the dollar bill as a prize. (According to the inflation calculator, $1.00 in 1903 has the purchasing power of about $30.00 today.)

The most unusual contest happened next. Area engaged couples who beforehand had shown an openness to the idea of getting married on the square, if given the opportunity, were identified and their names were placed in a hat. The name of the winning couple was drawn at 12:45. They received an all-expenses paid wedding on the spot, along with a "nice piece of household furniture"—sort of like Statesville's version of the Newlywed Game.

Throughout the week before the big celebration, game prizes were displayed in the front window of Sloan's Clothing on the square, and the whole town was a-buzz with excitement. The newspaper estimated there were at least a dozen men eligible to run (or walk) in the fat man race. The event closed with an evening dinner served by the library fundraiser ladies dressed in colonial costumes.

Stimson   **Greased pole climbing contest at Everybody's Day, 1907**   *Stimson*

Brady   **Everybody's Day floats**   *Stimson*

Brady **"Blackface" minstrel bandon the square**   **Big sales at every store**   *Landmark*

The first Everybody's day was a huge success. The event returned in 1904, this time sponsored by the county's Confederate veterans and the United Daughters of the Confederacy as a fundraiser to acquire a Confederate monument. The ladies of the county were encouraged to pack a picnic dinner (lunch) which could be sold on the streets. Cakes and Confederate song sheets were sold, and a supper closed out the evening. The Daughters raised $200.

In 1905 Everybody's "Day" was expanded to "Days" to include Friday events. A large parade was held and there were games and contests similar to those the previous years. The railroads offered reduced ticket prices for out-of-towners traveling in. Friday a large audience attended the laying of the cornerstone for the new monument honoring the Confederate dead.

A merry-go-round was set up in front of the courthouse on Wednesday, but court officials ordered the music system and steam whistle to be disconnected, "because Judge Cooke didn't like noise." The merry-go-round operator from Charlotte provided attendees a free sideshow when he was arrested for hitting a man with a stick and rendering him unconscious.

The big draw for the 1906 celebration was a balloon ascension by a pilot billing himself as "Professor Smith." At the time, Professor C. O. Smith was purported to be the only black aeronaut in the world. At 2:10 he ascended from West Broad in a 65-foot hot air balloon rig, performed some acrobatic feats on a trapeze, and then parachuted back to the ground, landing near where he took off. A second flight had to be cancelled when his balloon caught fire.

Smith was said to have made 4,311 ascensions over a 16-year span. He claimed to have landed in trees, live wires, rivers and on tops of houses, but had never broken a bone or received a serious injury. But shortly after his Statesville performance the professor was killed in a crash.

Proceeds that year were directed to the fire department. There was an alarm demonstration by the fire company; a bag of flour was awarded to the man bringing the largest family to town; and a rocking chair went to the oldest lady in attendance. The merry-go-round was back and there were concerts, a mule race, and other contests. But the bicycle race was cancelled because the streets were too crowded, a nice problem for a town to have.

During the week leading up to Saturday, the Edsall-Winthrope show put up a tent on West Broad for nightly theatrical performances. The troupe had performed several times previously in the Opera House on the southwest corner of the square and was a town favorite.

At a brief ceremony on the square, Captain Rowland was presented with a gold watch by the downtown businessmen in appreciation of his loyalty to the city. Carnival rides were set up in front of the courthouse, including a contraption called the "ocean wave," that appears to have been something similar to today's tilt-a-whirl.

Apparently, the blacksmiths in the area had missed the previous years' festivities because they announced they were joining forces and would be closing their shops to attend Everybody's Day that year. The fire company coffers were $200-$300 richer from the proceeds.

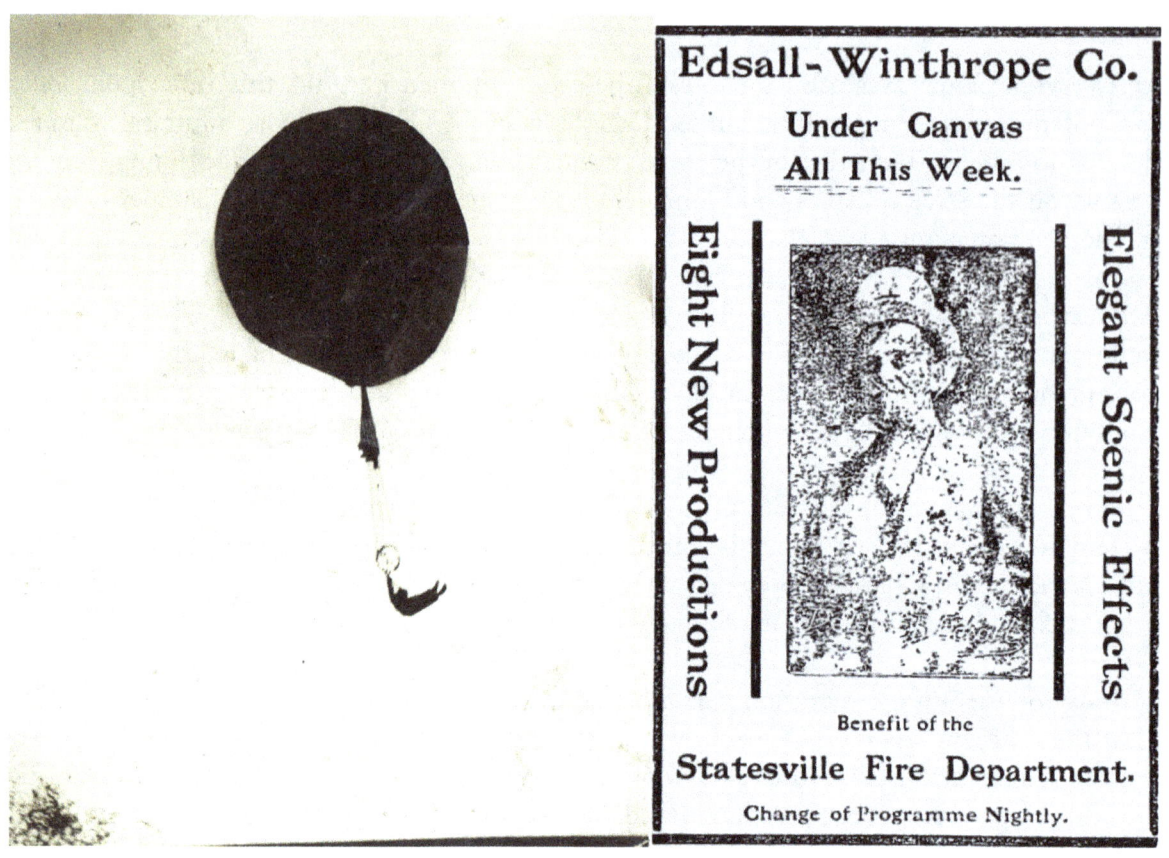

SHC Balloon ascension and the Edsall-Winthrope Co. show *SHC*

The "ocean wave" in motion *SHC*

42

Ferris wheel (that looks awfully close to the power lines) *SHC*

The 1907 Everybody's Day was believed at the time to be the largest crowd ever assembled in Statesville. Organizers estimated 8,000 in attendance, 5,000 of which were visitors. Outsiders had begun streaming in on Tuesday, and the trains were packed all week. The hotels and boarding houses were full, and many visitors had to sleep on the streets and in the back trade lots. The firemen were in charge again and maintained good order considering the size of the crowd. They earned $435 for their work.

The main draw that year was the "world's smallest woman," "Little Ina Brewer," aka "Ina the Dwarf." For most of her adult life, Ina traveled across the country as a sideshow attraction with the Smith Shows and Jones Carnival. But it was a homecoming for Ina. She was a western Iredell County native, and surprisingly, she had only been exhibited in Statesville once before the 1907 event. Ina was 36-inches tall and weighed 36 pounds. She died in Statesville in 1921 at the age of 30 and is buried at Pilgrim Baptist Church near Love Valley.

SHC   **Billed as "the world's smallest woman," "Little Ina Brewer"**   SHC

The first order of the morning was a Confederate veteran's reunion and speech by N. C. Secretary of State Col. J. Bryan Grimes, son of Civil War General Bryan Grimes, who had led many of the Iredell County men during the War. The vets then marched to the Opera House where they were served a meal by the ladies of the town.

Balloon ascensions were back in '07 with three flights from Center Street. "Professor" Smith, who had died in a fall shortly after his 1906 appearance here, was replaced by "Professor" Jack Casselle from Indiana. The professor's first feat took him up 2,000 up, and after performing a few stunts on the rigging, his parachute deposited him south of town at the "Willow Hole Bridge," which was along the branch, at the foot of the hill before starting up to the depot.

Many lucky men went home with hats on their heads that year. The Wallace Brothers threw 200 new-old-stock straw hats from the third-floor window of their building (where Statesville Jewelry & Loan is now) into a swarm of a thousand or so up-reaching hands on the street. Sloan Clothing on the square got rid of a similar amount of old hat inventory the same way.

Other festivities included a Ferris wheel, merry-go-round, knock-down-the-babies, Maude the Kicking mule, punching machines, dunking booth, striking anvil, palmist's tent, fortune telling machine, glass blower stand, roving bands, balloons, and confetti. And someone in a bear costume roamed the streets alongside the usual clowns.

The town's one-horse fire wagon with yellow umbrellas bearing the inscription, "Statesville—Best Town in N.C.," carried a load of pretty girls through the streets. The fire companies, both white and "colored," conducted races and demonstrations, and a mule race was run between the square and Tradd Street.

Fire Chief Buck Conner and a load of pretty girls *SHC*

The 1908 installment was re-marketed as "Homecoming Day," a part of "Fireman's Week." It was coupled with the John Robinson Circus the same weekend which brought in approximately 10,000 spectators. Balloon ascensions, this time conducted by a name-less female aeronautic acrobat, surprisingly without the title of "professor," made some balloon trips. She suffered some minor injuries on her final flight.

After a six-year successful run, Everybody's Day gradually faded away. In 1909 the two major outdoor social events were the floral parade, sponsored by the DAR, and the Confederate Memorial Day parade.

In later years, the Fourth of July became the big day for celebration on the square. From newspaper reports of the period, one could speculate that the big Fourth of July celebration in 1919 contributed to the second wave of the Spanish Influenza.

That was the town's first opportunity for public assembly after the pandemic broke out the year before. Ten thousand spectators poured into the downtown that year to celebrate. And there probably wasn't a lot of social distancing going on. Balloon demonstrations were replaced by an airplane flyover by Lieutenants L. C. Mallory and William Turnbull stationed at Pope Field at Camp Bragg in Fayetteville.

Floral parade entry, 1909 *SHC*

4th of July parade with concerts on the square, 1915 *Landmark*

Chapter 7

1900s–1940s

1900s-1940s

If there is such a thing as a "heyday," Statesville can boast of having enjoyed several of them, one in the 1880s, one during the Everybody's Day years, a third in the teens and '20s, and probably the biggest in the 1950-60s. During each of those times, the downtown shopping district experienced tremendous foot traffic and expansive retail success.

During most of the early and mid-1900s, shoppers could find just about anything they were looking for within hollering distance of the square. Clothing, shoes, household goods, farm supplies, groceries, furniture, hardware, toys, jewelry, guns, tobacco, alcohol, livestock, wagons, and even automobiles could be found within a few doors of the square, as well as medical, banking, insurance, funeral, barber/beautician, and real estate services. In the 1940s, five drug stores could be found within one block of the town clock.

Joining the wide array of locally owned and operated retail establishments filling downtown storefronts were regional chains such as, Belk's, Spainhour's, Smithey's, Butler's, Larkin's, Gaylord's, Diana Shop, Gold Shop, Smart Shop, Fashion Shop, Gables, Peggy's, People's, Lester's, Stelen's, Gilmer's, Cato's, Purcell's, Kimbrell's, Stratford's, Leonard's, Kiddie Shoppe, Three Sisters, Efird's, Eagles, Raylass, Jewel Box, Heilig-Meyer's, and others.

Even some national chain stores could be found downtown over the years, including A & P, Rose's, Sears, J. C. Penny, F. W. Woolworth, Montgomery Ward, J. J. Newberry, Scottie's, Piggly Wiggly, Singer, etc., as well as Western Auto, Advance, Firestone, B. F. Goodrich, and Good Year automobile-related franchises.

In the early 1900s, a community billboard on the square kept shoppers aware of downtown activities, hours of operation, etc. In the spirit of fairness, merchants were expected to maintain the same opening and closing times. The billboard was also where merchants posted names of deadbeats who had not settled their accounts—public info and public shaming all in one place.

The city celebrated entry into the 20th century with the installation of four new state-of-the-art automatic horse watering troughs at the square, two on Broad and two on Center. With the new system, water rose to an adequate level and cut off automatically; and as water was removed, it was automatically replaced. It was a technological marvel of that time.

The public watering troughs were mostly for the convenience of visitors, but locals could use them sparingly. Longer term watering services were available for a cost at the livery stables scattered around town. It was said that the troughs also helped prevent horses from being abused on hot days by drivers who were too lazy to draw water from the town wells for them.

A 25,000-gallon cistern buried under the square was abandoned and filled with dirt in 1903. One of four underground reservoirs in town, it had been there for firefighters to draw water from in earlier days but had become obsolete when water lines and hydrants were installed. It took workers three days and over 100 loads of dirt to fill it.

The plan to dig a cistern on the square had begun in 1876 but was tabled, since a water source without an engine to pump it would be of little use. That discussion led 28 men to volunteer for the town's first "hook and ladder" fire company. A cement-lined cistern soon followed.

On a Saturday afternoon in 1901 a bicycle thief struck the square. Frank Sherrill had ridden his "wheel" to work and parked it in front of his store in the Miller Block. A well-dressed man jumped on it and took off.

When Mr. Sherrill sounded the alarm an hour later, the thief had already gotten a good head start. Bicycle shop owner and early wheel enthusiast N. M. Fleming along with Sherrill's young son gave chase. The trail led them to near Turnersburg where the two spent the night. The next morning, they continued to Harmony where they finally caught up with the criminal, the son of a well-known citizen, and recovered the bike. Bicycle theft was once a nagging problem in town.

In 1904 a major ruckus was caused when the city allowed the Pierce Amusement Co. to set up a free, week-long street fair around the square. Permission had been granted with conditions that the fair activities didn't unreasonably obstruct the streets and sidewalks. Little did the town leaders know that a merry-go-round, Ferris wheel and other large attractions would be brought in. Shop owners loudly complained that the fronts of their stores were blocked with the paraphernalia, but by that time their complaints were too late. The entire square was completely blocked, and vehicle traffic was gridlocked in all directions the entire week.

Pierce's most elaborate thrill-seeking contraption was a two-story tower with a ribbon-like circular ramp. A not-so-young gentleman billed as "Minting the Marvel," rode a one-wheeled cycle up and down the steep incline to the pleasure of the crowd.

Other attractions were hidden inside canvas tents but weren't free as Pierce had advertised. There was an admission fee and the city got 10% of the take while the Hospital Fund got another 10%. The next year, the aldermen denied Pierce's request to return to town.

Gaither   **"Minting the Marvel" unicycle show 1904**

Pierce Amusement Street Fair   *SHC*

In 1905 when the United Daughters of the Confederacy group was searching for a site for the proposed Confederate monument, one group of ladies wanted it to stand in the courthouse yard, but another group insisted it grace the center of the square. At the August 7 Board of Aldermen's meeting, a Daughters committee petitioned the city for permission to place it on the square while another committee presented a similar petition in opposition to the idea. After hearing both sides, the aldermen voted to deny the use of the square, and the granite soldier ended up in the yard down the street.

Major infrastructure improvements came to Broad and Center Streets in 1906 when the aldermen voted to replace wooden sidewalks with cement walks. Also, that year, L. C. Henkel, and a group of local businessmen, approached the city with a plan to build a streetcar system to run from the square south to the depot and west to the college. Passengers would pay five cents in each direction. Henkel got the city's blessings to build and operate an electric trolley system. Afterall, neighboring progressive cities of Salisbury, Spencer and Charlotte were already operating street cars. There was even talk of running a line between Yadkinville and Winston.

An earlier partnership between the city and the Statesville Land Development Company to build a streetcar system in 1891 had not materialized. Henkel's franchise eventually expired in 1909 without any tracks being laid. By that time, the public's attention was turning to another method of moving people around town—the automobile.

In the early 1900s when traveling the state, Judge A. L. Coble described his hometown this way, "Statesville has all the modern improvements, except street cars. Even has high taxes."

The Landmark editor wrote, "Statesville was putting on airs Friday night. The streets were crowded and a brass band paraded Center Street playing selections. The only thing lacking was the hum of the street cars, which it is said will be forthcoming when the power is obtained." But the town was fortunate to have resisted the lure of the streetcar bell since the trolly craze would have most likely been short lived.

Wagon loads of dirt and a road packing machine were brought in to improve the square in 1908. The intersection was raised slightly to keep "frog ponds" from forming in wet weather. That year, on the night before the national election, over 1,000 local Democrats assembled on the square with torches, tin horns, and megaphones and then marched through the streets to drum up support for their party's candidates.

Later, the board of aldermen voted to pave Broad and Center from Meeting to Tradd and from Water to Front. A paving material known as "Tarvia" was used. The plan called for 20-foot sidewalks and 80-foot streets. Two 20-foot-wide driveways were planned from Front Street to the Depot with a 20-foot grass parking area in between them.

The tarvia system begins with a thin bed of concrete which is then covered with small gravel. The rock is topped with a tar mixture that is heated in a rolling steam boiler. Years later, a Hotel Iredell advertisement boasted that the city was spending $100,000 to add Bitulithic pavement.

Stimson   **Tarvia paving operation on Broad, 1912**   *Stimson*

City rock crusher that supplied paving materials   *Stimson*

Also, in the 19-teens, town aldermen addressed requests from business owners to raise or lower the sidewalk levels in front of their stores to reduce the number of steps customers had to maneuver to enter. Owners on the west side of Center from the square to Court Street wanted the sidewalk grade built higher, and those on the east side wanted the sidewalk lowered. Each would have improved customer access by eliminating the need for one or two entrance steps. A level grade from the sidewalk to the store floor was good for business.

After much discussion, the board voted to leave the grades the same and property owners were left to make their own adjustments when they remodeled. Even today, a slight incline can be found at the front doors of those stores on the west side. The board also voted to place thick prism glass over the basement window holes in the sidewalks instead of metal grates. Some of those glass sidewalks were still visible up into the 1980s.

During that same time, the highlight of the spring season was the county commencement parade. High school seniors from across the county dressed in their finest attire and marched from the depot to the square. A separate parade was held for African American students, also ending on the square.

A regular occurrence in the early days was a run-away horse or mule, often attached to a wagon or buggy. And the paper reported in detail who the owner was, who was responsible for allowing the escape, whose property was damaged, and who was injured.

In 1912 a six-year-old girl held onto a horse as it galloped at a good clip back and forth across the square. Luckily, some men lassoed her steed, and she was uninjured. Later, a horse pulling the "bus" belonging to the Statesville Inn got spooked by the empty coach rattling behind it and ran at an increasingly high rate of speed across the square, turned over, and caught fire. Bystanders quickly unhitched the horses. A lantern hanging inside the vehicle was the culprit.

That year Sherman Ramsey appeared before the Mayor's Court for exceeding the speed limit across the square in his automobile. The mayor reminded him that the speed limit was eight miles per hour (why not seven or nine or even ten?). Ramsey pleaded innocent because he didn't believe he was going that fast, and the charge was dismissed.

In the summer of 1913, a portable bandstand was located on the square from which the Statesville Mechanics Band, led by Charles H. Turner, gave free weekly performances—kind of like an early "Friday After Five" concert series.

The Statesville Mechanics band with director Charles H. Turner on the right *Rickert*

In an effort to ease horse, wagon, buggy and automobile traffic congestion, the city installed a metal plate in the middle of the square in 1913 with "KEEP RIGHT" embossed in large letters. Some merchants, including druggist Polk Gray, capitalized on the opportunity for a little light-hearted fun at the city's expense. He included a snarky traffic sign reference in his weekly ad.

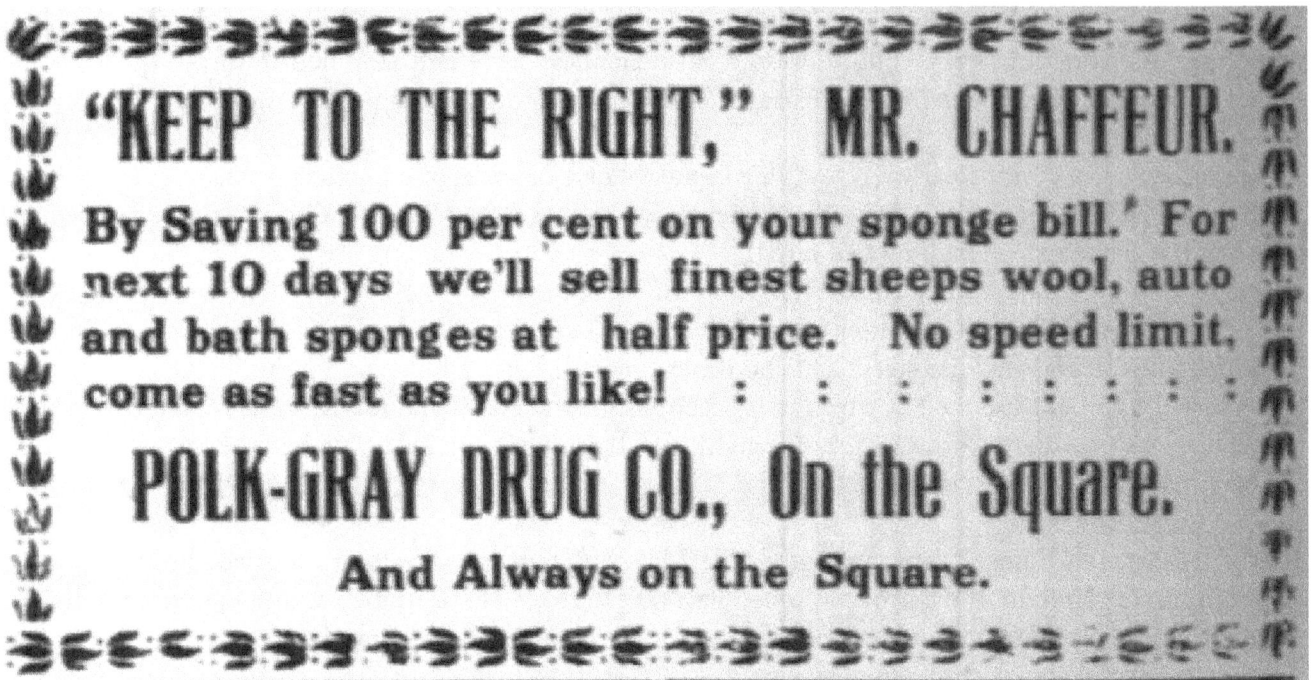

Polk Gray Drug advertisement, 1913 *Sentinel*

Another reaction to the "KEEP RIGHT" sign was a brief push to move the Confederate monument from the courthouse to the square. The idea was initiated by James Tharpe. Tharpe argued that the city had been "enforcing the law of the road about driving to the right and making the proper turn," and that it was a disgrace that what amounted to a dry goods box was being used for a marker in the center of such a beautiful town square. He said he had grown tired of seeing this box in such a prominent place and confessed that it was he who had, under the cover of darkness, removed the box and replaced it with a large urn holding a live plant.

Tharpe believed that the streets were sufficiently wide to hold the soldier monument, and besides, as the trees grew in the courthouse lot, the monument would become increasingly hidden from view. He also argued that the new People's Bank headquarters under construction next door to the courthouse would block the view. Tharpe, himself, had the perfect view of the monument from his 5&10 cent store and produce stand across the street from the courthouse. He was an interesting character whose 15 minutes of fame up to that point had been that he once owned and sold a valuable four-legged chicken.

Tharpe further suggested that an iron railing or iron post and chain system would fully protect the monument and would even add to the artistic effect. He said his proposal was supported by the Daughters of the Confederacy who had informed him that they were eager to see the monument on the square and would cover all expenses of moving it.

It only took a letter from Mayor J. C. Steele to put the "move the monument" campaign to rest. Steele countered that there was not enough room for the monument on the square, especially if the cannon and cannonballs, which were a package deal with the monument, were included in the move. He also didn't believe that the new bank building substantially blocked the view of the monument. And as for the tree growth, he said, "a beautiful grove of green leaves is the next prettiest thing to a beautiful girl surrounded by ornamental Flowers."

During the discussion someone else suggested that a tall marble water fountain with a circular horse trough at the base be installed at the intersection to block riders and drivers from making turns. Steele was quick to ixnay that notion as well. He didn't think a horse trough on the square was a fitting tribute for the center of such a beautiful city; and besides, Salisbury had just removed the fountain from their square because it was impeding traffic.

Not many people could (or would) argue with J. C. Steele, especially on monument-related matters. He, himself, was a Confederate veteran and was mayor when the monument was purchased and dedicated. And he was solely responsible for obtaining the cannon and balls from the War Department to flank the monument. There would be no monument without J. C. Steele, and it wasn't going to be moved without his blessing.

When Bert Bristol took the reins as mayor in 1917, his first official act was to change the speed limit for automobiles. There had been an ongoing battle between the buggy and wagon drivers and the automobile drivers. The former complained that their horses were becoming nervous wrecks and the lives of both them and their animals were being put in jeopardy by the reckless actions of the later.

Bristol set the speed limit at 15 miles-per-hour, and 10 miles-per-hour in alleys and when crossing the square. Speeds were calculated by the best guess of the police officer on duty and were usually upheld in the mayor's court, all the more reason to keep on the good side the of cop covering the downtown beat.

That same year, the city purchased seven "silent policemen" for the major intersections, including the square. These were substantial devices implanted in the ground in the middle of the intersection to slow drivers down and point them to the right.

In 1918 a man calling himself Dr. Speigel set up a stand on the square selling patent medicines. After a few days, he was notified that he owed sales taxes to the town for those sales. It wasn't a surprise when the tax collector discovered the doctor had quietly left town the next morning. The square was a great place for grifters to make a few sales and then skedaddle before the law got wind of them or before customers wised up to their scams and useless products.

Later in 1918, a military band from Camp Green in Charlotte was giving concerts on the square for the War Savings stamps campaign.

And on Sunday afternoon, October 20, 1918, international evangelist and Statesville native Rev. Caesar Allison, Jr., D.D. spoke from the square. The title of his sermon was "You Must be Born Again." Rev. Allison started the "colored Baptist church" in Statesville in 1874 before hitting the road for the Lord. He would return home between coast-to-coast tours and often hosted evening mini revivals on the square.

Rev. Caesar Allison, Jr., D.D. *Stimson*

Statesville's 1919 Fourth of July festival was the largest ever. It began with a parade featuring Confederate and "Great War" veterans riding in automobiles, followed by the Red Cross and the Mooresville and Statesville bands. People were ready to escape the lockdown brought about by the Spanish Influenza pandemic, and the 4th celebration was their first opportunity to leave their homes to enjoy and celebrate freedom again.

After the parade, the crowd gathered around a large stage on the square which was the center of the activities for the day. At noon, Lieutenants Mallory and Turnbull's airplane made its appearance. It circled high overhead then dived so close to the ground that the pilots could be seen waving from the cockpit, and its engine could be heard above the band. For 15 minutes it performed dives, somersaults, loops, and tail spins to the cheers of the spectators. There had been rumors that the pilots might attempt a landing on a nearby highway, so spectators had been warned not to rush to the scene if a landing occurred.

After the air show, Mayor Bristol delivered his 4th of July speech. Then some soldiers just back from the war in France spoke, including Lt. John Scott who expressed his appreciation to the town for the warm welcome being extended to returning soldiers. The ladies of the town then served a noon meal to 1,200 soldiers and guests. The town was decked out in red, white, and blue bunting and an army tank was brought in for the boys to climb on. Band concerts flooded the square and life after a deadly war and a deadly pandemic was once again good.

Soldiers returning from the Great War march down West Broad at Meeting Street *Stimson*

Red Cross float, 4th of July 1919 *Stimson*

In 1920 an automobile rally organized by the state Good Roads Boosters club packed 245 clattering machines into the four blocks around the square. A hundred years later, car shows continue to be a popular form of entertainment.

In the March 14, 1921 issue of the *Landmark*: "The city has hit on a scheme that may get the citizenship of the town up early in the morning. Saturday morning about 7:30, city authorities brought to the corner of the square nearest Kelly Clothing Co. cans containing about 65 gallons of blockade (confiscated illegal) liquor. The muzzles of the cans were turned first to the north and then to the west. Along the gutters of the west side of North Center and the north side of West Broad, a comparatively raging stream of liquor flowed. Some little boys and some grown men got into action along the stream, dammed up the flow and hustled to the backlots for Coca-Cola bottles or other receptacles which they filled from their improvised ponds."

The *Landmark* printed the following front-page story in June 1921: "For the 'Cop's' Comfort—Statesville has gone another step toward being more citified. Friday there was placed on the square a booth for the use of the traffic officer, a place in which he may stand protected from the weather and direct the movements of automobiles with a 'Go' and 'Stop' sign. A move in the right direction and a convenience to the 'cop' who is on the job."

A few months later it was announced that the "cop box" was being removed and would be replaced with a lighted box that didn't take up as much space and didn't require, well, a cop.

In an inventive show of school spirit, when the Statesville High football team defeated Lincolnton High 23-0 in 1921, students and cheerleaders, led by the team and their coach, formed a triumphant walking procession from the school on West Front Street to the square where each individual player received a rousing cheer.

On the 12th anniversary of the Boy Scouts in 1922, a re-induction ceremony was held on the square where Mayor Bert Bristol was made an honorary "tenderfoot" scout. He of course returned the favor with a stem-winder speech.

The square was the place to find 500-600 boys on May 3, 1924. The youngsters were marching in the Loyalty Day parade at the culmination of Boys Week, "a celebration of the potential manpower of the community's boys." A review stand was built on the sidewalk outside the First National Bank building manned by over 30 politicians, preachers, and business dignitaries. Local troops led several divisions of boys by the stand, including athletes from each of the sports teams at the high school and the boys from Barium Springs Orphanage. The community band performed lively march tunes while the spectators cheered each group of boys.

It was on a lazy spring evening in 1926 that an unusual flurry of cars passed by the square headed north. The paper later reported that a liberally attended chicken fight had been staged just north of town at which gate receipts were no meager sum. The number of out-of-state cars passing through was enough to attract the attention of the usual "stand-arounders" on the square who reported it to the editor.

In December 1926 store employees were asked to park a few blocks away from the square ten days before Christmas to allow shoppers ample parking spaces. Probably every year since, shop owners have to be reminded to leave the front-door parking spots open for their customers.

The Salvation Army held its first open-air service on the square in January 1927 to raise money for the needy in town. Also, on a Christmas shopping night that year, an impromptu fist fight on the square between two young boys drew several hundred spectators.

Arguably the darkest and most divisive day in the history of Statesville was Monday, July 4, 1927. That was the day the city hosted the annual convention of the Knights of the Ku Klux Klan of the Carolinas, attracting several thousand Klansmen from across North and South Carolina and Virginia.

Most downtown stores were closed for the 4th holiday, but the shopping district was still packed with out-of-towners and curiosity seekers. Hospitality stands with ice water were placed at all four corners of the square to welcome the robed conventioneers. Official Klan bands from Winston-Salem, Gastonia and Maiden were brought in by bus to perform. For the convenience of the visitors and their families, the

Patriotic Order of the Sons of America voted to leave their lodge hall in the Miller Block on the square open for guests to rest during the day.

At 1:00 the official ceremony, featuring members in formal regalia, took place at the convention headquarters at the Iredell Tobacco warehouse, 211-215 North Center, where the CVS store now stands. There were programs and speakers during the day and the women's auxiliary groups provided food.

At 8:00, the Knights saddled up for a horseback parade in full regalia, quite a spectacle for the people of town who came out on their porches and balconies to watch. They pranced across the square and stopped at the courthouse for the keynote speech from Dr. W. A. Hamlet of Atlanta, editor of the *Kourier*, the official propaganda organ of the Klan. Then at 9:30 the line proceeded to what's now the old Country Club area on Salisbury Road for the obligatory burning of the fiery cross and the climactic fireworks show.

The newspaper reported that the congestion on the streets was the greatest in the town's history. A "solid mass of humanity" lined the parade route causing a 15-minute standstill between Water Street and the square.

The Ramsey-Bowles Department Store had an unusual take on the spectacle. In their weekly ad they wrote, "It's commonly reported there will be 5,000 Ku Klux Klansmen here today. We would like for someone to introduce us to the white-goods buyer for this organization."

Underground trash receptacles were installed on Broad and Center Streets in 1929. The lids were flush with the sidewalk and operated by a foot pedal mechanism. A trash wagon made rounds once a day to empty the cans. The aldermen also passed an ordinance that year prohibiting peddlers from selling produce from their trucks parked on the main streets.

And in compliance with the tree conservation movement that was prevalent at the time, the Merchants Association voted in 1929 to end the tradition of placing decorated Christmas trees around the square. A replacement theme was not announced, but two years later the Scrooges had retreated (make that re-tree-ted), and the cedar Christmas trees were brought back.

In 1930 some of the electrical and telephone poles were removed around the square and new 600-candlepower lights were installed. That winter, 50 unemployed men were hired to join 30 city workers to shovel snow from the streets and sidewalks one block in each direction from the square.

In the summer of 1931, the North Carolina Firemen's Association Convention brought in 1,200 members from across the state. The day included firefighting demonstrations, races of all types, a bathing beauty contest, and a street parade. Broad Street was roped off down to Meeting Street for a 9 p.m. street dance to wrap up the festivities.

In the spring of 1932, another wedding took place on the square—well, sorta. Miss Emily Powell and Mr. James Stewart decided they wanted a different kind of ceremony. So, they tied the knot in the jump seats of an airplane just as it passed over the Statesville square. Rev. B. E. Morris from Western Avenue Baptist Church officiated his first and only aerial nuptial service, and Emily's sister was the sole bridesmaid in attendance.

Only six Civil War veterans participated in the 1932 Confederate Memorial Day ceremony and parade, one of them being 87-year-old A. D. Troutman who described in detail to those gathered on the street about being the last living member of a group of 100 local volunteers who mustered on that same square in 1861. He recalled the battles of Gettysburg and Petersburg as a calvary-man under Gen. Robert E. Lee and his imprisonment prior to his surrender at Appomattox.

The Merchants Association came up with an interesting promotion for their 1932 "Dollar Days." They hired "Professor Nemar" to put on a show. For an hour, while completely blindfolded, the professor drove a brand-new Ford in congested traffic up and down Broad and Center Streets.

Nemar to Drive Blindfolded Through Traffic on Business Streets Saturday

Professor Nemar hits town (surprisingly he didn't hit anything) *Daily Record*

In a 4:00 exhibition on the square, a committee of local citizens had blindfolded the "psychologist" by placing a silver dollar over each of his eyes, sealing them with adhesive tape, and then using 25 or 30 handkerchiefs and four or five layers of heavy black cloth to cover his entire face. As he drove around town, the professor would occasionally park his car in front of a business and, while still blindfolded, enter the store, and return with products that he would give away to lucky persons in the crowd, i.e., a tube of lipstick to the prettiest girl, stockings for the oldest woman, a comb and brush set to the baldest man, etc. Nemar's Ford was closely followed by another car carrying "Madame Nemar" who purportedly exercised mental control over Nemar and directed his car by telepathy. Adding to the theatrics, the Nemar vehicles were followed by the Bunch Funeral Home ambulance in case there was a problem.

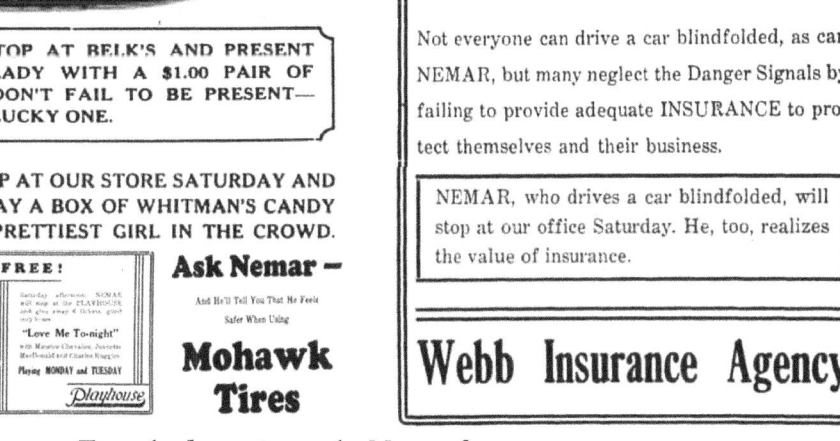

Daily Record **Everybody got in on the Nemar fun** *Daily Record*

The first big doin's on the square in 1933 was the President's Day celebration. The day started with a parade led by the Statesville High band, followed by the "presidential car" carrying a man dressed as president elect Roosevelt and the local calvary unit led by Captain Godfrey Kimball. After them came the local Boy Scouts, students from Barium Springs Orphanage, the American Legion, floats, and veterans. There was a "rube Band" playing "Happy Days are Here Again" and plenty of clowns along the way.

"Rube band" *Rickert*

At 12:30, people crowded into the square to witness, via the magic of radio, history being made. The swearing in of President Franklin D. Roosevelt was broadcasted live from Washington, D. C. An Atwater-Kent radio and loudspeaker system were set up by the Morris Battery & Radio Shop to carry the ceremony and the inaugural events that followed. Beforehand, the crowd was encouraged to "throw aside political partisanship for the day." No word on how that went.

1934 brought the usual parades. One difference in the American Legion parade was that all parked cars were removed from the parade route one block in each direction from the square. This allowed for the floats to get through easier. The annual May 10 Confederate Veterans parade was down to two survivors in attendance. As always, the parade proceeded to the Fourth Creek Cemetery. The high school band and Boy Scouts led the United Daughters of the Confederacy, the local calvary unit, and the War Mothers. The Children of the Confederacy carried flowers to decorate the graves of veterans.

The 1937 Shriner's parade from the Grace Hotel at Sharpe Street to the square drew a large crowd. The Oasis band and Oasis Drill and Bugle Corp. performed a concert and drill on the square.

New Year's Eve 1938 was called the liveliest in the town's history, as the square was thronged with revelers. The chimes of First Presbyterian Church, factory whistles on all sides of town, car horns, and tin horns joined the chorus led by the town clock at the stroke of midnight. Hundreds walked the streets making noise with anything they could find. The warm, noisy, boisterous welcome lasted for an hour into the new year.

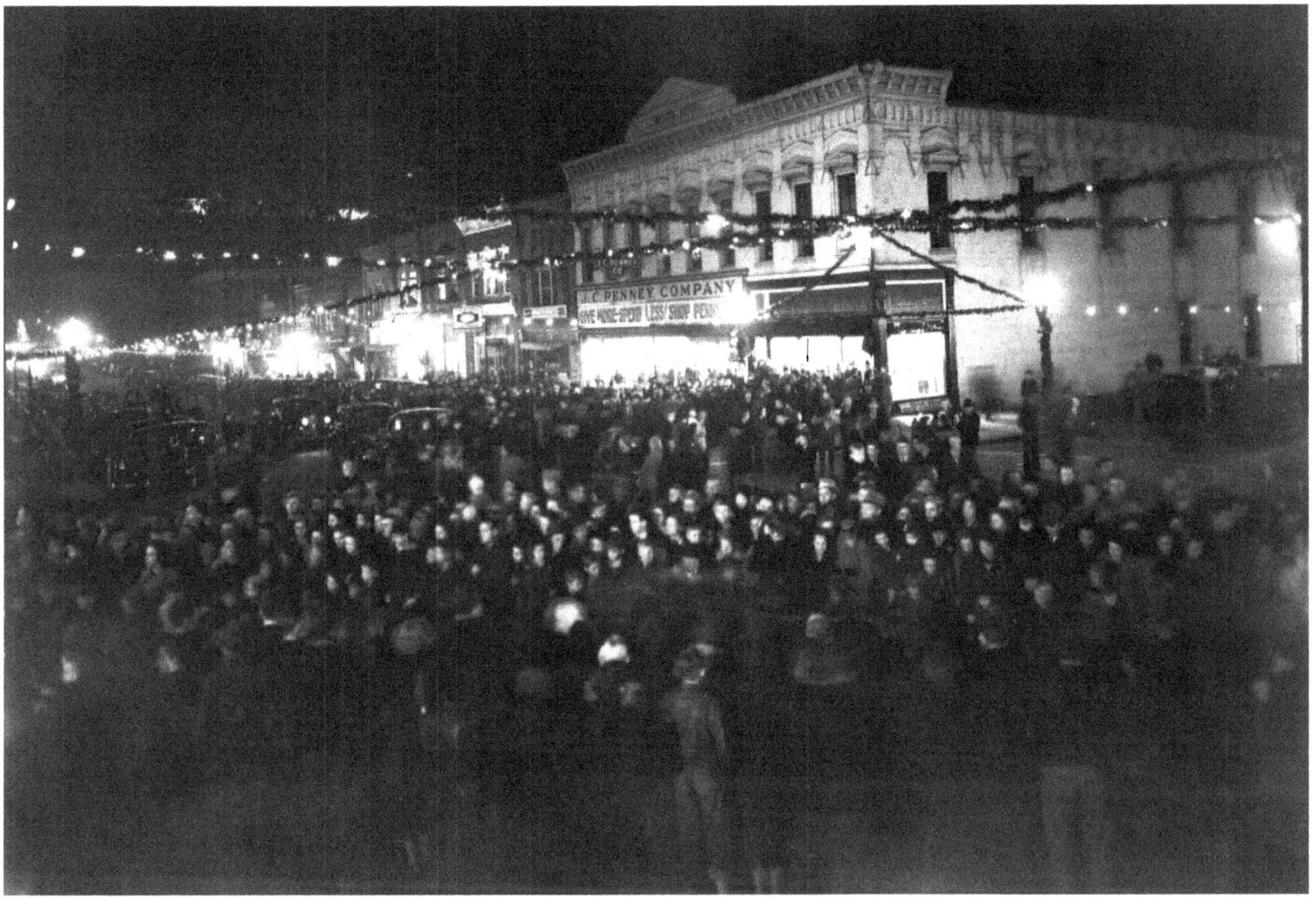

Celebrating on the square *Stimson*

The city ushered out 1938 in an equally enthusiastic way. Three thousand lights were strung on the two main streets when the Christmas Parade rolled through. Fire chief "Red" Gaither brought the department's flood light truck to the square and lit the place up like daylight. The parade, organized by the Junior Chamber of Commerce, started after dark to cash in on the light show. Prizes totaling $120 were given to the best float, best window decoration, and to the most students from each county and city school.

The Record

THE STATESVILLE RECORD

LARGEST CIRCULATION OF ANY NEWS PAPER PUBLISHED IN IREDELL COUNTY

MR. MERCHANT

STATESVILLE, N. C., FRIDAY, NOVEMBER 18, 1938 — TUESDAY AND FRIDAY

PARADE TO BE HELD HERE NEXT FRIDAY NIGHT

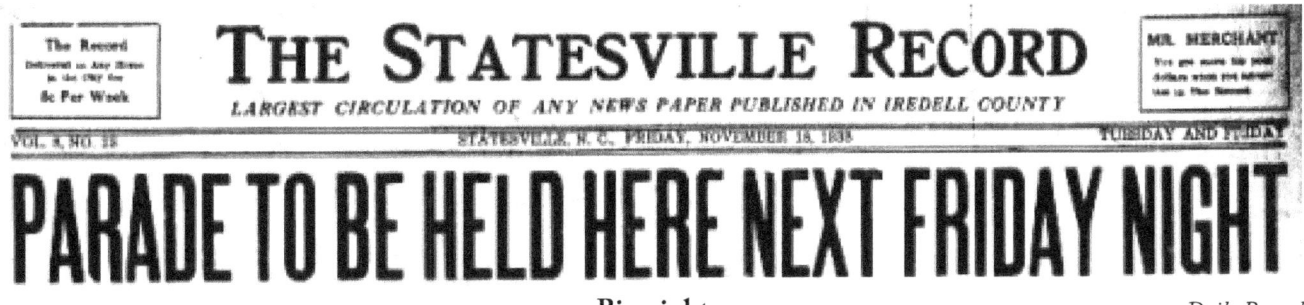

Big night *Daily Record*

There had been many traffic accidents on the square before the crash in April of 1939 that had everyone scratching their heads. That pile-up involved two bicycle riders, both traveling at a high rate of speed and making illegal left turns. One was the Postal Telegraph messenger on his way to deliver a telegram, and the other was the delivery boy for Hawkins Drug. Both claimed to have the green light; both ended up with wrecked bikes, and one with a hand laceration. But, if we're counting, Holmes Drug holds the record for most delivery bicycle wrecks with three.

Forever looking for a reason to throw a parade, Statesville found a new one April 28, 1939. The town was getting its first minor league baseball team—the Statesville Owls. The lineup started on the square and headed north to the brand-new baseball stadium behind the high school. It included police department units, the high school band in their new uniforms, the National Guard, Boy Scouts, Owls players, politicians, and the fire department. The procession ended in time for the dedication of the stadium and the game between the Owls and Newton-Conover.

In 1940 Tom Cooper, candidate for governor, parked his sound truck on the square and blasted his message through the streets to the displeasure of many shopkeepers within earshot.

Also in 1940, an alert citizen noticed that most of the cars parked up town that showed evidence of being from out-of-town had parking tickets slipped under their windshield wipers. He wrote to the paper remarking how this was a bad way to treat visitors to our town. He then discovered these weren't regular parking tickets. Each had a message printed on it that said "Howdy stranger. Make yourself at home. You are Statesville's guest, and the one-hour parking rule does not apply to you. Park here as long as you please. Ask the traffic officer or any citizen for any assistance or information. Of course, you will observe the marked parking lines for your protection. Come back soon." The cards were signed City of Statesville, J. Wesley Jones, mayor and W. S. Thomas, chief of police. A classy example of Statesville hospitality.

On October 27, 1941, World War I patriot and all-American hero Sergeant Alvin York spent a day in Statesville to promote the blockbuster movie "Sergeant York" staring Gary Cooper that was opening at both the Playhouse and State Theaters. Statesville was the fifth city in the country to premier the movie, following New York City, Washington, Nashville, and Los Angeles. Major I. C. Holloway, manager of the Playhouse, had served in the same division in France as York and was able to convince the powers in Hollywood to make Statesville an early release city.

Several thousand spectators braved the rain to welcome York at a speaker's stand built on the square for the occasion and to watch the mayor honor the hero with the key to the city and a declaration proclaiming, "Sergeant York Day."

SHC   The crowd awaits the arrival of Sergeant York   Tharpe

The 1941 Christmas parade took a different twist. As usual, it was proclaimed to be the biggest and best ever, but this year, the word "Christmas" was removed from name of the event. With the country at war in Europe, the Junior Chamber of Commerce and Merchants Association came up with a new theme for the parade, the "Friendship Day" parade. An American flag so big that it took 25 Boy Scouts to carry it was one of the highlights of the event.

Although there were no specifics given for the name-change, one might speculate that in addition to being a show of respect for the war effort, it was also a show of solidarity with the community's Jewish friends. It was billed as "a great unity celebration to bring together all the people of Iredell County." Organizers discouraged "those who are grouchy and grumble all the time" from attending Friendship Day.

The downtown decorations also looked different. The federal government had issued a nation-wide nighttime blackout, so street lighting was forbidden. Garland and tinsel were used instead. The blackout also forced the parade to be held for the first time on Saturday morning instead of Friday night. The upside was that 2,000 school children were able to participate in the festivities.

Non-electrical decorations, 1941 *Beck*

An Armistice Day parade was held in August of 1942. It formed at Mitchell College, paused at the square, then headed for the high school stadium where political speeches were delivered, and military maneuvers and demonstrations were performed by the 193rd Field Artillery Unit from Fort Bragg.

Armistice Day parade *SHC*

The friendship theme was a thing of the past and the Christmas parade was back in 1942 and the "grouchy grumblers" were undoubtedly invited back. Store owners agreed to close their doors at 3:00 p.m. to build enthusiasm for the parade. When they reopened at 7:00 that night, each of their stores had been transformed into its own Christmas wonderland. The town's first "singing Christmas tree" adorned the square and piped festive music into the streets.

The square suffered a major catastrophe on the night of February 17, 1943, when the N. B. Mills building, the most beautiful and ornate structure in town, burned. The Eagles 5 & 10 store that had just opened there was a total loss as was the federal ration board office upstairs. The fire started from an unknown source in the basement. Fortunately, a change in wind direction allowed firefighters to save the Efird's building next door.

With building materials and manpower in short supply due to the war effort, the Mills family immediately petitioned the federal War Production Board for permission to rebuild, but their request was denied. For the next five years, Statesville would, once again, be blighted with a vacant lot on the square.

Remains of N. B. Mills Building, 1943

Stimson

In a show of support for the local War Bond sales drive, a patriotic rally was held on the square on a September Saturday morning in '43. An armored car, jeeps, howitzers, and a 155-mm "Long Tom" cannon were on display, and a 30-piece Army band performed. A large thermometer was placed on the square to track the bond sales.

In order to enable more parents to attend parent-teacher meetings, bus service was run from the square to D. Matt Thompson School on P.T.A. nights in 1943. The bus left at 7:08 to get parents there for the 7:30 meetings.

In 1944 racketeers selling maps and magazine and newspaper subscriptions, that they had no intention of delivering, had become a problem on the square. They aggressively accosted everyone passing by. Shoppers were warned to avoid giving money to anyone selling products on the square. But some suckers couldn't resist. Eventually the scoundrels were run off.

On a fall morning in 1944, a great ruckus arose when a mutilated human figure was found suspended from wires in the center of the square. The newspaper sent a reporter to investigate and found that it was a stuffed dummy depicting a Monroe High School football player that had been hoisted there by some spirited Statesville High School students as a symbol of what their team planned to do to their opponent at the game that night. The students were planning to hold a pep rally on the square and then set fire to the dummy. And they followed through with the plan. The rally started with a "snake dance" parade (of course) from the library on West Broad to the square. After some chanting, cheering and effigy burning, students proceeded enthusiastically to the game. It is unknown whether the fire department was standing by.

Joining cities around the world, Statesville stopped what it was doing on Tuesday, May 8, 1945, to celebrate Victory in Europe day (V-E Day) and the end of World War II. Factory whistles blew, church bells rang, and people walked the streets cheering, laughing, and crying. Assistant police chief Charlie Rumple sounded the city's air raid siren. The downtown was filled with noise as drivers drove back and forth across the square with horns blasting. Stores closed at 10:30 a.m. and the area churches opened their doors at 11:00 for services to give praise and thanks for the end to six years of war.

In 1946, with no war to fret about, the citizens refocused their complaints on how long it took them to drive through town. Congestion had gotten so bad that traffic was backing up for a block in all directions. In February the aldermen banned turns on the square on Saturdays and there was an increased effort by police to clamp down on double parking on Broad and Center. Later in the year, all turns were prohibited 24-7 and a policeman was posted there with a whistle to wave traffic through. Left turns to and from Center at Court Street were also made unlawful.

If traffic wasn't enough to get folks riled, some started complaining about the mailbox on the square. It seems that patrons were having difficulty placing letters in it because it was the community congregation place for old men to stand around and gossip. According to a complaint to the newspaper, sometimes up to four men were leaning on the box at a time making it inaccessible to the public.

Earlier there had been complaints about the green mailbox outside Holmes Drug that was used by downtown postal carriers for short-time storage while they were making their rounds. It was a typical looking postal box but lacked the usual blue paint and deposit slot; but that didn't stop patrons from trying to figure out a way to slip a letter into it. Apparently, the gossipers didn't lean on it.

Also, that year, another strategy to reduce traffic congestion was to move the city bus stops from the square to the front of the courthouse. The extra-long bus parking spaces remained for a while, and it didn't take long for motorists to put the former bus stops to good use.

The Penny Brothers Allstar String and Brass Band presented a free Saturday morning concert on the square in the summer of '46. It was an advertising gimmick they used to lure crowds to their sales. After the concert, the brothers, who called themselves the state's original twin auctioneers, encouraged the crowd to follow them down Center and then over to Meeting Street where they auctioned off 50 residential building lots.

The Penny Brothers worked frequently in Statesville   SHC

On Easter morning 1947, the 20-member-strong Statesville Community Band assembled on the square at 2:00 a.m. for a holiday music concert. They then boarded a Statesville Motor Coach bus that carried them around town performing holiday spiritual songs at various stops. They ended the tour with a sunrise concert in front of Mitchell College.

On April 8 and 9 a truck carrying a traveling museum of captured secret WWII weapons parked on the square for public purview. It included a suicide weapon developed during the war. The free exhibit was sponsored by the Navy Club of U. S. A.

Another truck parked on the square for a couple days later in the month displaying property from the War Assets Administration. A few weeks after that, the U. S. Army mobile recruiting station was parked there for three days signing up recruits and reservists.

In 1951 the Crusade for Freedom motorcade parked on the square for a day giving demonstrations on how America was fighting Communism behind the Iron Curtain. Several hundred spectators witnessed the launch of a helium balloon filled with pamphlets. It was designed to burst at 30,000 feet and scatter the fliers over several miles.

WWII Secret Weapons traveling museum *Daily Record*

On the civilian front that year, shoppers complained about a racketeer from Newton accosting them scalping raffle tickets for a new automobile that was parked on the square. Later that month the world-famous magician MacDonald Birch performed at Mac Gray Auditorium to raise money for the school's free lunch program. Birch escaped from a sturdy wooden crate constructed for the occasion by G. L. Wilson Building Company. The crate had been placed on display on the square for a week before the performance so the public could test its sturdiness and ensure there were no sliding walls, fake floor, or hidden compartments.

CHALLENGE!
THE G. L. WILSON BLDG. CO.
Challenges Birch to Escape From the Strong Packing Box Displayed on the Square
BOX WILL BE RENAILED ON THE STAGE BY A COMMITTEE FROM THE AUDIENCE
BIRCH
Accepts the Challenge
TEST TO TAKE PLACE ON THE STAGE
High School Auditorium
April 21

Daily Record   **MacDonald Birch the Magician**   *Daily Record*

A gust of wind had shoppers scrambling around the square one fall afternoon when it removed a gentleman's hat along with the stack of cash he had been carrying under it. A policeman helped him gather his hat and money and the scene settled back down to normal.

During the 1947 Christmas season, the Merchant's Association turned the "burnt corner," the former Mills Building corner, into the largest and most elaborate Christmas display in the city's history. The cost was estimated at $3,000 with city aldermen donating a third of the cost. A raised stage was built for a nativity display and smaller stages held bands and carolers. For the first time since the beginning of the war, the city was allowed to provide power for lighting holiday decorations. Santa pulled up on top of a big red fire truck on December 9 and made the place his headquarters until the big day.

Chamber of Commerce president, Lonnie Mills, made a New Year's resolution for 1948—to put a new building on his family's property on the southwest corner of the square that had been vacant for five years. A. W. Bunch vowed to do the same on his lot on the southeast corner of West Broad and Meeting that had been empty for 3½ years. Mills fulfilled his resolution but was a few months late. Unfortunately, the buildings shared the same non-descript architectural style. "Sidewalk engineers" keeping an eye on the Eagle's store construction on the square wondered aloud why designers didn't put any windows on the West Broad side of the building. Decorative faux windows were added in recent years.

And on the weather front, Gloria Holmes and Minnie Sain fried an egg on the sidewalk in front of Holmes Drug in July 1948.

Egg frying on the square *Daily Record*

The Christmas parade that year, advertised as being a mile long and, as usual, the most elaborate ever, crossed the square twice, once on Broad and again on Center. It included five bands, 11 beauty queens, the 50-member local National Guard unit and 16 gigantic balloons trucked in from Charlotte.

A tractor-trailer stage was parked on the square for the crowning of Miss Merry Christmas, Sibyl White from Scotts High. Stores closed at 4:00 for the 5:30 start time and reopened immediately afterwards. The winner of the shop window decoration contest was postponed until the next day because the sidewalks were too crowded for the judges to get around to all the stores. Attendance was estimated at 35,000.

Tharpe   **Christmas 1948, National Guard keeps the crowd back while Santa crowns the queen**   *Tharpe*

Tharpe.   **Hungry hippo**   **Sibyl White Miss Merry Christmas '48**   *Tharpe*

In 1949 the Statesville Lions Club parked a truck on the square for their annual broom sale. The Lions had already purchased property beside Statesville High School for a new football stadium, and broom and doormat profits went to start the construction. Their broom stand on the square became an annual affair that lasted many years.

The brooms had been made by blind craftsmen at the Guilford Industry for the Blind in Greensboro. Campaign chairman James Epperson said, "blind people made the brooms, but the profit from their sales will be used by those with the ability to see football games." Before grading began on the football field, G. L. Wilson Building Co. had to move Free Nancy Creek from the middle of the site to the base of the hill where it flows today.

Lions Club broom sale *Tharpe*

The square was also where the Civitan's sold their fruit cakes, the Red Cross thermometer tracked blood donations, and the Heart Fund, March of Dimes, Easter Seals, United Way, etc., launched their campaigns. And it was the perfect location for Girl Scouts to hawk their cookies each year. The rule of thumb was, if you wanted it to be seen or heard, put it on the square.

The '49 Christmas parade was even bigger and better, of course, with 600 musicians, seven bands and 24 beauty queens from Iredell and Alexander Counties. The big balloons were back, but with different characters, and the new twist was a floodlight system that illuminated the parade from the college to the square. An organ with loudspeakers was placed on the roof of the Playhouse Theater building to blast holiday music to the city and as far as three miles away.

In a stunt to draw attention to the importance of voting, the Statesville Jaycees posted "Squawky the Duck" on the square on the Saturday before the 1950 primary and election. Squawky typified the person who doesn't register or vote but complains about the government.

Over the years the square has been the scene of numerous catastrophes, car wrecks, struck pedestrians, etc. But an especially serious one happened in 1950. Statesville fireman Lee Black attempted to jump on the hook and ladder truck as it crossed the square. It had just pulled out of the station a half-a-block away while Black was up the street. Black's hand slipped off the rail and he fell under the dual rear wheels of the truck. He waved for the driver to continue without him. He suffered a fractured pelvis and shock and remained in the hospital for three months.
Eighteen years later, the city's new 11-ton American LaFrance fire engine started what was at the time said to be the costliest accident in the city's history. The truck was rushing through the square to a fire when it took out six cars in a chain reaction crash.

An exact replica of the Miss Liberty Bell in Philadelphia passed through town promoting U. S. savings bonds and was displayed on the square from 3:30 until 6:00 on a Tuesday in 1950. A welcoming ceremony was held at 5:30 sponsored by Carolina Motor Company.

Liberty Bell replica on display *Daily Record*

It wasn't long after new benches had been placed on the square that "assistant custodian of the square," Pete Beck, was inviting the public to enjoy a seat there, but requesting they quit spitting on the sidewalk and sticking their chewing gum on the benches. Pete was given his title by the newspaper editor but was more often called "the mayor of the square." He was actually a city bus driver, and his route began and ended at the square. His riders used the benches while waiting for the bus, so he felt it was his duty to keep them clean for his customers. He continued keeping the seats spic-and-span after they were moved down to the front of the courthouse.

Beck   **Ray "Pete" Beck**   *Daily Record*

Truckload of clowns, circa 1940   *Ramsey*

Chapter 8

1950s–1980s

1950s-1980s

In 1950 city leaders began fielding complaints about the poor downtown street lighting. Mayor Pro-Tem Ben Ramsey admitted that "the lighting system uptown is so poor it makes the square an ideal parking place for courting couples." The *Daily Record* editor took it upon himself to count the number of burned-out streetlights between the square and the Vance—a dozen. He reported that after the stores turned out their lights at night, the streets were dark.

The dark streets may have been a contributing factor to the theft of the "No Left Turn" sign one morning from its securely bolted spot in the middle of the square. At 3:30 a.m., someone drove up, unbolted it, and drove away with it. Officer "Red" Lane who was on patrol near the post office witnessed the larceny, but by the time he ran to the square the thieves were gone.

The Statesville square was even the subject of a play called "Broad and Center," a comedy written by Dr. Charles Darby and performed on the Mac Gray auditorium stage in 1951. The show was set on the square where real-life citizens were characterized by actors as they walked across the stage. The audience was challenged to figure out the identities of the citizens the actors were mocking.

The performers were a who's-who of local leaders, including eight ministers who dressed as convicts and sang "The Prisoner's song." Judge Fred Hedrick sang several songs, as did police officers, the city manager, the high school principal, etc. Some controversial subjects were included in the script such as the recent election, high electric rates, traffic congestion, and rivalries between downtown businessmen. The Lion's Club sponsored the fun night.

On October 11, 1951, there was quite a stir in front of Statesville Drug store. Movie star Penny Edwards was in town promoting a new feature film showing at the Playhouse Theatre. At 1:00 a throng of spectators assembled on the square where Edwards was interviewed live on WSIC radio and given a key to the city.

Earlier that morning Ms. Edwards had surprised the students at Statesville High with a visit. She had starred in "That Hagen Girl" with Shirley Temple, "Two Guys from Texas" with Donald O'Connor, "Ziegfeld Follies," several Roy Rogers movies, and was at the time working on a film with John Wayne entitled "Wings Across the Pacific." Her TV roles included, "Wagon Train," Bonanza," and "The Red Skelton Show." She was also involved in several commercials, appearing as "The Lux Girl," "The Palmolive Girl," and "The Tiparillo Girl." And for a few brief moments, she was, "The Statesville Girl."

According to Edwards biography, enormously popular cowgirl Dale Evans chose Penny to replace her in her husband Roy Rogers' movies (Evans was pregnant), predominantly because of Penny's strong religious background. Edwards was once romantically involved with Ronald Reagan in the late 1940s when he was between marriages to Jane Wyman and Nancy Reagan. She was 17 years younger than Reagan and her religious upbringing reportedly eventually stopped her relationship with the future president.

Tharpe   **Movie star Penny Edwards in 1951**   *Tharpe*

Tharpe **Trying to catch a glimpse**   **Penny's morning appearance at Statesville High parking lot** *Tharpe*

The Iredell County Health Department parked the mobile X-ray unit on the square regularly in 1952 to give free X-rays for tuberculous screening to anyone 15-years old and older. In the first two days, 1,437 procedures were administered.

Yet another traveling exhibit was parked on the square for a few days in May 1952. This one carried an animated "wax copy" of a famous Leonardo di Vinci religious painting. The free tour was sponsored by the Lion's Club. Donations were encouraged to help the blind in the county.

"Babe in Manger" *Daily Record*

In May of '52, South Center was closed from the square to Court Street for two days for the Iredell County Dairyland Festival that included two parades, dances, and livestock exhibits. Local businesses pledged $5,000 to support the event.

Cooper Street was also closed. Tents were erected to hold 300 cows, reminding old-timers of the days when that area was surrounded by stockyards and livery stables. Approximately 18 candidates for public office participated in a cow milking contest. A Friday night square dance exhibition by Sam Queen and his Soco Gap dance team drew several thousand spectators with local celebrity Dwight Barker and the Melody Boys supplying the stringed music.

The Dairy Festival beauty queen competition drew contestants from 14 counties. Pens built in the lobbies of two banks and the Vance Hotel became homes to three lucky calves for the week.

Tharpe   **Dairyland Festival parade**   *Daily Record*

The festival brought to town cowboy movie star Don "Red" Berry and his host of western musicians for three stage shows on the square and then two impressive romps through the streets on his horse, first in the kid's pet parade, followed by the big parade.

Earlier, in the day Berry ate lunch at Barium Springs Orphanage where he told the children there that he, too, was an orphan. His parting cowboy-esque words of encouragement to them were, "always be kind to others and you'll get along alright in this world."

One attendee who got to meet Red remembered that he reeked strongly of alcohol.

Tharpe "Red" posing for a fan

"Red" at Barium Springs *Tharpe*

Cowboy movie star Don "Red" Berry *Tharpe*

A wrecked car was parked on the square for a week preceding the annual Red Cross blood drive in 1952. Signs proclaiming, "Don't Spill Your Blood, Give it to the Red Cross" adorned the car and city policeman "Red" Lane (not to be confused with "Red" Berry) spent the afternoons sharing with curious observers the gory details surrounding the accident.

Policeman "Red" Lane discussing the wreck *Daily Record*

In 1953 the fire and police stations were moved from North Center Street, just a half block from the square, to the new station on South Meeting Street, three blocks from the square. In order to make up for the increased distance, a police telephone call box was installed on the northeast corner beside Holmes Drug to help shorten emergency response time.

In 1953 the *Record & Landmark* declared war on nefarious extracurricular nighttime activities on the square. In the front page "Down in Iredell" column, the editor wrote: "We would suggest that officers could better spend their time cleaning up the necking parties and smooching displays which go on in cars parked under the full glare of street-lights around the square." "Let's not teach our children it's alright to neck on the square."

The editor was fired up by a letter he received from an out-of-town visitor and her husband who had taken a Sunday evening stroll around the square. They wrote: "The thing we saw was sickening. At 9 p.m. we counted over 15 cars in one block with from one to three couples in them, parked and doing obvious petting." (It would appear, at least, that the streetlights were finally working.)

The editor agreed. On Sunday evenings "in car after car there is flagrant, open, public necking, with the participants oblivious to passersby, coming up only occasionally for air." "Youngsters by the dozens, breathing down each other's necks in hot intimate contact, and we walk by, turn our heads and say, 'thank God for Statesville where we know how to keep the Sabbath.'" That sarcastic comment was in reference to the new city ordinance that forced movie theaters to close on Sundays "for fear they might corrupt the morals of the youth."

A mother quickly countered with a letter stating that she was glad teens were parking and courting under the safety of "the brightest lights in North Carolina." "Who has ever heard of a couple being murdered under the streetlights of Statesville?" She had a point there. A host of teenagers also took exception to the "peeping Tom" visitors and joined in the letter writing fray to suggest there was nothing to do in town on Sunday nights except to engage in unwholesome conduct on the square. That same "there's nothing for teenagers to do around here" complaint has been a reoccurring theme around Statesville, and probably most small towns, since the beginning of time.

The public necking war at least gave the "no turn on the square" drama a brief respite, but the ire of the civic controversy connoisseurs quickly turned to a new problem—loud mufflers. As gutted mufflers, Hollywood mufflers, and straight pipes became popular among the hot rod crowd, police were urged to better enforce the difficult-to-enforce noise ordinance. A young writer to the paper said, "You can't drive through town without violating some law, and if you don't bypass the square, some policeman will see those twin pipes and be down on his hands and knees to see what kind of muffler you have and whether it's making too much noise."

Other writers argued that the trucks and buses passing through town made even more noise than a car muffler. They must have been really steamed when a week later, the Atlantic Greyhound company parked one of their new "Scenicruiser" highway coaches on the square from noon until 3 for public inspection. And then at 3:00, city officials and civic leaders were given a 30-minute cruise around town in the huge noise maker.

For the 1955 August Dollar Days, the fire department ladder truck was parked on the square and gift certificates were dropped from two stories up into the eager hands of shoppers. The Greyhounds football homecoming pep rally was held on the square again that year and team captain Butch Allie had the honor of torching the, by that time traditional, straw stuffed mannequin representing the Thomasville team.

In January 1956 the March of Dimes parade against polio began and ended at the square, with a march around town in between. Love Valley's founder, promoter, and real-life cowboy Andy Barker was the marshal (I bet Andy could whup "Red" Berry).

In September, the downtown was turned over to the state's Shriners for their first official convention in Statesville since 1941. They had a parade, and the Oasis Temple Patrol performed one of their crackerjack shows on the square. A few weeks later, the season opener SHS football game was celebrated with a "snake dance" to the square followed by a rally and impromptu pep band concert. They repeated the process for the homecoming game.

For the '56 Christmas season, the city borrowed 21 35-foot poles from Southern Bell Telephone to support the 14,000 downtown Yule lights city workers hung (up from only 2,500 lights the year before). Cowboy TV and movie star William Boyd, better known as Hopalong Cassidy, was the parade marshal. Ah, the sight of Hoppy leading the pack and Santa bringing up the rear was stuff children's dreams were made of (not sure Andy could whup Hoppy).

On the Superior Dairies car **Christmas Queen Glenda Wilson** **Hoppy and his fans** *Love*

July 30, 1957, marked the beginning of Statesville's first, and possibly only, 10-day mustache growing contest. The contest culminated on the square on Saturday, August 10 where a group of ladies inspected the contestants and determined the winner based on beauty, poise, and perfection. Before the event, the newspaper took the liberty to doctor photos of some of the towns contestants to get an idea of how they might look after ten days. The event was part of Old-Fashioned Bargain Days.

Sheriff Charlie Rumple, 4th from the left; policeman Casey Jones, 5th; radio announcer Garrett Allen, 8th

Master promoter Andy Barker chaired the Christmas parade committee in 1958. And he didn't disappoint. He promised "more surprises than could be found under the mistletoe." A month before the event, he announced that the theme for the parade would be, of all things, turkeys. Twelve turkeys would be roosting on one of the floats and released one at a time at various intervals along the parade route. The persons who caught them got to keep them. Then at the end of the parade, a band concert would be held on the square during which more turkeys would be dropped out of second-story windows onto the crowd below. As they fluttered and flapped their way to the street, lucky winners would gobble them up and take them home.

Andy's plan got folks talking…a lot. Businesses included turkey references in their advertising, civic groups held turkey dinners, and the grocery stores pushed turkey sales. The scheme to pump some excitement into the yearly event worked. As promised, the Dunbar High band from Mooresville did provide music immediately after Santa's sleigh passed by, but the newspaper's recap of the evening's festivities made no mention of turkeys. Whether Andy delivered on his turkey plan is not known, but he did deliver an estimated 40-50,000 parade watchers.

Saturday, May 2, 1959, was "Straw Hat Day." The first 100 men to show up at the square wearing a straw hat got a free ticket to the Playhouse Theater.

Later that year, 22-year-old WSIC announcer, Bob Marlowe, attempted to set the national record for the longest radio broadcast from a mobile studio. He parked the station's Volkswagen bus on the square at noon on Friday and settled in for the long haul. By 8:00 Monday morning he had broken the state record of 68 hours, set by an Asheville disc jockey. Dr. John Stegall was brought in to examine the marathon man, one of five medical exams he received. Dr. Stegall reported that the patient was in good shape except for a swollen tongue and sore throat. The doctor recommended that Bob lay off the cigarettes, so he switched to menthols for a day. On Monday afternoon during a baseball game broadcast, colleagues had to pour ice water over the announcer's head when it appeared he had blacked out.

Bob said he felt like a monkey in a cage. People surrounded the van day and night. WSIC employees made sure he was never alone more than five minutes at a time. He had been warned that going that long without sleep could cause temporary insanity. He said at one point he did see a man with green hair walk across the square, but was assured by onlookers that the man really did have green hair. And, unlike today, not many people had green hair in 1959.

Newton **The van with colleague Jeff Watts**

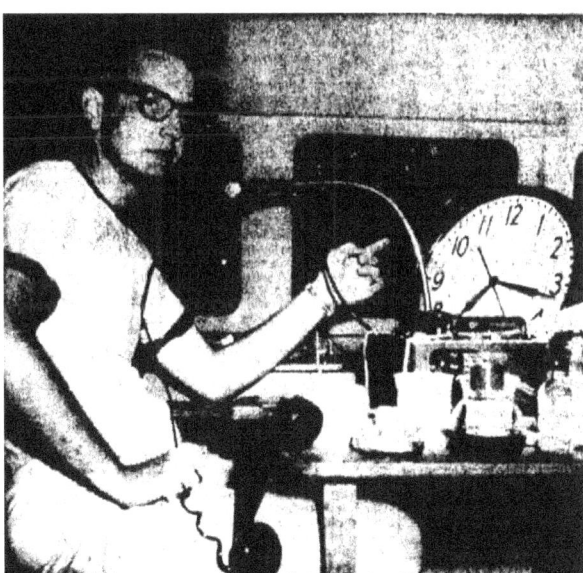

Bob the "Marathon Man" *Record & Landmark*

On Tuesday, September 1, at 7:00 a. m. Bob set the national record. He continued for another four hours and 31 minutes before falling asleep. He was carried by ambulance from the square to his home where he slept for 19 ½ hours.

The city's first "walk-don't walk" lights were installed on the square in 1960, the year the city earned first place and the grand prize in the American Automobile Association National Pedestrian Protection Contest with the highest score ever obtained by a city, regardless of size.

Fuller Sams, owner of the theaters in town was the master of innovative marketing. In 1960 he and Miss Helen Johnson, manager of the State Theater, conducted an experiment to determine if the people of Statesville had a "touch of larceny" in their hearts. Coincidentally the movie "A Touch of Larceny" was starting that week at the State Theater. With the help of *Record & Landmark* reporter Sylvia Carson and photographer Tom West, four wallets were discretely dropped onto different busy downtown sidewalks, including the square, to see what would happen. Tom hid in a car and snapped photos of each finder. The wallets contained small amounts of cash, change, keys, and Helen's contact info.

In each instance, the wallets were returned either to Helen or the police station within minutes, and each time the finder refused to accept the money as a reward. One girl even ran all the way to the police station. It's good they were honest because the paper published photos of the four picking up the wallets in the next day's paper and praised them for being model citizens.

The Statesville Owls minor league baseball team sponsored a "mystery man" contest in the spring of 1962. The mystery man mingled near the square between 10:00 and noon. The first person to identify him won some prizes, including tickets to the game against Newton.

Old Fashioned Bargain Days in 1963 transformed the downtown into a cowboy movie shoot. Six covered wagons and a stagecoach from Love Valley were parked on the streets for shoppers to paw over. And a greased pig was released for some lucky person to catch and redeem for prizes.

A booth was built on the square for military recruiters in 1964. In January a lady Ice Capades member joined the Navy recruiter there and attracted a lot of interest. But it was "Bunny Days" that captured the most attention. Two human-sized stuffed bunnies were enclosed in glass cases on the square for three weeks before Easter and then given away to two lucky shoppers. And over 750 smaller bunnies were given away during the Merchants Association promotion.

Yet another traffic engineer was hired in '64 to study the bottle neck at the square. He recommended that the "no turns" restriction in effect on Saturdays be extended to Fridays between 4 and 9 p.m. So, city council put the plan into place.

Dancing "Go-go girls" were positioned on the square on a Thursday in 1966 to raise money for the Iredell County United Fund's one-day drive, probably leading to more snarled traffic. Each time the donation thermometer rose another thousand dollars, music would play, and the go-go girls would dance. The girls must have worked hard because over $52,000 was raised.

The first murmurs that the face of downtown Statesville was about to forever change came in 1966 with an announcement of a new shopping destination east of town—Newtowne Plaza Shopping Center. The anchor would be Kings department store, a national chain operation from Newton, Mass. offering a wide array of moderately priced products. Could it be possible that the downtown might not be the main shopping district in the county forever? Just might.

Ralph Sloan, an elderly downtown businessman, local historian, and respected gentleman philosopher presented a plan to save the downtown business district from the invasion of shopping centers. In a *Record & Landmark* front page piece, Sloan wrote:

"For a long time, I have been concerned about what would happen to the Uptown area if shopping centers hit Statesville. In a letter to you several years ago, I compared my idea of a shopping center to a terrible monster, reared up and about to devour the business section. I would like to advance my idea as to what should be done."

"First, buy the property lying on Tradd Street between Water Street to a point just East of the Curlee Appliance store and make it into a gigantic parking lot with covered walkways leading to Center and Broad Streets. Second, on North Center, make a two-way underground vehicular tunnel with a large subterranean roof under the square as a waiting room for car passengers to embark and alight and with stairways leading to the surface on each corner of the square."

"And third, make a mall beginning at the AARP Church alley and running to the intersection of Meeting Street, and beginning at a point halfway down North Center from the square and extending southward to Front Street. This area would be covered with transparent plastic at a height of about 25 feet."

All traffic would be prohibited from Cooper Street to Meeting, and the traffic ordinarily on Center would be underground. The area under this roof could be completely air conditioned in the summer and heated during the winter period. The openings into the mall section would be closed, with quick opening doors at each entrance in case of emergency."

"The closed passages to the parking area would also be air conditioned. The ground area under the mall would be landscaped with fountains, trees, plants, flower beds, and grass, and with benches scattered all around. Anyone with a degree in imagination can visualize the beautiful sight it would make and the great comfort it would afford shoppers who would be drawn to Statesville from miles around."

He concluded, "Afterall, Statesville is not quite dead and such a rejuvenation would give it a new life."

A roof over the streets around the square had been a pipe dream for a handful of futurists since the early 1900s. Sloan's prediction of a dying uptown was laughed off at the time, but he would soon be proven right.

One must wonder what would have happened if the major parts of his plan had been implemented. Would the threats to the vitality of the city's shopping district by outlying shopping centers have been delayed or thwarted? Probably not, but interestingly when architects designed the 2010 "streetscape" plan, some of Ralph's tamer ideas were included.

By the close of 1966, the downtown exodus had begun as 12 storefronts near the square were vacant.

Sadly for baby boomers, there were no Christmas parades in 1963, 1964 or 1965. But the tradition was reignited in 1966. That year Santa arrived via the Batmobile.

In 1967 "little pixies" were the downtown Christmas theme. The "grand pixie," called the Christmas Imp, was a giant 15-foot nightmare inspiring creature that was prominently placed to stare down shoppers as they crossed Center Street at the square. The Merchants Association said the pixies were chosen with children in mind, but Alfred Hitchcock couldn't have picked a better creature to scare little kiddies. City employee Robert Turner had the embarrassing task of hanging the worst Christmas decorations in the history of the town.

Robert Turner hanging the Christmas Imp *Tharpe*

One of the town's most popular shopping promotions was Moonlight Madness. On a Friday night in the fall, stores would close from 6-7:00 p.m. to mark down their prices. At 7:00 they would open their doors and magically the isles would be packed with customers until 10:00. Moonlight Madness began in 1967 and continued into the mid 70s when the idea was borrowed (or stolen) by the stores at Signal Hill Mall.

Moonlight Madness organizers *SHC*

In 1968 city workers began cutting 4-foot square holes into the sidewalks on Broad and Center, one block in each direction from the square. Downtown merchants placed dogwood trees in the squares as part of a major beautification initiative. This wasn't a new plan. In the early 1900s the city streets had been lined with tall elm shade trees. The newspaper editor pushed the dogwood project suggesting that it takes more than bricks and mortar to draw people to the heart of our city. It takes a touch of beauty, a bit of comfort and an air of hospitality. The dogwoods helped with that.

Dogwood planting *SHC*

In the early 1970s both North Iredell and Statesville High Schools held their homecoming parades downtown with special activities on the square.

In 1972 a giant candle replaced the traditional Christmas tree that hung in the middle of the square. WBTV cowboy personality Fred Kirby was the Christmas parade marshal riding his horse Calico. Fred was a familiar face around town. He appeared at live theater shows and at store grand openings from time to time.

In July 1973 the square was the backdrop for the Iredell County Rescue Squad to show off their emergency equipment. And the Fantasyland Train depot was located on the square as part of Old-Fashioned Bargain Days. The miniature engine, "Cinderella Coach," followed by "Happy Pumpkin Coach" and "Little Caboose," could haul 54 small passengers per trip around town. It was so popular that the Merchants Association brought it back the following summer.

SHC   **Old Fashioned Bargain Days**   *SHC*

Charlotte broadcaster Doug Mayes came up with a new feature for the 6:00 WBTV newscast in 1974. He would visit Carolina communities and invite folks to "get what's on your mind off your chest." He spent several hours on the Statesville square on April 9 listening to the concerns of locals. Whew! Fortunately, and surprisingly, nothing controversial resulted from his visit.

Record & Landmark   **Charlotte TV man Doug Mayes "On the Square" feature 1976**   *Record & Landmark*

During the late 70s, Ralph Sloan was back at it pushing an updated draft of his plan to ensure the long-term vitality of the downtown area. Again, he proposed a roof, or "bubble" as he called it, over the four blocks surrounding the square. His plan included a tunnel down Center Street from Water to Sharpe Streets. Steps at the square would lead to underground restrooms and waiting areas similar to those in a railroad station. An above ground public transportation system would provide access to and from the square from outlying parking areas. Sloan believed the avant-garde system he had promoted for years would relieve traffic congestion, provide shoppers with a unique shopping experience, and save Downtown Statesville.

The 1977 Christmas parade featured two crowd favorites, WBTV personalities Fred Kirby and Ty Boyd. Boyd was a native of Statesville and SHS graduate. Santa broke character and danced on the square with a clogging troupe. Of course, both the kids and adults loved it.

The community was inspired by one particular participant in the 1,200-strong March of Dimes Super Walk through the downtown on a blustery Saturday in 1979. Local Vietnam War nine-times-decorated, and triple-amputee hero Dale Wilson, completed the four-mile walk on artificial legs and crutches.

The late 1970s saw stagnant business traffic and lots of empty buildings in need of repair, despite a brief effort to breathe life back into the downtown in '78. A revitalization committee was formed, and a new theme was born— "Olde Town Statesville." But within a year, the only change was the parking configuration on Broad Street from parallel to diagonal. The committee threw in the towel admitting that "the merchants expected the committee to do something, and the committee expected the merchants to do something, and it ended up with nothing getting done." For the next several years, high interest rates and bankers who labeled the downtown as "depressed" made it difficult for potential new merchants to get funding.

Although the storefronts on the square remained occupied, there were many vacant buildings in the shopping district during the early 1980s. Signal Hill Mall had become the shopping destination of choice and most of the downtown businesses were smaller family operations selling specialized products. By 1982, 22 vacant buildings dotted the concrete landscape.

But that year a downtown improvement master plan was implemented by Statesville Main Street director Hillary Greenberg. The plan included improvements in parking, lighting, signage, vegetation, public amenities, code enforcement, and pedestrian traffic. The following year the Downtown Statesville Development Corporation (DSDC) was formed by a group of 31 community and business leaders. With DSDC came a ray of hope.

By 1984, drawing from a meager pot of grant and corporate money, the DSDC began making headway, one building at a time. In two years, 30 new businesses had opened. The group's goals were straightforward—to spark interest in the downtown by rehabilitating buildings, recruiting businesses, increasing shoppers, and improving communication between merchants.

Their first major project was saving the old Belk's department store building at 109 South Center. It was days from being condemned and demolished. The next year, the future of the downtown focused on the City Center building. And the status of the Vance Hotel was included in every discussion and every plan.

1986 data showed that Statesville was becoming a national model for downtown revitalization.

Many of the community activities around the square during the 1980s revolved around the Dogwood Festival. The city had planted 200 white dogwood trees (and a few pink ones that were accidentally slipped in) on Broad and Center. The trees transformed the city into "The Dogwood Capital of the Dogwood State."

In 1983 the Weekend in the Village festival, a fall event highlighting arts and crafts, food, and live music became a popular and successful yearly event. It was organized by the Statesville Merchants Association and Main Street organizations with the help of the Statesville Parks and Recreation Center and the Statesville Civitan Club. Broad and Center Streets were closed for the 200-vender event.

In 1984 it appeared that the Grinch would once again steal Christmas in downtown Statesville. The Merchants Association had become inactive and had decided to get out of the Christmas decoration business. But in November, DSDC leaders stepped up to save the day. They spent $3,800 on 1,100 strands of white lights for the dogwood trees and 17 artificial trees. A Christmas tree and giant strands of garland on cables were hung over the square. There were even whispers of a downtown economic renaissance.

In 1986 Old Fashioned Bargain Days morphed into Old Fashioned Fun Month and in 1987 Weekend in the Village added a car show and a petting zoo. In 1989 the Center Stage on the square hosted a variety of talent including the Davidson Brass Ensemble, Tilley's Dance Academy, Statesville Little Theater, Donna's School of Dance, North Iredell High Chorus, Dixie Wheelers Square Dance club, Academy of Dance Arts, Donna Bustle and Rene Roberts, Suzuki String Players, Academy of Fighting Arts, the Catalinas, and the Carolina Dogwood Festival Queens.

Grand marshal for the 1987 Dogwood parade was Kim Morgan Greene, star of 25 episodes of "The Colby's" TV show on ABC and 23 episodes of "Days of Our Lives." That was also the year the hands on the town clock stopped turning. It would be 1989 before repairs would be made to return her to her glory.

After a five-year successful relationship with the North Carolina Main Street revitalization group, the city dropped its formal affiliation with the organization in 1988.

The 1989 Weekend in the Village offered jazz, rock, country, bluegrass, and steel drum music on the square stage including local favorite the Franklinn Hammerr Band. A Hometown Parade was the highlight of the June 1989 Old Fashioned Bargain Days promotion. The decade closed out with a colonial theme in "Old Town Statesville's" big Christmas parade.

In the late 1980s it would not have been unusual to pass a movie star of two on the square. For a half-dozen years beginning in 1988, six movies were filmed in town. You might run into Phyllis Diller, George C. Scott, or even Brad Pitt.

And happier days were on the horizon.

DSDC photos

Chapter 9
The Circus

The Circus

The most fun time of the year for any town was when the circus rolled in. Circus promoters were experts at pumping up excitement in the community. They usually started a few weeks before by plastering posters on every vertical flat space they could find. Then on the day they arrived, usually by rail cars, they held an elaborate parade through town.

In 1908 the John Robinson Circus, one of the most elaborate traveling menageries on the road, came through Statesville, complete with a parade across the square. Robinson's promotional materials promised a $300,000 free street parade that included: 300 horses, 100 ponies, 50 cages and dens, 19 tableau wagons, two steam calliopes, a steam organ, a drove of camels, four brass bands, a wild west troupe, a brigade of ex-U.S. soldiers, and a 50-member band.

SHC   **John Robinson Shows 1899 and 1908**   SHC

The circus was an almost yearly occurrence for Statesville. Eager boys and girls (and adults) gathered to watch the parade of wagons carrying an endless lineup of exotic animals, clowns, and freaks pass across the square to the circus grounds, which was for many years along Light Street on the hillside north of the Fourth Creek Cemetery. Promoters knew the free parade would incentivize townspeople to find a way to scrounge up the 25 or 50 cents for a ticket into the big top for the 1:00 or 7:00 performance. Each company used their own marketing twist to entice ticket buyers. Their show was either the biggest, grandest, longest, oldest, etc.

Colossal Shows Circus parades down Center Street in the early 1900s *SHC photos*

Some of the shows that stopped in Statesville   *Landmark photos*

 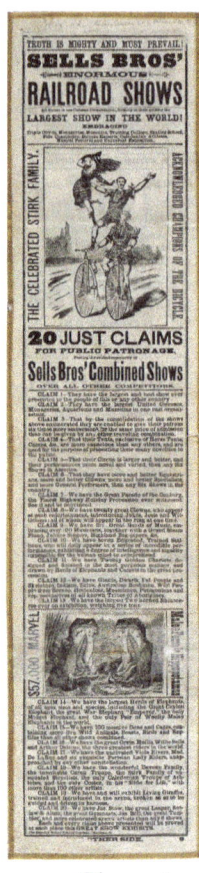  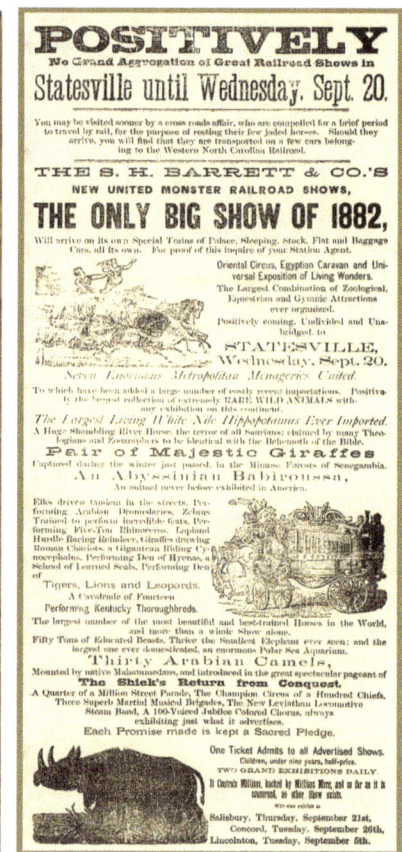

Shows in the 1880s *SHC photos*

1939 circus parade crosses the square *Ramsey*

Chapter 10
Characters Found
Loitering Around the Square

Characters Found Loitering Around the Square

No town would be complete without a cadre of unique and colorful characters to grace its street corners. And Statesville has had its share. For the purpose of this chapter, I narrowed the list to three of my favorite public figures who would have been found routinely hanging around the square on a typical day—three interesting citizens I wish I had had the opportunity to meet.

Actually, there would be at least one other personality I should add to this cast of captivating characters. That would be "Casey" Jones. As a child, I had many opportunities to meet the beloved celebrity while accompanying my mother on her weekly shopping trips. For a young boy, "Casey's" sticks of Juicy Fruit chewing gum would stick in my memory forever. "Casey" was so special that he has his own chapter, Chapter 14.

This writer is aware that the descriptions of the following characters might butt up against the boundaries of both decency and political correctness. For that, I apologize. These short narratives are not meant to be cruel or demeaning. They are not written to ridicule the subjects, but instead are an attempt to recognize their uniqueness and applaud their courage to stand up to the challenges they faced. They are written from a historical perspective, not a clinical one, in hopes that the unconventional contributions of these individuals to the Statesville community won't be forgotten.

"Judge" Manlius Watts

Manlius Watts   *SHC*

Manlius Watts was a fascinating character who spent most of the later days of his life loafing outside the J. C. Turner & Son store on the northeast corner of the square. He was referred to as "the Judge" by both his large cadre of friends and his smaller group of foes. It's not apparent how he earned his title, just as there are few details about his early life, other than those he sprinkled into the colorful stories he told about being a slave as a young man.

To suggest that Manlius was an employee of the *Landmark* newspaper might be a little bit of a stretch, but theoretically he was. He was an errand runner for them. Most of his assignments involved taking the racks of news type from the type setter's office over Turner's store, down to the street level, and then down the basement steps to where the printing press was located.

The editor of the *Landmark* wrote the following about his former employee: "As far back as my memory goes, I can recall Watts as an adornment to the streets of Statesville. He was not a native, but where he came from and when he came, I never knew. He never worked a steady job, only eking out his existence with the nickels and dimes he could pick up running errands. For a time, he assisted in furnishing the motive power that ran the *Landmark's* printing press, then operated by hand. The *Landmark* was a weekly newspaper, so Manlius was not required at the office except a few hours two days a week. However, he was generally around every day."

"Belonging to the idiotic fringe of humanity, he was of the type that is ever inviting jabs, divisions and practical jokes. These he resented just enough to furnish a static delight to his tormentors. Usually placid and normally a harmless creature, he was capable of flaming anger. This fact was demonstrated more than once. The *Landmark* office was located on the square in the second story of the building. The press room was in the basement. One sunny summer morning, Manlius was standing as was his wont, in dreamy restfulness, in perfect peace and contentment with himself and all the balance of the world. One of the youngsters in the composing room, happening to glance below, saw Manlius standing there, and a cruel inspiration seized him. He rushed to the water bucket, picked it up, ran with it to the open window, and dashed the entire contents on Manlius' head. Quickly reaching for a rock. Manlius looked up to the window and shouted, 'You damn shark face!' 'You want me to kill you?'"

"Manlius liked liquor, but he was not a drunkard. He rarely bought a drink of whiskey. If someone gave him a drink, he enjoyed it immensely. One Saturday night two youngsters who were very fond of mountain dew were feeling pretty good. They already had more than enough inside them, but they sent the 'Judge,' as Manlius was called, to the bar for more. When the Judge returned, they not only rewarded him with coin, but they gave him a liberal portion of the liquid fire. Somewhere, they had resurrected a high-top hat, something of a style worn by a smart aleck or the blooming toffs of London. As a crowning act of generosity, they presented the hat to the Judge, who quickly removed the wretched makeshift lid that he was wearing and placed the topper on his head. This done, he was dismissed, and the incident forgotten."

"A while later however, loud laughter was heard coming from a grocery store as well as the excited voice of someone delivering an impassioned speech. Looking in, the Judge was seen talking with vehemence in the midst of a laughing crowd. He was pulling vigorously on a cigar, his high hat at a 45-degree angle, his head bobbing, and his arms gesticulating wildly. The crowd charged him with being drunk. This he very vigorously denied. A store clerk said, 'You know very well you are drunk. If you're not, what's making you talk so well tonight?' 'Mother wit' an multeity of the brain!' was the swift reply. 'I got sense. I don't have to be drunk to talk!'"

Manlius was, indeed, a smart man. That was evident to R. L. Flanigan, a local entertainment promoter, and Orin Turner, the 'son' of the J. C. Turner & Son dry goods partnership where Manlius hung out. They recognized the wisdom of the Judge and offered to become his manager.

For years, Manlius had graced the square with regularity, telling stories about ancient times around Statesville when he was the property of slave owner Fielding Watts. Flanigan and Turner saw how much people loved listening to the stories and seized the opportunity to cash in on the old man's tales. They first posted fliers around town and sold tickets for Manlius to deliver a lecture at the Iredell County courthouse. That evening turned out to be a financial success, so they dressed Watts up and booked him as a lecturer at other venues in town, and then as far away as Chapel Hill.

For ten cents, spectators could listen to the Judge boast about how as a slave he brought $1,500 at a public auction when his master sold him to J. S. Miller. He was proud that he had brought such a high price. To him it was affirmation of his value as a human being. Another common theme of his lectures was the sorry state of America's younger generation at the time.

A September 4, 1899, lecture at the Statesville Armory Hall paired the Judge up with "Professor" Sam Allison, a local black singer and fiddle player. Manlius was dressed by his handlers in a fine purple linen outfit for the occasion. "His shirt bosom shone like white marble and his collar was a veritable tower of whiteness, and upon the Judge's right shoulder was perched a large piece of honeysuckle." After the performers had taken their seats on the platform, "Professor" Allison introduced the Judge: "Judge Watts told me a few days ago that he was going to tell the people something they did not know was in him, and now is the time to hear from him." The Judge then delivered his speech entitled, "Old Times in Statesville."

The newspaper said that Judge Watts "spread hisself, he did." His speech was somewhat rambling, but he moved along nicely until toward the end when some questions were asked which the judge considered foolish. He expressed the wish that every poor soul might become reconciled and get great credit and "relitude." "The Judge tells us that the cause of the four-year war was the Negro race." He made a puzzling claim of meeting "a painter on the mountainside when he had nothing with which to 'revour' him."

Manlius then ended with a cryptic statement warning that the people who "hid his axe" were "going down to everlasting and everlasting 'reternity' where the fire never 'squenches.'" Approximately 75 people were in attendance that evening, and the $7.50 cash proceeds were divided equally between the two performers. Judge Watts was able to live on his part for the rest of the year, "as he is a plain man, and his wants are few and simple."

The news type printing racks for the March 6, 1900, edition of the *Landmark* were toted to the *Landmark* basement press by someone other than Manlius, for the newspaper that day contained his obituary. The paper reported: "Manlius was probably the oldest and best-known colored man in the community. Just how old he was nobody knew, but it was his boast that he had 'been here a long time' and he had unquestionably been here a long time, for some of our citizens who are well advanced in years recall that he was regarded as an old man when they were little children. Manlius was evidently a giant in his younger days. He never married and so far as known, had no near relatives. In recent years he made his home with the family of Bill McKee. While he was polite and civil when not crossed, he was always independent and indifferent."

"For the past 15 or 20 years he had done little work, so little that one wondered sometimes how he lived. He had few if any vices, except an indisposition to work. He was not a drunkard, nor was he ever accused of crime. He had a dislike for the younger generation. He thought they had no manners and little sense, and he never lost an opportunity to express his contempt for them. Like the aged of all races, he lived mostly in the past, and to him, the old days were better than these days."

"Within the past few years, feeble health made Manlius more dependent, and realizing his helplessness, he abandoned his attitude of independence and began to seek aid from his white friends. And he had many friends among the white race. For the past two or three winters some of these, moved to pity by the old man's condition, had kept him supplied with the necessities of life. During his last illness his wants were contributed to and when he died his white friends chipped in and buried him." The calendar pictured above featuring the photo of the "Judge" was printed on the *Landmark* press and sold to help care for Manlius during his declining days.

His obituary ended with, "Poor old Manlius! He apparently knew little of either the joys or sorrows of his mundane existence. Let us hope that he has gone to a better country."

Keener Snead
Mention the name "Keener Snead" to any Statesville native over 50 years old and they will smile and shake their head. Snead was a legendary figure in town in the 1940s, 50s and 60s, and if you didn't know him, you knew of him. Usually the word "lowdown" preceded his name.

Like Manlius Watts, Keener Snead was a smart man in his own unique way. He had a folksy type of smarts not unlike that of Yogi Berra and a wit reminiscent of Ernest T. Bass. He was constantly making simple, yet profound, statements that would be quoted everywhere, from the front page of the newspaper to the grocery store line, and eventually to the kitchen table.

Keener Snead (sometimes spelled "Sneed") was born in 1911 or 1914, depending on which records you're reading. An early census report lists his occupation as a boiler cleaner. Later he worked in several of the town's furniture factories. He was married to Nettie Shumaker for a short time, but for most of his life he was a bachelor. During his 60 or so years of existence he lived in a dozen or more houses, usually rental mill houses in the south end of the city.

Keener could be found on most days walking the streets of Statesville, loitering on the square, or blocking the entranceway to a business. Everybody knew him and spoke to him in passing. Those who tried to strike up a conversation with him quickly found that his language was rather crude, and he didn't mind unleashing a snarky or vulgar comment. This was obviously a self-defense tactic Keener had developed, since typically he was the one on the receiving end of sarcastic and unkind comments from others. It seems that his personality, like that of the Judge, was such that it brought out the cruel side of people.

Today the treatment Keener received on the streets would be considered "bullying." Back then it was "just poking a little fun." Even the editors were quick to get in on the "fun" by quoting Keener on the front pages like he was a Roosevelt or Kennedy, careful not to cross the line of being cruel, but always with an air of superiority that editors in those days were adept at using.

But Keener dished out about as much as he received. He was often his own worst enemy. He would drum up a verbal confrontation with a stranger by uttering some random inappropriate comment. Then if the stranger made the mistake of responding, Keener would let a few cuss words fly and walk away. Keener was a lot of things, but he wasn't a fighter.

Some of the comments made toward Keener alluded to his widely known lazy streak. Like Manlius Watts, his aversion to work was unmatched and unapologetic. Every public job he had was short lived. Usually, he was let go for not showing up at work.

But the most common comments about Keener related to his hygiene, or lack thereof. This writer remembers the first time he saw the legendary Keener Snead. My father sat me down in Troutman's Café on East Broad and ordered me a Coke. Dad looked over at the counter and said, "See that man on the stool? Do you know who that is?" I was thinking maybe it was the governor or even the president. "That's Keener Snead," he whispered.

He knew that I knew that name very well. I had heard it all my life. My mother used it almost every night. She would say, "Get in that bathtub, boy. You smell like Keener Snead."

Now my mother was a very loving and kind lady, and she would never be disrespectful to anyone, especially a socially challenged gentleman without a tub. And certainly, she would never teach her child to be unkind to someone less fortunate. But she, like everyone else in town who had walked down the streets of Statesville on a hot summer day, knew the odor that surrounded Keener Snead. Apparently, his aversion to bathing was as strong as his aversion to work. And it was that quality that old timers in this town remember most about Mr. Snead.

Keener was fond of taking in a movie on Saturday afternoons. He would always get to the theater early to get a seat in the middle of the front row. And of course, the half dozen or so seats surrounding him were always empty. Some quipped that he "had an air about him."

Another remembrance of Keener was on the school playground. When a boy called an adversary a "Snead," those were fighting words.

And Keener wasn't a stranger to officer "Casey" Jones, the policeman who protected the square, not that he was ever dangerous or that he was a thief. That wasn't the case at all. It just seemed that Snead had a way of attracting trouble. He was arrested at least two times, once for carrying a concealed knife, as most men did, and once for not keeping his dog tied up.

Each time, the newspaper reported his arrest on the front page along with Keener's response to the charges. The concealed weapon case ended this way.

THAT'S THE DEAL — "Ok," said Keener Sneed as he left Recorder's court this morning. "That's the deal."

But the deal he was talking about was not quite the deal he had been trying to sell Judge C. B. Winberry.

Sneed had been brought into court on a capias for non-compliance with an order requiring him to pay some $70 in court costs. He had paid it down to $47 and then stopped. Asked what he was going to do about it, Sneed stood up to address the court:

"I'm a-going to pay it off," he said. "And I'm a-going to pay you $20 interest."

"Yes," said Judge Winberry, "but when?"

"Just as soon as I make a check," Sneed said, explaining to the court that he was employed at a local veneer plant.

Judge Winberry then sent him out with an officer to call the employer to see if he would advance $49 to cover the costs. The officer came back with the report that Sneed had "been so sorry and laid off work so much" that he had been fired.

"Yes," Sneed explained, "but I'm a-going to go back to work tomorrow. And I'm a-going to pay it off like I said. And I'll pay you $20 extra for coke money."

"Well," Judge Winberry said, "you just forget about the interest and the coke money. Beginning Monday, April 4, and every subsequent Monday until this is paid off you had better be in here with $10 to pay on this. Otherwise, I'm going to send you to the roads."

"Ok," said Keener. "That's the deal."

TOO MUCH ROPE — Keener Sneed played his luck so long that this morning he found himself securely bound to a 15-month road sentence.

It all began about a year ago when Sneed was arrested on a charge of carrying a concealed weapon. Judge C. B. Winberry, who is always willing to listen to a man's story, gave Sneed the road sentence, suspended on payment of $50 fine—which is the minimum—and court costs.

Sneed assured the court he would go to work and pay the fine; but he said he would have to have a little time, which Judge Winberry granted.

The defendant, however, was brought back into court in November, 1948, for failure to comply. It was then that he made his most eloquent appeal.

"You're going to get your money," he told the court. He added that he was willing to pay $20 interest and, on being informed that the court could not accept interest, added that the court attaches could take the extra $20 for "cigars and coke money."

Consequently, Judge Winberry gave him a little more time; but when it developed that in more than nine months the defendant has paid only $40 on the total of $77 due, he was brought in again. This time he lacked something he had had before—the support of his mother. She had sent word to the court that Sneed was not using the money he earned as the court had ordered, but was keeping up "another woman."

Asked for an explanation, Sneed again assured the court that "you're going to get your money."

"I can pay you $10 today," he said. "I have already fixed that. And I'm going to work tomorrow. . . ."

At last, he was right. Judge Winberry ordered the sentence into effect tomorrow.

1949 *Statesville Daily Record*

Long story short, Keener served time on the chain gang because he couldn't pay off his fine for carrying a knife. It's unknown why his "keeping up another woman" was relevant to his case, or whether it meant a woman "other than his mother" or "yet another" woman, but it was mentioned in the newspaper several times. After all, Keener was quick to let it be known that he was quite a lady's man.

Most of the stories about Keener Snead can't be repeated in the presence of decent people, but the one that has been quoted most over the years originated from a prominent local physician who was treating Keener at the county health department. It is still told 75 years later in unmixed company whenever Keener's name is mentioned. The doctor, whose name will be withheld for this discussion, duly warned his patient, "Keener, your girlfriend has been with every lonely man in town." But Keener missed the doctor's thinly veiled warning, and without taking offense, just scratched his chin and responded, "Well, Statesville ain't such a big town."

Sue Poe
And then there was Sue Poe, the "Queen of Key Row." Sue lived in the little shanty town along the 200-300 block of East Front Street. The row of shacks was owned by the P. B. Key family who ran whiskey and tobacco factories in town, thus its name. "Key Row" was known as a place where one might find illegal alcoholic beverages, promiscuous women, and a good fight. After years of neglect and complaints, Key Row was razed in 1922 and replaced by several automobile-related businesses.

Sue Poe was Key Row's most notorious resident. She was known for her enormous girth and for her penchant for drinking and public fighting. In the early 1900s, she had the reputation of being "the meanest woman in town". Costume partygoers dressed up in her likeness, but never in a flattering way. And as was the case with Keener Snead, people cleared the sidewalk when they saw Sue Poe coming. And also, like Keener, she spent several nights in the county pokey.

One day she got into a spat with her next-door neighbor, Mitch Cowan, because she thought the tree he was cutting was in her yard. She beat him with the limb he had cut from the tree. Then her two children, Otis and Carrier, pelted him with rocks, leaving him with a bloody eye. Both Sue and the kids were arrested, and the public took great pleasure in following their court cases in the paper and amongst the gossip circles.

Sue was also involved in an occasional altercation on the downtown streets. Because of her temper and size, officers dreaded arresting her. Each time the paper reported her arrest, they were quick to estimate her weight, usually as "between 250 and 300 pounds," or "closer to 300 than 200 pounds." One article called her "ponderous." Another compared her to a "kicking mule."

Even Sue's love life was open to public inspection and ridicule. The following article in the *Statesville Sentinel* sarcastically covered her unique marital dilemma that had arisen when Sue's sister-in-law moved in with Sue and her new husband, Billy Wilson. The article is proof that bullying was alive and well in those days and that newspaper editors were a cruel lot.

MATRIMONY DOES NOT MEAN HAPPINESS ALWAYS.

Susie Poe Finds Troubles Although Her Heart Is Filled With Love.

Sue Poe, a lady of color who is well known around town, always had the appearance of a terrific battleship sailing out upon the waters in quest of an enemy. Her very bearing denoted strength and her actions further substantiated this fact when "Mitch" Cowan, colored, was helped to the court room to testify after he had angered Sue, (but that was the Sue of old and not the Susie Poe) Wilson of today. A change came in her life when Dan Cupid, colored, shot his arrow of love into this gigantic heart and with it the love powders of meekness. Those that attended the wedding of Sue to her dark complexioned man of choice, were surprised when that 300 pounds of grace came down the aisle leaning upon the arm of her 125 pound understudy. Her very walk denoted grace as she shed tears of innocense as the thought of leaving perhaps a home to go out into the world with a man. It was no doubt a great sacrifice for one of her mature years, but when love leads we all follow.

However, love does not always mean happiness. Did her dark skinned better half that had wielded the magic wand over her forsake his won treasure? Oh, no, but it seems that fate caused Susie to have to live with her sister-in-law, and as you know, sister-in-laws are not always as loveing as husband dears. At any rate the first chapter was brought to the public the other night when a physician of the city was called to the negro settlement. After he had alighted from his car and gone into the house and began a "post-mortem" examination of his patient, his attention was arrested by loud groaning and wailing. The very earth seemed to shake and a retreating Rumanian army driven before the terrific fire of the Germans would have seemed as nothing to this suffering element.

The house shook as the groaning object dragged upon the porch. The door was pushed open and the 300 pounds of suffering humanity squeezed through that three and one-half foot entrance. Every step was taken with pain and suffering as eyeballs protruded from their accustomed sockets and rolled around in quest of the occupant of the car outside.

All out of breath this suffering lover managed to answer the Doctor's inquiry as to who she was and what was the matter—"I is Susie Wilson and Doctor I's pizened". Poisoned, that caught the doctor's attention but he seemed to falter and seeing this required further explanation. "Don't you know me, this is Sue Poe, now Susie Wilson". That was enough to start the medicine chest to work to save this valuable personality. After giving heroic treatment an investigation was started to ascertain the cause of this poisoning "It was that huzzy sister 'n law ov mine—she's been trying to pizen me ever since we wuz married, she tried to put talcum powder in my bread one time en I caught her. We got to watching each other, caze she knowed I'd pizen her if I got a chance en I knowed she would pizen me. Last night when I turned my back while making break that huzzy put it in and I eat it". Put what in? "Rat pizen, thats what. I drank a gallon of milk and melted a pint of lard and drank it, caze I heard that was what to do—did I do the right thing, doctor?" The docter fully agreed with her.

Love why hast thou a sting?

Statesville Sentinel, **March 8, 1917**

Chapter 11
Public Transportation Serving the Square

Public Transportation Serving the Square

When I think about the town's early public transportation system, I'm reminded of an amusing anecdote that was told for years by employees of the J. C. Penney warehouse on Salisbury Road. In 1948 a bigwig from the New York City home office arrived in town late one night. He was scheduled to tour the company's newest facility the next day. He had flown to Charlotte and taken the Greyhound to the Union Bus Terminal at Front and Center. He got off the bus, stepped to the cabstand a few feet away and told the driver to take him to the Vance Hotel. He crawled in back and the driver promptly drove him about 100 feet and let him out at the Vance. "That'll be 25-cents the driver said," small town public transportation at its finest.

Even though the town's streetcar system never materialized in the early 1900s, Statesville did have several organized public transportation systems over the years. Early on, there had been a horse-drawn jitney service to get rail passengers and freight from the depot to the hotels. With the advent of the automobile, mechanized jitney services offered a more regular schedule.

In 1915 an enterprising young man was parking his automobile hack on the square and would provide a ride to any point in the city for the same price as his horse-drawn bus competitors. A year later, the Jitney Transfer Company, operated by Will Miller, established several six-day-a-week horseless jitney routes. One car, most likely a Ford touring car, left the depot for the square on the hour from 7 a.m. until 10 p.m. via West End Avenue and Front Street, and from the depot to the square by way of Davie Avenue and East Broad on the half hour. Another car left the depot for the square and North Center on the quarter hour and then for the square and Walnut, Race and Mulberry Streets a quarter before the hour. The cars would stop for pick-ups at any point with a hand signal from passengers. The cost was five cents.

A line was later added to run down "the Boulevard" and was "liberally patronized." Drivers rang a bell along the way to alert potential passengers of their approach. In 1917 a 12-15 passenger bus was added to the jitney line and the ticket price increased to ten cents between the square and depot, and 15 cents to points beyond the square. In 1921 the price went to 25 and 50 cents to and beyond the square, and 50 cents for calls after 9 p.m.

Jitney bus parked beside the Vance Hotel *SHC*

Miller even built a jitney passenger station near the square in the alcove between the Johnson-Belk storefronts. The transfer station was fitted with heat, lights, seating, and even a phone. Passengers were encouraged to ring number 504 to call for a car.

Jitney station in alcove between the two Johnston-Belk storefronts before sides were merged *Stimson*

The company name was changed to Statesville Auto Transfer Co. in 1918. "Jitney" was a dated reminder of the horse and wagon days. The company was crucial during the Spanish Influenza pandemic of 1918-1920 shuttling nurses around town to care for patients. By 1921 the town's team of drivers had grown to 17. In 1921 Miller got some competition when the "New Jitney Service" began operating.

But the end was near for the jitney lines. They would be gone within the year, and by the mid-1920s, five taxicab companies were providing door-to-door service and for the next decade were the town's only transportation system.

The year 1937 brought a new era for public transportation in Statesville. The Statesville Motor Coach company picked up where the jitney companies left off and began regular routes around town bringing affordable, convenient, and dependable transportation to shoppers, workers, and students.

Winston-Salem investors Moody White, C. B. White, C. W. Caudle and Allen Banner were the owners. They were also the drivers. Mrs. Annie Rives was the first passenger to pay the 5-cent fare from West Front Street to the square.

The coaches ran every 30 minutes from the end of Boulevard and West Front to the square and from the end of Davie Avenue to the square. Another loop ran from the square out West End Avenue and one took in the Diamond Hill area.

Parking spaces were painted on Center Street at the square for loading and unloading passengers. Later, to cut down on congestion, buses unloaded on the square at West Broad then turned the corner onto South Center and reloaded. Eventually, the loading and reloading operation moved to a more pedestrian friendly area in front of the courthouse.

The 5-cent fare was the same price the jitney drivers had charged 20 years earlier. Their maximum fare was 7-cents. The square was considered a transfer station, so riders could travel all the way across town for a nickel. The buses operated from 6 a.m. until 10:30 p.m., or later if there was a need.

Tharpe **Unloading and loading on the Square** *Stimson*

SHC **Loading and unloading at the courthouse** *Tharpe*

In 1940 Statesville Motor Coach began service to and from Troutman and Loray, and in 1942 a route was added to the Fairview community on the Turnersburg Road. That route was later expanded to include Harmony and Union Grove. The next year, service to Taylorsville was added, but the state required the owner to get approval from the regional Greyhound bus franchise to run their routes on NC Highway 90. A leg was even added to bring shoppers and workers in from Elkin.

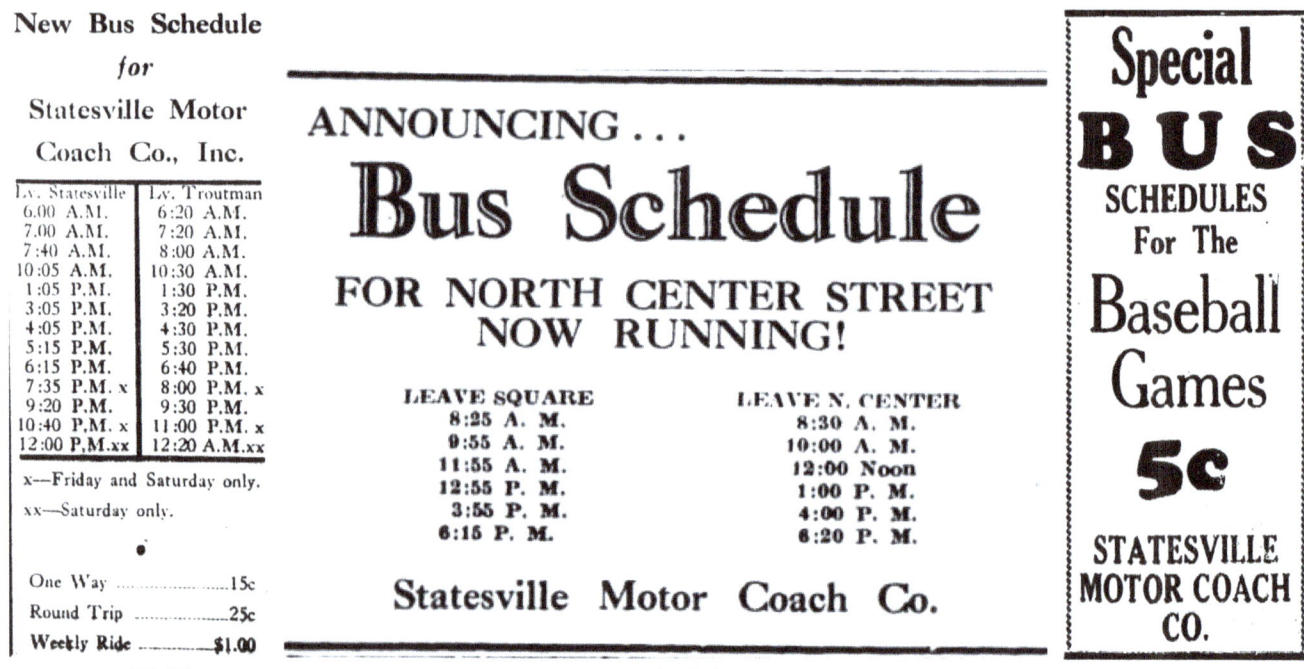

Daily Record **To Troutman**　　　　1940 schedules　　　　*Daily Record*　　　*Daily Record*

In 1946 two new 32-passenger green and cream-colored GMC coaches were added to the Statesville Motor Coach fleet bringing the number of buses serving the square to eight. A new 27-passenger Ford was added in '48. The company purchased six benches for passengers to use while waiting for the bus, four at the courthouse and two on the square beside Eagle's 5 & 10.

Statesville Motor Coach Co. GMC　　　　*SHC*

In the 1950s the Downtown Merchants Association arranged with the bus company to provide free rides to the square for shoppers attending "Dollar Days." This wasn't the first such partnership. In 1915 shoppers from neighboring Catawba County could show their sales receipt to the toll bridge keeper at the river and get a free pass back home. The keeper just added the toll to the merchant's association tab.

The Statesville Motor Coach route to Taylorsville was abruptly shut down by the N. C. Utilities Commission in 1950. The commission said the Parkway Greyhound Bus Co. owned the exclusive franchise for that route and was "able and willing to provide adequate service." While the company was fighting with the commission, they put in a request to raise their fares from 7-cents to 10-cents, or three tokens for 25-cents. The commission ordered the company to show proof of losses under the current rates, and they did. They showed a $1,721 loss and their request was approved, which would enable them to make a $600 profit for the next year.

But the agreement stated the company would still have to carry children to and from school for 5-cents, and hundreds of kids took advantage of that special rate each day. The school ticket price eventually went up to two for 15-cents and then to 10 cents each. In 1961 it cost a dime each way for adults then the price increased to 20-cents in 1967. The school bus tickets were ten cents each way until 1972 when they rose to 30 cents for a round trip ticket. Eventually the school system paid for busing and competitive contracts were awarded to the lowest bidders.

SHC   **Up to 20-cents in 1967** *SHC*   *SHC*

In the mid-70s as the major stores left downtown, local bus ridership began to dwindle. Statesville Motor Coach began relying less on hauling shoppers and more on hauling school children. Owner Sidney White explained to a senior's group how he had been forced to cut many routes. He said the bus business was changing because the public had more money than ever before, so many families had two cars and relied less on public transportation.

Also, shopping locations were no longer concentrated in one area and the hours of operation varied widely. He was alluding to the fact that Newtowne Shopping Center and Signal Hill Mall were now vying for the same customers as the downtown, creating the need for more expansive and less cost-effective bus routing by the provider. And automobiles were becoming more convenient than buses. "The times, they were a-changin."

Statesville Motor Coach at your service *Beck*

No child left behind *Plyler*

Chapter 12
The Square Egg

The Square Egg

From 1959 until 1965 the Statesville Merchants Association ushered in the spring shopping season in big way. A gigantic Easter egg was put on display at the square. It was a festive way to draw shoppers downtown, and it was a great way to occupy children's time while their parents shopped.

Big egg in front of Eagles 5 & 10   *Record & Landmark*

That first year, the paper reported a "live" egg was left by an Easter bunny and would break its shell at 10:00 on March 21st, thereby ushering in springtime. A physician checked the patient once a week to make sure it was in good condition. The checkups were always on Saturday in order to draw the most spectators.

Local obstetrician Dr. Harry Walker, accompanied by his nurse Vivian Caldwell, made the first egg-amination, as it was called. Afterwards, they delivered an official public report reviewing the hatching process.

During the incubation period each year, children were invited to enter by mail the "Egg Hatch Contest" to guess the mystery animal hiding inside. On the morning of the hatching, a huge crowd assembled to watch the delivery and see what critter emerged. The hatchling awarded a grand prize to the lucky guesser and passed through the crowd with smaller prizes to all the other little bunnies.

What will it be? *Record & Landmark*

In '63 a six-foot duck in a sailor suit crawled out *Record & Landmark*

In 1963, an intercom system allowed the animal in the egg to talk to visitors. Over 150 egg-cited, rain drenched children, and at least that many adults, turned out to watch the Easter bunny help the mysterious giant guest fight its way out of the canvas egg. Tracy Parlier and Harriet Louise Tsumas were the only two contestants that year to correctly guess it would be a duck.

In 1965, stores sent out live models to intermingle among shoppers to show off their latest spring fashions.

In 1966 the mammoth egg on the square was replaced with the "Wishing Well" promotion that invited shoppers to drop a coin in the well and make a wish to support the Easter Seal Association. A six-foot bunny hopped around town passing out registration blanks for a "Guess the Name of the Bunny" contest. Stores were open until 9:00 each Friday night.

The egg on the square made a curtain call in 1968, but with a little different twist. From the egg would hatch, not one, but two bunnies. One flop-eared hare passed out sugar-filled loot while the other distributed valuable merchant discount coupons.

In the meantime, kids 16 and under could visit stores to pick up tickets for the "Easter Bunny Contest" drawing for store discounts and prizes.

But, the chapter of this story that local baby boomers remember most, took place late on a Friday night in April, 1963 when the egg on the square promotion suffered a temporary catastrophy. Somebody stole the egg!

Police officers on patrol discovered the egg missing from its nest at 11:45 and began their search. Robert Forsyth, a local fireman working part-time at the Esso station at Tradd and East Broad, reported seeing the egg headed east on the back of a dark colored pickup truck, accompanied by two teenage boys riding in the back.

Early the next morning an unidentified man called the WSIC radio station to report a huge egg on the side of the road near the cloverleaf at I-77 and Hwy. 64 (I-40). The city scrambled to get a truck and crew to the scene, and the egg was returned to its nesting place. That year as the morning sun lit the square, the children of Statesville were treated to a different kind of Easter miracle.

George Snipes, head of the Merchants Association asked police not to worry about catching the culprits. I suppose he figured "No harm, no 'fowl'" (that was a yoke…I crack myself up). Snipes denied that his group was involved in the heist. He said that although it was great publicity and he wished he had thought of it first, downtown merchants weren't involved.

Police, despite having egg on their face, didn't pursue the case, but declared they would prosecute the pranksters if they found them. And although the names of the culprits most likely quietly circulated inside the halls of some nearby high school, the great egg heist of 1963 remains another of the city's most sensational unsolved crimes.

But, the statute of limitations has expired, and if by chance the culprit is reading this narrative, this would be a geat opportunity to clear your conscience so we can all shake your hand.

The following year the egg was enclosed in a large "vandal-proof glass case."

The Easter Bunny Contest rules — *Record & Landmark*

Chapter 13

Christmas on the Square

Christmas on the Square

As the song goes, Christmas is the most wonderful season of all. The festive display of holiday spirit on the square has been, and continues to be, one of the city's warmest and longest-held traditions. For many years right after Thanksgiving, the city staff turned the downtown into a winter showplace. Some years the colors were bright and tinkle-y, and other years they were more subdued. Some years there were wreaths, and other years candles. But whatever the theme, city workers and merchants worked hard to get the community ready for the season.

SHC **Whether overhead or in the middle of the intersection, the tree was always huge** *Ammon*

Beck **Some years with electric lights and some years without** *SHC*

SHS **Each year a little different theme** *Tharpe*

Christmas 1948

The worst Santa costume ever   **Santa's sled is a Turner Manufacturing golf cart**

Beauty queens   *Tharpe photos*

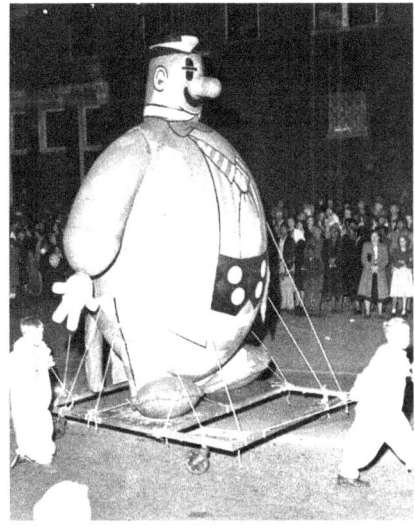
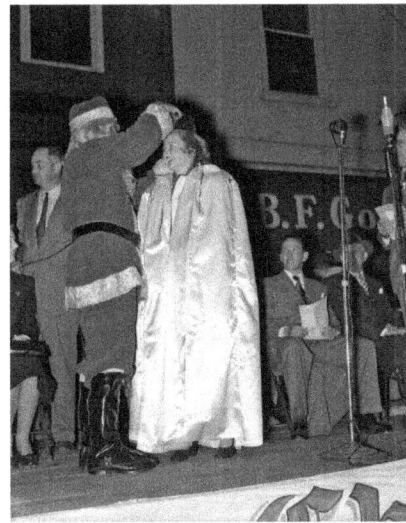

Wimpy in '48   Crowning the queen

You never know who you'll meet on the square Cowboys Pecos Pete (left) and Andy Barker (right)

Statesville's own Times Square   *Tharpe photos*

The jolly ole elf himself bringing up the rear *Stimson*

View from the judges stand *Rickert*

Chapter 14
"Casey" Jones — Keeper of Law & Order Around the Square

"Casey" Jones—Keeper of Law & Order Around the Square

Officer James Howard "Casey" Jones *SHC*

One of Statesville's most beloved characters was Statesville Police Department officer James Howard "Casey" Jones. "Casey" could usually be found tending to his beat on the square. He was the unofficial town greeter and goodwill ambassador. His official duties included maintaining both the peace and the traffic flow at Broad and Center. He was known for his cheerful and helpful attitude, always ready to chat, shake hands, or pass out a stick of chewing gum to a kid (I know of at least one child who looked forward to a stick of chewing gum every Saturday morning, and has the dental fillings to prove it).

Always fun-loving and good-natured, Casey was often the willing butt of the joke in the "Statesville Shots," the local gossip section on the front page of the daily paper. Once when he was hospitalized for a minor condition, a shortage of rooms forced the staff at Long's Hospital to place Casey in the maternity ward. When he got out, he was razed unmercifully by everyone from the newspaper editor to mothers on the street who would hand Casey their baby bottles when they passed him at the square. And he loved it.

Some remember the time Casey put a parking ticket on the windshield of C. L. Lineback's car. Lineback happened to be the city manager. Others reminisce how he kept a close eye on the teenage boys hanging out at Kid Sharpe's Pool Hall. Some remember his letter to Santa in 1949.

Letters To Santa Claus

Dear Santa:

I have been a good boy all year, helping direct traffic at the square and doing what I can for law and order. Anything contributed will be appreciated.

Yours truly,
Casey Jones, policeman

Daily Record   **1949**

NO SCENTS HERE—There was quite a dispute yesterday over which of two policemen led the now-noted "Goat train" through Statesville. Patrolman Ralph Hoover was first to claim the honor, but Patrolman Casey Jones made the same claim, and neither would back down.

We smelled around both of them for quite a while and finally decided it was a tie.

1950   *Daily Record*

Children in town all knew and loved Casey. When little Billy Ray Martin wrote his letter to Santa in 1949, he put in a good word for his friend Casey. He wrote, "I have been good enough to ask for a stake wagon and blackboard and anything else you would like to bring me. Be good to all the other boys and girls. P. S. Be sure to be good to Casey Jones because he is a good policeman and I like him very much. Love, Billy Ray Martin."

When school was in session, Casey doubled as a traffic safety officer at the Mulberry School and Davie Avenue School crossings where he had a huge fan base.

POSIES AND THE POLICEMAN—Casey Jones, Statesville police officer is one of the high points of the day for Mulberry street school students. They like him so much, in fact, they bring him flowers every day. Here he is surrounded by Elizabeth Wilkinson, left, Alan Eisele and two handfuls of roses. (Staff photo.)

GOODBY, MR. CASEY — Patrolman Casey Jones, who has helped Davie Avenue School children cross the dangerous intersections for another term, is shown here with a group of his charges saying goodby for the summer. Left to right are Jimmy Gilbert, Debbie Gilbert, Stewart Lindsey, Elizabeth Louise Hinton, Julie Ann Lindsey and Patricia Hinton. (Fry photo).

Daily Record   **The kids loved Casey**   *Daily Record*

When the Downtown Merchant's Association's "Old Fashioned Bargain Days" event came around each August, Casey was in rare form. He would patrol the streets and stores decked out in his comical "Keystone Cops" outfit, handing out favors and joy to all.

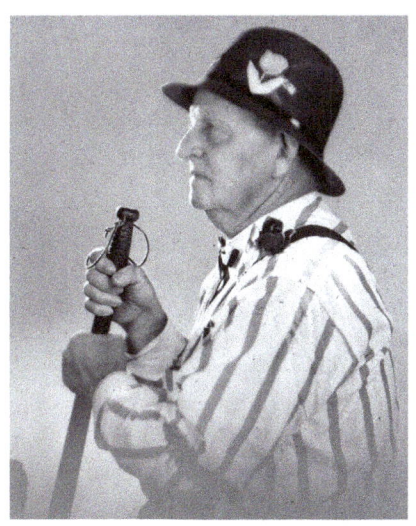  

Tharpe   **Casey Jones at your service**   *SHC*   *Tharpe*

Casey Jones went to work on the square in 1946, back when turns were outlawed. He retired from his beat there in 1961 but continued working parttime as the traffic control officer at Oakwood Junior High School. At his retirement ceremony he was presented with his department shield, the prestigious badge No. 1, and his nickel plated .38 caliber pistol.

When Casey died in 1965 at the age of 69, school children across the city went door-to-door taking up a love offering as a show of appreciation to his family.

The "Casey Jones Policeman of the Year," award was established in his honor by the Statesville Police Department in 1965 and is presented to, "the policeman who best lives up to the code expected of a police officer." The first recipient was desk sergeant Billy Watts.

Author sporting Casey's pistol and badge "No. 1"   *SHC photos*

Daily Record **Casey with a few of his fans**

Watching for boys playing "hooky" at Kid Sharpe's Pool Hall, two doors down from the square *Beck*

"Groomsman" Casey Jones, (center right) always a good sport, shakes hands with his "bride," Earl Fleming (an even better sport) in a "womanless wedding" for the Mulberry School PTA

Record & Landmark

BOLD THIEF

One Lewis Hedrick was arrested Saturday night on the streets near the police station for being drunk. Nothing unusual about that of course.

Hedrick was taken into the station to await a patrol car which would take him to the jail. Finally the car arrived and the officers took Hedrick and started out the door with him. One of the officers discovered Hedrick's overalls bulged too much in front and, suspecting he was carrying either liquor or some other illegal thing, he made a quick search.

It was only a sweater. Nothing extraordinary about that either, except it belonged to Patrolman Casey Jones and was stolen while Hedrick sat in the police station.

1947

GOT HIT IN FACE WITH DISH TOWEL—Well, I'll tell you eggzactly how it happened. Went in a local cafe the other night for a cuppa java. Talk came up as to whether a certain cute little waitress would hit your columnist in the face with a dish towel. We didn't believe she would, but just at that moment "Casey" Jones walked up and grabbed both my arms and she let go the towel and I got it in the mush. That's all there was to it and any other story is just so much wind pudding.

1947

APPRECIATION — This letter found its way to us through the chamber of commerce. It comes from "A grateful student at Mitchell college."

"This is just a note of appreciation to the City of Statesville for the warm welcome it has extended since I first moved here in September, 1960," it says.

"A special word of commendation is due Mr. Casey Jones, retired member of the police force. His loving 'hello' and deep concern for young and old are enough to brighten the darkest day. In my opinion, it is devoted individuals such as he who make Statesville truly merit the title, the City of Progress."

1962

STREET SCENE—They called Casey at half past four . . .

That creature who padded up the main city streets Sunday night in bedroom slippers and tucked-in pajamas was none other than Casey Jones, local policeman.

It seems that Casey was already in bed when he received a call that his brother, Marvin, had arrived in town. Casey hadn't seen his brother in 15 years, and when Marvin arrived from Iowa Sunday night, he figured no one would pay much attention to how he was dressed.

1951

Casey was a regular on the front page of the newspaper *Record & Landmark photos*

'Casey' Jones Struck By Car

Veteran policeman J. H. (Casey) Jones was hospitalized this morning after being struck down by a car as he assisted school children across North Center Street at the Water Street intersection.

The 61-year-old officer was admitted to Davis Hospital shortly after the 8:22 a. m. accident where authorities said he would be kept for at least 24 hours for observation.

1957

Casey Jones Fund Planned

A memorial fund will be received on Monday from Statesville school children and other interested persons at a Casey Jones Day.

J. H. (Casey) Jones, 69, well-known policeman, died yesterday at Davis Hospital. He was extremely popular with school children as he served as a crossing guard.

Mrs. Phillip Mills, 201 East End Avenue, said plans had been made for children and mothers to collect the funds on Monday as the children go to the various schools. Containers will be available and the memorial funds will be turned over to the Jones family.

1965

Casey Jones making front page of the newspaper (continued) *Record & Landmark photos*

Chapter 15
Sammy the Fire Dog

Sammy the Fire Dog

SHC

When Sammy the Fire Dog wasn't napping at the fire station up the street, he was roaming the square. The small Boston Bulldog just showed up one day in 1935 and was taken in by the firemen and the citizens of Statesville. He quickly became the city's most popular and beloved citizen. He was even listed in the city phone directory—Samuel Mascotte, occupation, fireman; residence, 120 North Center (the fire station).

Sammy had free reign of the town, but he could usually be found on the square coaxing pats on the head, loose popcorn, and the love of the community. He could walk into any café and get a free meal—and did so quite often. Sammy would follow the downtown cops on their night patrols and was always the first one on the front seat of the truck when the fire alarm sounded.

When Sammy disappeared in 1945, it was front-page news. Everyone suspected the worst. But he was found a week later, 15 miles away in the town of Harmony. The police investigated the disappearance as a kidnapping, but the case remains yet another of the city's unsolved crimes (Is it starting to sound like Statesville has a lot of unsolved crimes?).

Sammy was killed by a hit-and-run driver on the square, August 23, 1946 (yep, unsolved). He was 12 years old and had become, blind, deaf, and rheumatic (possibly from of all those café burgers and hotdogs). A special handmade coffin was built for him at a local furniture factory.

Sammy was given an elaborate sendoff by his firefighter colleagues and was buried with full honors under the driveway in front of the old fire station, his favorite spot to lie. His grave marker was set in concrete in the sidewalk. His front-page newspaper obituary said, "Sammy loved everyone, both young and old, but never lost his hatred for cats." He was a good dog.

In 2016, middle-schoolers Cooper Hall and Abby Schieck launched a campaign to establish some type of remembrance for Sammy. Seventy years to the day after his death, a marker was placed on a brick wall at the site of the front door of the old fire station, near where he was laid to rest.

SAMMY FOUND

The sun is shining and all is happiness at the local fire and police station this afternoon. Sammy, the bull dog mascot and companion of the guardians of home and law, has been found.

It is understood he was located in Harmony. How he had gotten out there, no doubt only Sammy and the Lord knows.

MORE VIGOR

Now that Sammy, the Boston bull mascot of city firemen and police, has returned, the fire-eaters have put more vigor into their work. This morning the whole crew on duty was seen energetically sweeping the pavement in front of the fire house . . . even dogs have their good points.

SAMMY'S WREATH

John McLaughlin, Jr., and Sally, children of Mr. and Mrs. John R. McLaughlin, listened to the story of Sammy's death. They liked him very much. But what could be done to show the love for a dog?

Today a nice wreath with Sammy's name is over his grave at the fire department. The McLaughlin children did it to show their respect for man's best friend, a dog.

As popular as Santa at the Christmas parade *Beck*

"Sammy" mascot at the Statesville Fire House, is a small French Terrier and very, very smart, according to the firemen, who all hold Sammy in high regard. He makes headquarters at the Benfields, next door to the firehouse, and when he wants to get into the house, he can almost, but not quite, let himself in. He stands upon his hind legs, and makes a definite effort to turn the knob, and of course, this brings assistance. When one of his friends say, "Well, Sammy want to go uptown and get a hamburger," he understands as fully as a youngster of his age would, what this means—he is seven years old—and acts accordingly.

When he is away from the station, and the siren sounds, he bolts for home like a streak.

He is very fond of riding the trucks, but of course this is not to fires, only on trial trips, or such. The firemen all say he is about the smartest dog in town.

Daily Record **1945**

1946-47 city directory

ANNIVERSARY

Today marks the first anniversary of the death of Sammy Mascot.

On this date—August 23—just one year ago, Sammy, the little Boston bulldog mascot of the Statesville Fire department lost his life when run over by a hit-and-run driver. A friend to the public as well as the firemen, Sammy was probably the most well-known and popular dog in Statesville. He is still strongly missed.

If you want to find out how strongly he is missed just read the inscription on the cold, concrete slab over his grave in the fire department driveway. Sammy now lies under the walkway where he used to sun and shade himself for more than 12 years. The inscription: "Sammy, killed by auto, 8-23-46."

Still missed a year later Daily Record

Chapter 16
No Left Turns

No Left Turns

DSDC

For 100 years, the Statesville town square was so sacred that it was protected by a special ordinance that lesser intersections could only dream of—left turns were strictly forbidden.

Until the steel plate sign was placed in the middle of the square in 1913 with the words, "Keep Right," there was no organized system for street traffic flow. For the next century, though, city aldermen kept the law on the books making it illegal for horse-and-wagon, and later automobile, drivers to make a left turn on the square.

In later years, most of the traffic through the square was local, since only highways 21 and 115 came up Center. The east-west Highways, 64, 70 and 90 were routed through the Front and Center Street intersection to avoid gridlock. Actually, N.C. Hwy. 90 begins/ends there still today.

But occasionally, on a Saturday night, a wet-behind-the-ears teenager would get up the nerve to challenge authority and go for it, joining an un-distinguished club of dare devils and rebels jeopardizing their driving records and their parents' insurance rates for a few seconds of glory. And one or two were even brave enough to burn a "donut" on the square.

At extra busy times, the hated "NO TURN" pylon was placed in the intersection. In 1927 all turns were outlawed at all times to protect pedestrians. The price of getting caught—$2.50.

The unpopular "NO TURNS" pylon *Tharpe*

But then there was that one famous left turn on the square. On the morning of May 1, 1868, a wagon picked up a prisoner at the old jail on East Broad. The wagon proceeded to the square, hung a left, and headed toward Depot Hill. That prisoner was Tom Dooley. He rode atop his coffin and sang along the way to the gallows.

Guess where the town's first traffic signal was placed in 1925. Yep. In order to keep traffic flowing and pedestrians safe, the first traffic signal was located in the middle of the Broad and Center intersection. It included stop arms and a bell that rang when it was time for the driver to proceed through the intersection. Now isn't that what we need today, a bell at stoplights to tell us when to stop texting and start driving. Before that, a brave policeman stood out there inside a wooden box armed with only a "stop" sign and whistle. That system was soon updated to a stoplight suspended over the intersection and the officers were happily relegated to the curb.

In 1929 that light was replaced with four modern light units on posts on the right side of each of the intersection curbs as was being done in larger cities. Underground conduits were run under the streets which eliminated some of the unsightly electrical and telephone poles.

The change meant that for a few days, as the old light and "no turns" signs were being removed, drivers had a ball flaunting authority. The paper reported, "During the brief respite, especially when no officer was watching, many motorists had a hilarious time shooting to the right or left and sometimes making a U Turn." "But with the new signs, the playhouse for motorists and freedom at the square ends. They must now settle down to keeping straight ahead while passing through the heart of the city."

One of the duties of the officer working the square was to watch for speeders and illegal turners. Without the help of a patrol car, he could stop lawbreakers by holding up his hand and blowing his whistle. And most of the time the perpetrator stopped. On a quiet Sunday night in April 1928 policeman "Friday" Mize was working the square when a driver turned left despite the warning sign. Mize signaled the driver to the curb and while schooling him on the importance of following the town's traffic laws, he discovered the man had been drinking.

As Mize walked around the front of the car to check out the passenger, the driver hit the gas, forcing Mize to jump on the bumper to keep from being run over. The car proceeded down Broad and turned right on Meeting with the officer hanging on yelling "STOP!" As they approached the cemetery, Mize was able to hold onto the hood ornament, slide across the fender to the running board and reach inside to cut off the switch. The High Point driver was handcuffed and got to spend some quality time in the Iredell County jail under a $500 bond.

When the policeman on the square wasn't watching for illegal turns, he tended to his unofficial duty of keeping count of the number of out-of-state license plates passing by. On a random Thursday in 1929 Police Chief Tom Kerr counted 43 "foreign" cars passing through the square. But officer Reagan who was working the Front and Center intersection had him beat. He counted 186 cars from 24 different states passing east-west by the Vance Hotel between 7 a.m. and 4:45 p.m. That didn't include the ones that slipped by during his lunch hour.

The local papers often ran snarky front-page comments about the traffic laws on the square. In 1935 they said, when somebody makes a turn, there's always some comedian who says, "Hey, you can't do that!" And after they do it, they say, "Darned if he didn't, though."

In 1949 right turns were legalized again on every day except Saturday. Experimental signs warning pedestrians to cross only on a green light were installed with hopes that an expensive synchronized light system could be avoided.

On special occasions in the 1950s and 60s officer Casey Jones would blow his whistle, hold up his hand and wave some visiting dignitary through.

Casey directing a rare legal left turn for movie star Penny Edwards *Tharpe*

It wasn't until 2012 when the new streetscape plan was completed that citizens could finally enjoy those beautiful 90-degree arrows on the square pointing north, south, east, and west.

Mitchell College student club initiation "protestors" *SHC*

DSDC **Can't miss it**

Snow left turn *SHC*

Disrespecting the "No Left Turn" sign was popular *Tharpe*

Then: Don't do it! *Rickert*

Now: Go for it! *SHC*

Chapter 17
Parallel or Diagonal? That is the Question

Parallel or Diagonal? That is the Question

Want to get someone's blood boiling? Tell them the city is bringing back parallel parking. Statesville has endured battles over parallel vs. diagonal parking for many years. During the early days of the automobile, diagonal was the vehicular parking queue system of choice.

1920s *Stimson*

1930s *Stimson*

But as the city grew and the streets around the square became more congested, city leaders began experimenting with parallel parking. The theory was that if cars were parked bumper-to-bumper, parallel to the curb, a second travel lane in each direction could be added, and as a result, the constant 5-6 car back-up at the Broad and Center stoplights would be eliminated.

The main problem with parallel parking was that it substantially reduced the number of "doorstep" parking places. Also, it was more difficult for inexperienced drivers to get situated into a parallel space which backed up traffic while drivers were making a second or third attempt to get it right. Also, two lanes of traffic in each direction required pedestrians to check four lanes before crossing the street instead of two, so there was the safety factor to consider.

Diagonal parking on the other hand had its distractors too. Although it was easy enough to pull into a space at a slant, sometimes when exiting, the driver's vision was blocked by the car beside it. This led to bump ups and people pulling out in the middle of the street and unnecessarily slowing traffic flow. It also cluttered the curbs with more parking meters.

SHC   **Diagonal parking, circa 1939**   *SHC*

In 1930, city officials had grown weary of complaints about downtown traffic congestion, so they "imported a traffic consultant" to come up with a solution. And the medicine the traffic doctor came up with was far worse than the disease. He suggested *two* parallel parking lanes, one of which required painted lines down the middle of Broad and Center Streets. The block-long lines allowed parallel parking in either direction down the **middle** of the streets, with traffic passing on both sides. Drivers could also use the traditional parallel parking spaces along the curb. A similar system was being used in Baltimore. The consultant also recommended that all high schools teach parallel parking, since the skill was difficult to master naturally.

The curb parking was timed by meters and designed for short visits to a store. Shoppers (and store owners/employees) could park in the middle lanes from either direction all day long. But, as the paper put it, the new parking system died "a-borning." "It was unable to withstand the violent storm of opposition" when police started directing people to parallel park between the white lines down the middle of the street. And as quickly as the plan was hatched, it was gone.

The Landmark continued, "Wednesday night, while the population was quiet in peaceful repose, the street men were busy changing the parking lines back to the old way, blotting out the white spaces in the center of the streets." "And this morning some sympathetic friend, looking for a way to remember the dead, placed a beautiful floral wreath in the center of the streets at the square. The police officers who discovered the flowers were at first puzzled, but later caught the motive that prompted the act." The only thing missing was a bugler playing "Taps."

"From the date of the inauguration of the 'new system,' there was a universal howl of disapproval. At least 90% of the people were opposed to the change, and many were almost violent in their opposition." But white paint isn't easily removed from pavement. For months, police officers had to gently redirect visitors who parked within the faint but still visible lines in the middle of the streets.

In 1953 the city brought in another traffic consultant to survey the situation. Traffic was once again backing up on the square and tempers were growing short. City council was pushing a return to parallel parking and was working to offset the loss of 100 spaces by leasing off-street lots. But the survey found that merchants were against returning to parallel parking. They believed that the inconvenience it caused their customers would hurt business. Shoppers might base their trade on a store's proximity to a parking space rather than the quality of the store's merchandise and service.

Furthermore, the consultant contended that ladies did most of the shopping and ladies could not parallel park (their theory, not mine).

The study also found that 200 cars a day parked the whole day without moving. These were mostly store employees. That age-old dilemma seems to never change.

Eventually, Mayor Garner Bagnal used his power of persuasion to convince the Merchant's Association to vote in support of the switch to parallel parking. In a special New Year's Day, Friday night, January 1, 1954, called meeting, council voted to buy new parking meters, lease off-street parking, convert Cooper Street to one-way headed north with angle parking on the east side, and implement parallel parking. Cooper Street had been built between Front and Broad in 1928 to provide drivers a cut through to dodge the square.

Sixty-five years later, Cooper would once again be made one-way, but this time headed south. So, today if you meet a car headed north on Cooper, it's probably going to be an old person.

East Broad, 1950s

Tharpe

In the years that followed, changes to diagonal and back to parallel have met somewhat less resistance. Whichever school you belong to, you probably have a strong opinion about parking. And I don't dare delve into the parking meter discussion.

Stimson **But sometimes drivers came up with their own hybrid parking system** *SHC*

Apparently even Sgt. Vic Serino had trouble *Tharpe*
squeezing the crime stopper van into a parallel space

Chapter 18
Mystery of the Misaligned Buildings

Mystery of the Misaligned Buildings

Local historian Red Watt had a keen eye for detail. He was fascinated by the fact that the building on the southwest corner of the square was built two feet closer to the center of the street than the one on the southeast corner.

In other words, if you're walking west alongside the "town clock building," and lay your head on the side of the building (go ahead people won't stare) and look across Center Street at the "gg's building," it's obvious that the square is misaligned. Actually, the buildings on the 100 block of West Broad are two-feet closer to the street than those on the 100 block of East Broad.

Watt, a trained civil engineer, had a theory to explain this oddity. It wasn't that the original town surveyors had made a mistake; he believed the property owners on West Broad were the culprits. He traced the problem back to the late 1850s, right after the "Great Fire of 1854" that devastated the town and burned down everything in the 100 block of West Broad. But luckily, the fire didn't touch any of the buildings on East Broad.

Watt believed that the first lot owner to rebuild, maybe intentionally, encroached two feet onto the sidewalk. And, since there were no town building inspectors, he got away with the ruse. Then as his neighbors rebuilt, they followed his lead and were also never challenged.

Possibly, by the time the mistake was noticed, it was too late to force the issue with the owners. Afterall, they were some of the town's most powerful men, and the aldermen would not have been enthusiastic about forcing them to tear down a new building and start over. The resulting encroachment affected the width of the sidewalk, but not the width of the street. So, since the 1850s, the West Broad sidewalk has been two feet narrower than the East Broad sidewalk.

It's difficult to determine which landowner was the first to build back after the fire, but most likely it was Joseph W. Stockton. By 1857 Stockton had begun construction on, if not the first building on the block, certainly the largest one. His Stockton Hall on the square was three stories high and included two storefronts on Center Street and another small storeroom facing the Broad Street side. The town's Opera Hall was on the third floor.

Stockton Hall *SHC*

After Stockton Hall was destroyed by fire in 1892 and N. B. Mills replaced it with his beautiful building, he lined it up with the others that had been built in the 70s and 80s. And then when the Mills building burned in 1943, the current building was built on the same footprint.

The two-foot shift didn't cause a noticeable problem on Broad Street, but it had a major negative effect on another part of town that is still an aggravation today. As the town built out to the south, lots all the way down to Front Street followed suit, relying on the original measurements of the front walls of the Broad Street buildings. As a result, all the buildings down to West Front were pushed two feet further to the north than those down to East Front.

To prove this theory, look at the intersection of Front and Center Street. The Vance Hotel lines up further north than the City Hall building, resulting in the awkward zigzag pattern drivers encounter when traveling from East Front to West Front, and vice versa.

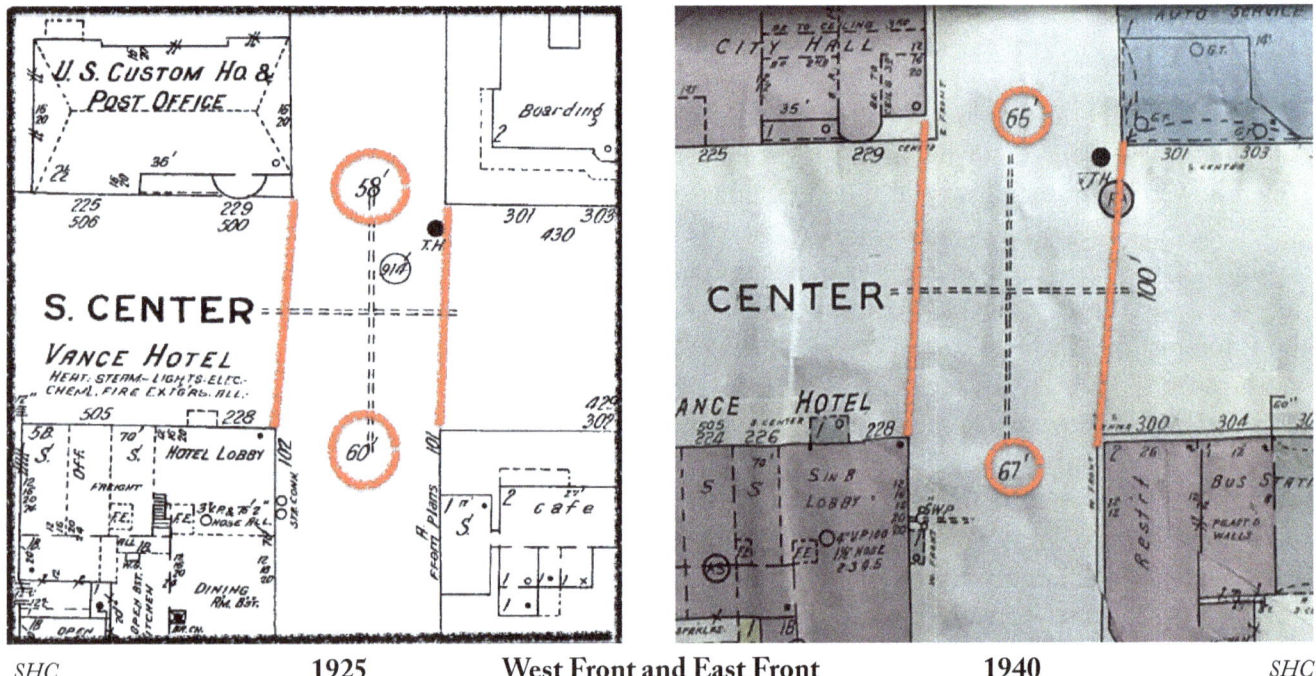

SHC   **1925**   **West Front and East Front**   **1940**   SHC

To further complicate the equation, Watt found that the old federal building (now City Hall) is not two feet, but actually three feet, further to the south than the Vance Hotel. Apparently somehow one or more landowners picked up a few extra inches here or there and added another foot along the way between East Broad and East Front. This additional foot made the traffic pattern zigzag at the intersection even more pronounced.

If ole Joseph W. Stockton was, indeed, the encroachment culprit, karma caught up with him in the end. When he built Stockton Hall, he was the third wealthiest man in town. After the Civil War, however, he had lost it all, including his downtown properties and his 14 slaves. He filed for bankruptcy, and as an old man was working as a clerk. The once wealthy landowner died nearly penniless.

"Streetscape" engineers verified the problem when they re-worked the streets in the early 2000s. After 150 years, the square was optically redesigned and returned to an actual square.

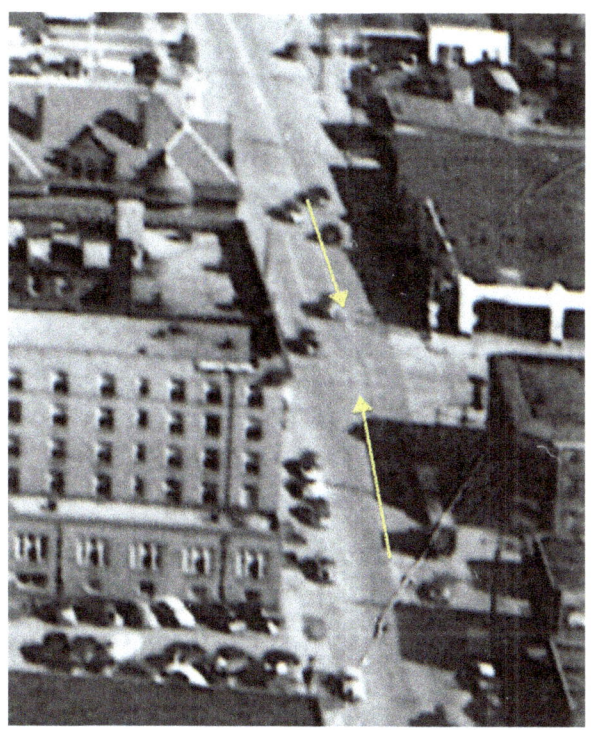 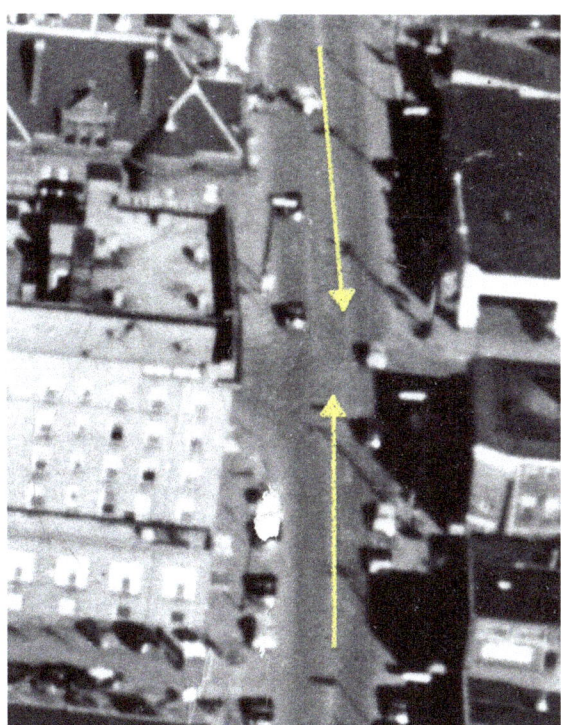

SHC   **The zigzag in the mid-1950s**   *SHC*

SHC   **Looking west from East Broad down the side of the bank building**   **Looking east from West Front down the side of the Vance Hotel**   *SHC*

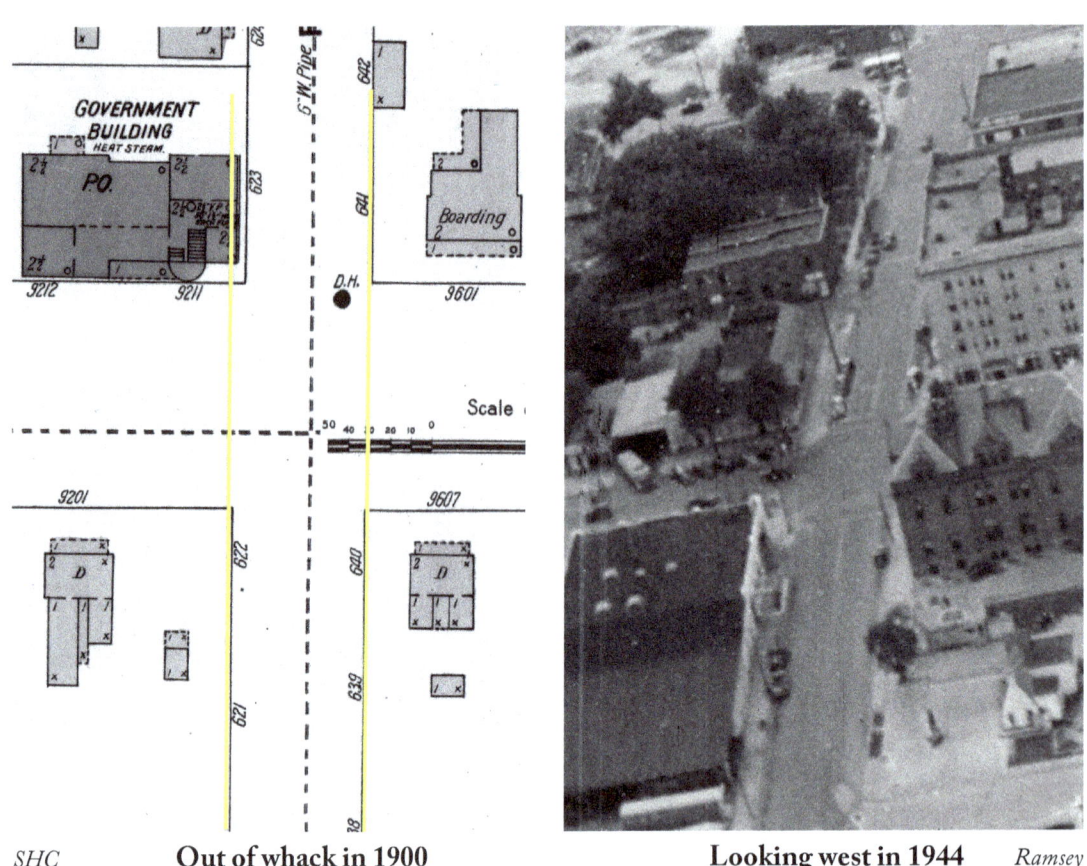

SHC   **Out of whack in 1900**   **Looking west in 1944**   *Ramsey*

View from the driver's seat in the left lane headed east   *Hill*

Chapter 19
Cruising

Cruising

Most everyone knows that the square was once a popular teenager cruising destination on Saturday nights back in the 1950s, 60s and 70s. But do you know who the first cruiser in Statesville was? In December of the year 1900, Clarence Steele, son of local industrialist J. C. Steele, purchased the first "horseless carriage" in town, a steam powered Locomobile and started the cruising trend. The paper reported that Steele's "thing" was "as dangerous as a mule and about as unpredictable."

Clarence Steele and his horseless carriage *Lackey*

After a few weeks of watching Clarence putter around the neighborhood, J. C. took a fancy to the machine and started taking it out for an occasional spin himself. Those in town who were resistant to change, complained about him cruising around town scaring their horses.

It was only a short matter of time before the beast got away from Mr. Steele, resulting in the town's first automobile accident. He was parked on the square and had invited a friend, John Dunlap, to climb in for a ride. J. C. put 'er in reverse but then couldn't figure out how to stop it. The "Loco" sailed across Center Street getting faster and faster.

Luckily, a pole in front of the telegraph office stopped the runaway before it plowed into the bank building. Mr. Dunlap bailed out before the crash, but J. C. rode the bronc till the end. Dr. Laugenour's horse that was hitched nearby was spooked and broke loose and galloped down the street adding to the excitement.

From then on, it was said, the elder Steele relied on a more reliable means of transportation to town, either behind a horse or "riding Shank's mare" (walking).

Mayor J. C. Steele could cruise wherever he liked, even on the courthouse lawn   *SHC*

By the 1920s, cruising became an organized hobby, with touring groups springing up across the country. On Saturdays as many as several dozen "touring cars" would caravan to Statesville and neighboring towns. The passengers would disembark, visit, shop, eat and get home before dark.

As gasoline rationing disappeared after World War II, young drivers took to the streets again on weekends to cruise, park and socialize. Over the years, the cruising "loops" changed. Depending on the time period, J. C.'s Toot-N-Tellem, Randy's, the Rotonda, the Big Rebel, and Newtowne and Signal Hill shopping centers were included in the loop to the square and up to the college.

Cruisers were usually welcome downtown as long as they were spending money with the local merchants and weren't littering and causing a ruckus. But as downtown stores started closing at 5:00 each day, and as shopping moved to the suburbs, cruisers had little opportunity to contribute to the financial health of the downtown shopping district.

In 1989 cruising was officially banned by the city council in the Signal Hill area because of repeated complaints from merchants, compounded by congested traffic conditions caused by young people driving around and sitting around in their cars. So, the cruisers moved their processional back to the downtown and Mitchell College area causing West Broad to take on what city manager Pete Connet called "a block party atmosphere." The circle drive in front of the college made a perfect turn-around point and the empty parking spaces around the square was a perfect congregation spot.

But a few months later, city council voted to eliminate cruising throughout the entire city. Signs were posted from the mall area to Mitchell College. Drivers passing a police checkpoint three times within two hours between 6 p.m. and 4 a.m. would be fined $25. As might be expected, keeping up with the parade of cars and trucks was an impossible task for police officers.

Councilman C. O. (Jap) Johnson chaired a committee to look at the problem. He said it had simply become unsafe for people to come to town at night, even to go to the post office. He said he had gotten calls late at night, saying, "Listen to this racket." "Public drunkenness, public urination, loud profane language, vandalism, and traffic congestion were results of cruisers." And "90 percent of them don't even live here." "We can't let other people take over the town."

A second resolution at the same meeting, also aimed at cruisers, restricted use of on-street and city parking spaces after business hours. That solved the problem of adolescents sitting on the hoods of their cars and yelling at their friends as they passed by.

Approximately 35-40 cruisers showed up at the council meeting. After the unanimous vote, one young man stood up and said, "Communism!" and stormed out of the room. Another turned to the councilmembers and said, "It's a sorry way to treat kids in this town." The youngsters vowed to boycott downtown and Signal Hill businesses, but the city manager said their efforts had little effect. The age-old rite of passage into adulthood known as cruising all but disappeared after that.

1940s *Tharpe*

1950s *Tharpe*

Among the last of the cruisers
Left to right, Todd Josey, Mark Handy, Craig Gifford,
Tricia Christenbury, and Mike Galliher

SHC

Chapter 20
The Northeast Corner

The Northeast Corner
101 East Broad
McRorie/Polk Gray/Holmes Drug

The building on the northeast corner of the square is often referred to as the McRorie building. But today, many remember it as Holmes Drug Store which was located there from 1932 until 1997. The Polk Gray Drug Store was located there for 22 years before Ralph Holmes bought the place, so a drug store operated from this corner for 87 straight years.

The McRorie building is one of the oldest (most likely the oldest) business structures in the downtown district. Although some say it was built in the 1880s, it is believed to date back to 1854, making it only the second structure to stand on that corner.

The editor of the *Landmark* noted in the 1890s that the newspaper had called the place home since its birth in 1874, so it has definitely been there for nearly 150 years or longer.

When county commissioners sold the lots for the town of Statesville in 1790, this corner had the distinction of being designated "Lot Number 1." George Robinson bought it on August 25, along with Lots 44 and 45. He paid 25 pounds for the three parcels that included the entire east side of the 100 block of North Center Street.

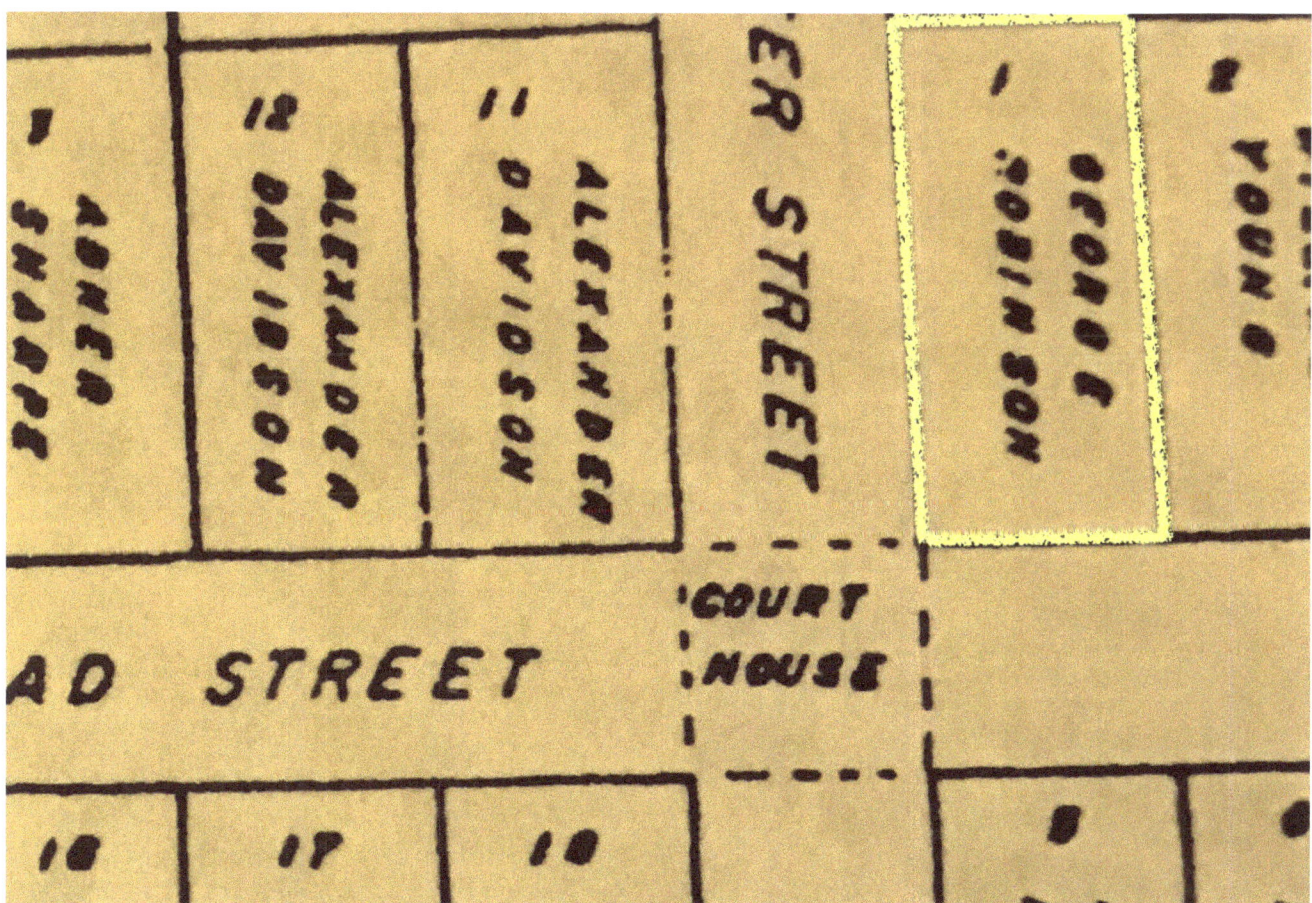

Original Landowners, 1790 *Watt*

175

Robinson made his home on the corner lot, and it would be several years before his dwelling would be replaced by a business structure, although like most townsmen, his home at times doubled as a western outpost tavern for passing travelers. The 1800 census reveals that the tax value of his home was $175. He had five family members living with him plus one slave. There were only 11 families in the entire town at the time, and the population totaled just 68.

George was a nephew of Fergus Sloan the gentleman who sold commissioners the land that would become the town of Statesville. Legend says that when Sloan moved here, he brought with him a huge liquor still, the first still in the state. No wonder, a hundred years later Statesville had become the liquor capital of the southeast.

Robinson was a town commissioner and purportedly the meanest man in town. He was arrested at least 24 times for assault or fighting, etc., on up into his 70s. And his wife faced the judge at least once.

By 1834 T. M. and J. A. Young had purchased Lot Number 1 from George Robinson's widow and were running a store there. Thomas M. McRorie entered the picture in 1845 when the Young's sold their store to him.

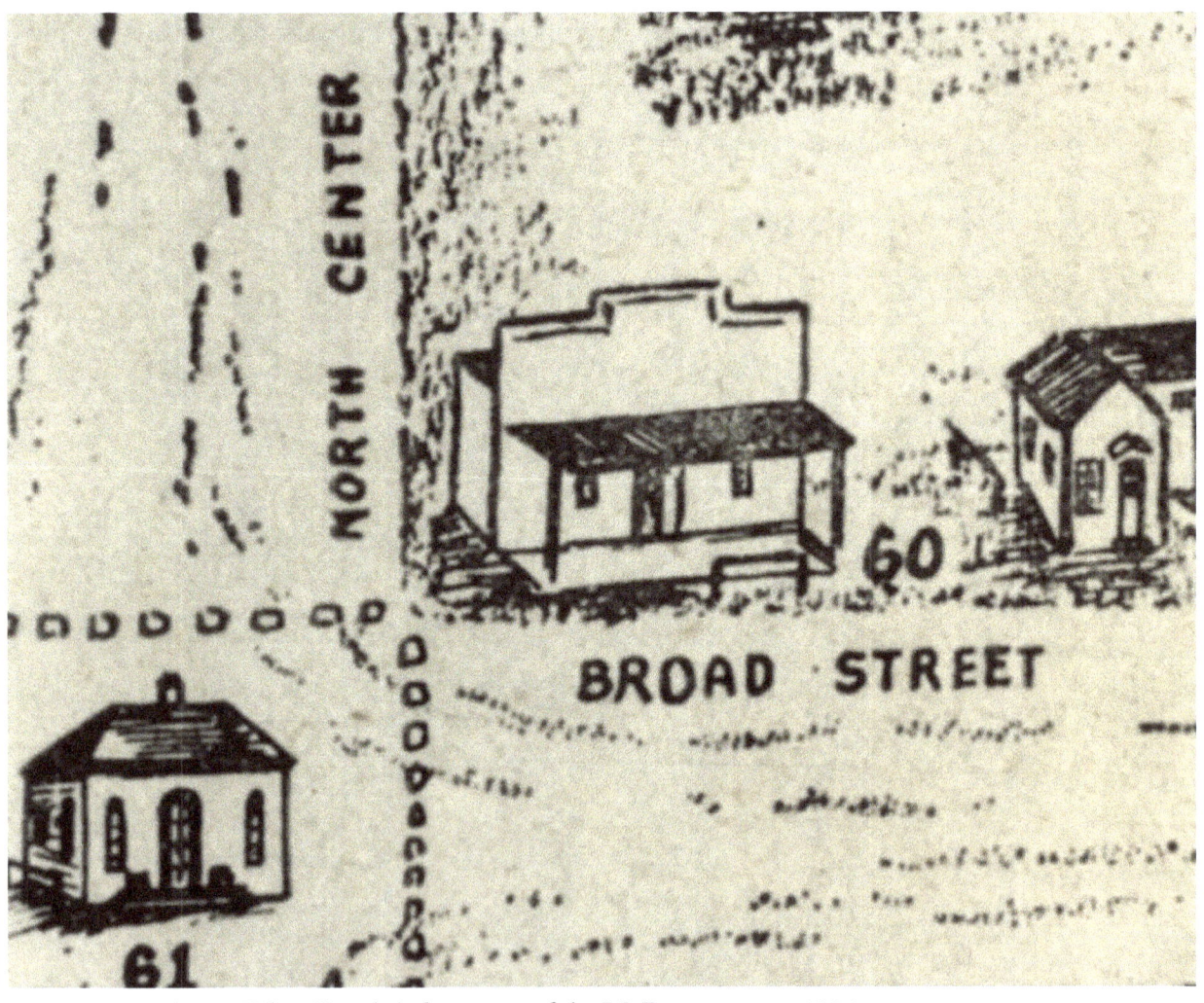

Artist Edrie Knight's depiction of the McRorie corner, 1834 *Record & Landmark*

When the "Great Fire" of 1854 struck the village, the McRorie corner miraculously escaped the flames. All of the wooden homes and businesses on both the north and south sides of West Broad burned, along with those on the west side of South Center. The brick courthouse on the square was also destroyed.

1858 and 1859 *Iredell Express* ads

McRorie ran a general merchandise store on the corner lot Number 1 up until the Civil War. The original store was not made of brick. At some point it was rolled back to the rear of the lot and used as Jamison's boarding house. The brick building that stands there today was built at that time, most likely just before the War.

McRorie had served as clerk and master of equity for the Iredell County court system in the 1830s and 40s. He was also a charter trustee for the Concord Female College and an elder in the Presbyterian Church.

It would appear that McRorie was a dapper dresser. The silk vest he wore on his wedding day in 1837 was put on display in the front window of the Forester-Privette clothing store in 1927 for the enjoyment of window shoppers.

McRorie died inside his store in 1862. His wife had preceded him in death, so his entire estate was sold at public auction, including his furniture, cooking utensils, horse, 540 acres of farmland and 24 slaves. The store, along with an adjoining vacant lot and storehouse, sold for $6,123. It was purchased by Simon Hammershlag, a Salisbury clothier who was looking to expand into a more profitable market. He must have decided Statesville wasn't the right fit for him because six months later he sold out to the Wallace family for $7,500 and opened a store in Asheville. The Wallace's sold the property, described on the deed as "the old store house lot," to Samuel A. Sharpe a short time later.

After McRorie's death, various business ventures operated out of the building. Charles A. Carlton & Bros was selling groceries and farm-related supplies on Lot 1 from after the Civil War until 1877, and dentist T. J. Corpening had an office upstairs. Like McRorie, Carlton had held a government job while involved in retailing and was better known for his insurance and real estate services. He was the County Treasurer from 1868-1876 and was a charter subscriber to the Statesville Air Line and A. T. & O. Railroads.

Carlton had served as a deputy sheriff as a young man and was as charter subscriber and cashier for the early Statesville Bank. In 1865 he was wounded and captured by General Stoneman's troops as they passed through town on their tear across the state. The Yankees confiscated $10,000 in bank funds that Carlton was trying to hide, but for some reason returned the money to him before leaving town. Charles and his brother P. C. carried the first store goods offered for sale in town after the War.

E. B. Watts and C. S. Morrison operated a store on the corner for a few years. J. B. Gill bought Morrison's part in 1886 and the firm became Watts & Gill grocery. The next year the name changed to just E. B. Watts grocery. Watts was known as the pioneer delivery wagon man. He had the first one in town. His wagon was the object of much attention as passersby stopped to marvel at its beauty. The *Landmark* editor chronicled the advent of Watts' wagon as a sign of progress.

```
For Variety, Quality and Quantity no stock in the city is Equal.
       We are receiving Fresh Goods daily.
A Choice Stock of Canned Fruits, Vegetables and Meats.
                The finest line of
Pickles, Chow Chow, Sauces, Catsups, &c., &c.,
              ever on this market.
New crop Raisins, Figs, Currants, Prunes, Citron, Nuts, &c.
                Received to-day.
ROYSTER'S CANDIES AND CRYSTALIZED FRUITS,
       FRESH CAKES, CREAM, OYSTER AND SODA CRACKERS,
  PINE APPLE AND CREAM CHEESE.
      A Specialty, Fine Teas and Coffees.
The Wholesale and Retail Trade will find it to their interest to examine my
         stock and prices.  A call solicited.
J. K. WATTS,  }
H. P. GRIER,  } Salesmen.    E. B. WATTS.
W. E. SLOAN   }
```
1888   *Landmark*

Watts closed up his business in 1890 and moved to Winston-Salem and W. P. Turner and A. P. Barron moved into the popular storeroom under the *Landmark* office. They sold "heavy and fancy groceries." In 1893 W. P.'s brother, J. C., bought out Barron's share in the company and continued to operate it as W. P. Turner & Co.

> You will find at W. P. TURNER & CO.'S a full stock of
> # HEAVY AND FANCY GROCERIES,
> Consisting of LEGGET'S OAT MEAL and FLAKES FRY'S CHOCOLATE MAILLARD'S COCOA, CROFT & ALLEN'S PRESERVED COCOANUT, JOHNSTON'S PINEAPPLE, SPANISH QUEEN OLIVES WORCESTERSHIRE SAUCE, HARVEY'S HAMS, BREAKFAST STRIP and LARD, No 1 MACKEREL and WHITE FISH, Standard Brand of CANNED FRUITS and VEGETABLES Try our KEY WEST CIGAR. We deliver goods free of charge in city limits. You will find us at the stand lately occupied by E. B. Watts. Call and see us.
> Very respectfully,
> April 10, 1890
> **W. P. TURNER & CO.**

1890 *Landmark*

For several years, Turner's store was a county tax collection headquarters. G. P. Austin was the tax collector and also had an office there for his fertilizer business. Turner's was also a central collection spot for donations for the poor and downtrodden members of the community.

In 1895 D. F. Jenkins opened up a grain and grocery business in the storeroom adjoining the rear of the Turner store.

William P. Turner died in 1902 and brother John C. and his son Orin L. bought the W. P. Turner store and changed the name to J. C. Turner & Son. John was a city alderman and, like Carlton, was a Confederate vet who also served as Iredell County treasurer.

For about 30 years the city scales were located on the McRorie corner of the square. The scales had been moved there in 1882 from the tobacco warehouse. The scales were available to the public for a small fee that was collected by the downtown policeman on duty. It was utilized mostly for weighing wagon loads of farm products and animals but was also used by merchants to determine shipping weights without having to ride down to the express office at the depot. Slips with the official weight signed by the weighmaster would be provided to the buying and selling parties.

It made sense for the city to offer this service. It prevented farmers and merchants from getting ripped off by shysters using inaccurate scales and thus cut down on fights, shootings, cuttings, and general ill will. After all, when dealing with farm commodities, pounds and ounces translated into dollars and cents.

In 1910 the scales were moved from the square to the old steam electric plant on Light Street.

In 1905 druggist Polk Gray bought the Nathaniel P. Tunstall Drug Store that for many years had operated from the wooden store building at the northeast corner of North Meeting and West Broad. In June 1910, Gray moved the company a block east into the newly remodeled former J. C. Turner & Son corner. A new electric sign was installed, one of, if not the first, in town. At the same time the owners divided the second floor of the 31' by 71' structure into offices.

In 1913 the United States military recruiting station had an office there.

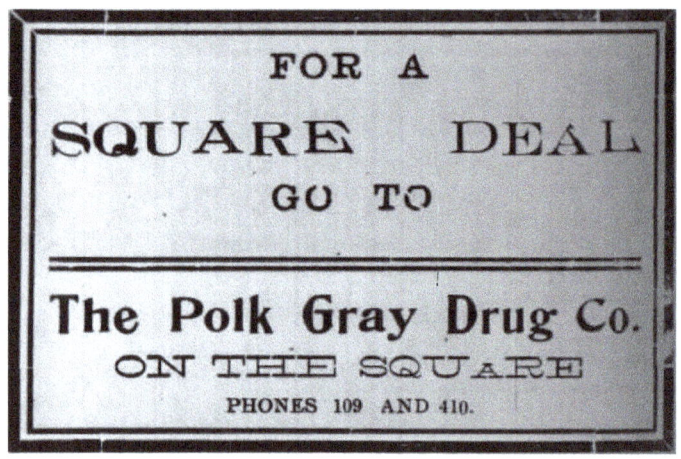

SHC   **1910**   *SHC*

"The Polk on the Square"—Polk Gray Drug Co. token   *SHC*

Prescription bottle   *SHC*

180

Polk Gray Drug soda fountain *Stimson*

Polk Gray Drug interior view *Stimson*

In the teens, Dr. Charles Cruse had a veterinary office in the rear of the store, and Dr. Forest Carpenter was treating two-legged patients upstairs.

A few years before Gray moved in, the *Landmark* newspaper and print shop moved out of their long-held upstairs perch in the McRorie building. A writer to the paper in 1932 described the *Landmark* office when the paper was first starting out there. He recalled that the editor J. B. Hussey and his family lived in the same space as the paper office. The press equipment and printing supplies shared the same cramped room as the cooking, living, and sleeping equipment belonging to Mr. and Mrs. Hussey and their two children. Larger presses were located in the basement. After the type was set into blocks in the upstairs office, a runner (for many years Manlius "Judge" Watts) would carry them down the staircase to the ground level and then outside and around to the side of the building to the basement door on Center Street.

When *Landmark* owner and editor Joseph P. Caldwell sold out to Rufus R. Clark and became editor of the Charlotte Observer in 1892, he sold the printing operation of the paper to John A. Brady. Brady maintained his shop on the square for the next quarter century.

The paper office served as the town's own "Ripley's Believe it or Not." It was the place where folks dropped off for inspection odd, unusual, and record-breaking objects from across the county—all sorts of artifacts, antiquities, curiosities—including reptiles, animals, insects, eggs, fish, the biggest or most oddly shaped fruits and vegetables, etc. Even ole Jim Tharpe's four-legged chicken was on display there in 1898...and then someone else dropped off a second one in 1899. And the particulars of each were carefully described in the next issue of the *Landmark*.

Agricultural products, floral arrangements, and baked goods for competition at the county fair could be dropped off there, as could lost and found items. And, of course, the newspaper was the central collection point for citizen complaints of every type. The office was also occasionally used as a public meeting space. The school board was meeting there in 1896.

It would have been within the walls of the second-floor *Landmark* office that editor Caldwell created and chronicled the legendary "Santer," the mysterious beast that roamed Statesville, Iredell County and beyond for more than half a century. It would have also been from the upstairs corner window that Caldwell's successor, Rufus Clark, stared off into the distant sky while reading telegraph reports of the Wright brothers experiments and forwarding them to his eager readers. The square was a great place to sit and dream even back then.

When the paper moved down West Broad Street to the upstairs offices over Brady Printing in 1906, owners John M. Sharpe and R. E. Nooe began remodeling the former newspaper office. The Iredell Telephone Co. office moved in to serve their 100 phone customers and remained there until they built a new headquarters at Center and Water in 1910. Tobacconist G. E. French also moved his office into the improved space. That same year, a new storeroom was built in the rear of the building, 104 North Center. In later years the Carolina Café, City Café, and the Singer Sewing Machine Company occupied that spot. From 1921 until 1950 Dr. J. H. Nicholson's dental office was located upstairs, and Drs. Eugene Yount and Lauren Gibson had offices too.

In 1932 Polk C. Gray suffered a heart attack and a month later announced the sale of the popular Polk Gray "Polk on the Square" drug store to Ralph T. Holmes and F. M. Youngblood. Holmes was a Harmony, NC native who was living in Charlotte and traveling for the Burwell-Dunn Drug Company at the time. Youngblood was from Concord. The name of the new company was Holmes Drug.

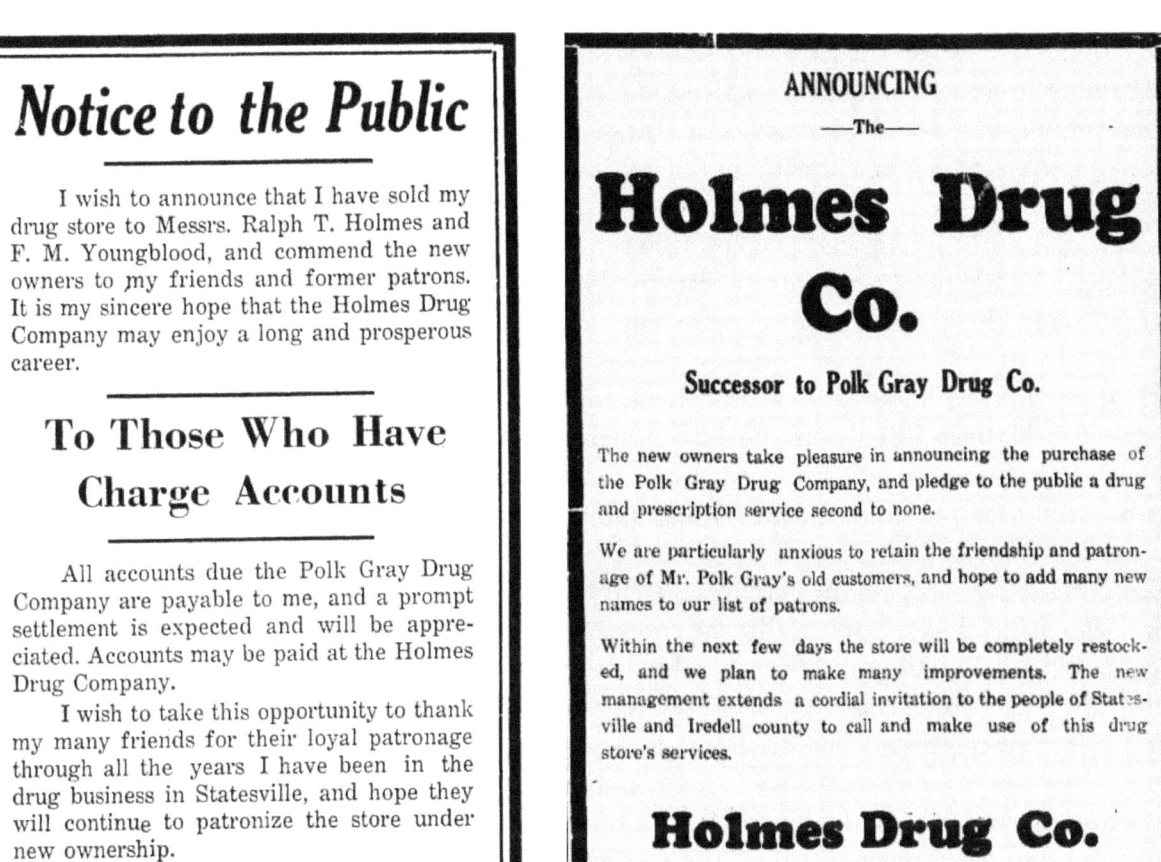

Holmes Drug "On the Square"

The exterior of the building was painted and upgraded with the name change, but the interior remained the same. Photographer Elbert Ammon moved his studio into an upstairs office space. At one time, as many as six doctors operated out of the Holmes building, including J. M. Alexander, J. L. Pressley, J. H and C. R. Nicholson, and Lauren and McKamie Gibson.

The National Farm Loan and Statesville Production Credit organizations opened offices there in the late 1930s. In 1940, Ben Stimson opened an auxiliary photography studio upstairs, resulting in friendly competitors Ammon and Stimson working out of side-by-side offices. Stimson's West Broad location was his portrait studio, and the East Broad office was for commercial work.

On August 6, 1933, the National Recovery Act loosened some government red tape to help curb the nation's economic downturn caused by the Great Depression. This resulted in Holmes Drug having the honor of being the first drug store in town to open on Sunday. The new regulations allowed one of the five downtown drug stores to be open each Sunday. Holmes was the first in the rotation. But even then, the hours were strictly limited to 9:00-11:00 a.m. and 3:00-6:00 p.m. to avoid conflict with church services. The city's "Blue law" regulated Sunday activities that officials deemed as unnecessary. They continued to protect the Sabbath into the 1970s.

Ralph Holmes carried on the altruistic traditions of McRorie, Turner, the Landmark, and Polk Gray as the central location for community services and information. He sold passes to the circus, subscriptions to organizations, and a wide array of raffle, theater, ballgame, and dance tickets—sort of a homegrown predecessor to Ticketmaster, but without the service fees.

Hurst Turner American Legion Post 65 utilized the charitable services of Holmes Drug for active members to pay their dues and new members to enlist. The Holmes's also collected live rabbits for the annual rabbit dinner put on by the legion for former service members.

In 1947 they collected hundreds of second-hand comic books for patients at the Veterans Administration Hospital. The Holmes Drug staff provided a great service to the community, and in return for their generosity, potential customers streamed into the store and patronized the soda fountain. Later, when the Miller brothers took over, they continued that hometown spirit for nearly another 35 years.

Holmes Drug pharmacists in the early years were Charles Mills, a hold-over from Polk Gray, and Lester Fisher. Later came Fleet Scroggs, Bryant Stone, Bagwell Goode, C. G. Leslie, B. R. Phifer, William Sappenfield, Boyd Kunkle, James Fletcher, Fred Lowry, James Connell, and the last owners Jim and Joe Miller. Mills was a loyal employee of Polk Gray and Holmes drug stores for 35 years, and the Miller brothers filled prescriptions there for almost as long.

For a period of time Holmes employees used a motorcycle to deliver prescriptions around town. Ralph's wife Annie, who was the president of the company, also worked in the store. She prepared pimento, ham, chicken salad, and egg salad sandwiches at her home each morning and brought them in to sell at the soda fountain.

Beck **Circa 1940** **Largest and smallest at Holmes** *Daily Record*

In 1947 an interesting pair made a personal appearance at the store, Senor Felix Manse, one of the world's largest men and Senorita Margauria Leyton, the "world's smallest woman." (Hmm, I wonder if she knew about our own "Little Ina" Brewer?) The couple was promoting the Cole Circus that was in town that week. Their visit was broadcast live on WSIC radio.

During the city's "Straw Hat Week," a contest was held in front of Holmes Drug to improve the public's perception of straw hats. A hat was frozen inside a block of ice. Contestants guessed how long it would take the block to melt, and of course the winner got…a straw hat. A few months later girls were frying an egg on the sidewalk out front.

Holmes' pharmacist William Sappenfield set a company milestone on March 31, 1955, by filling the one millionth prescription in the company's 45-year history. W. R. Watts was the lucky customer.

Tharpe **A typical day at Holmes Drug** Tharpe

Since the drug store building was bordered on the north and east by other buildings, throughout the years, owners constantly had difficulty finding a convenient system for loading and unloading supplies and merchandise into the store. There was no designated loading zone nearby. It wasn't until 1956 when Ralph Holmes was hauled into court for not paying his overdue parking fines that the city got serious about helping ease the problem.

The judge threw the case out after a discussion with the police chief. The chief verified that two years earlier he had, indeed, told Mr. Holmes, that since his store lacked a loading zone, he could disregard any parking tickets he received. And Mr. Holmes did just that. Holmes Drug was granted an emergency loading space exclusively for their delivery vehicle shortly after the trial.

Holmes Drug was known for its well-stocked women's cosmetics counter, but it is probably best remembered for its soda fountain. The place was equally packed throughout the day with ladies trying out the exclusive line of Helen Rubenstein products and boys and men lined up at the soda fountain for one of Mrs. Holmes sandwiches and a made-to-order fountain concoction—sometimes a cherry Coke, but more often a freshly squeezed orangeade.

In 1963 the Iredell County Republican Party opened a "permanent headquarters" over the store. Rep. James Broyhill attended the opening ceremony. The Republicans remained there into the late 70s, probably because the building was owned by some prominent Republicans (see below).

It was also in 1963 that Ralph and Annie Holmes sold their venerable company to brothers W. James and Joseph L. Miller. The Holmes couple continued their association with the store as it closed in on filling its million-and-a-half prescription. Ralph was still working for the Miller's when he passed away in 1974. The Miller's continued providing the same friendly, personal, customer service and the same awesome orangeades.

A top-to-bottom renovation was given to the old building in 1966 by the Miller brothers. In 1972 the store took in the prescription records from their competitor a few doors down when Purcell's Drug closed their operation. In 1997 Jim and Joe ended the 87 year long tradition of being the "druggist on the square" when their company was purchased by the Revco drug chain.

SHC **Owners Joe and Jim Miller**

Jim and Joe SHC

Record & Landmark **1963**   **Advertising ashtray**   *SHC*

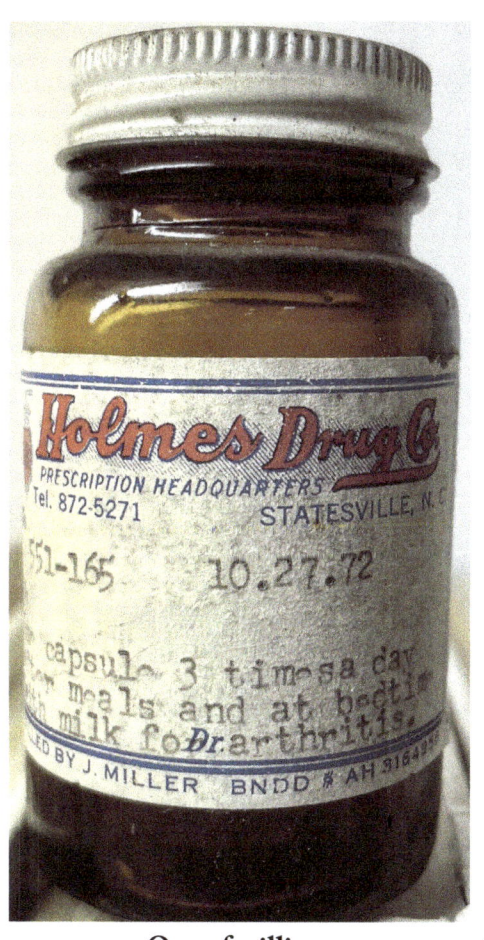

One of millions   *SHC*

187

An interesting sidenote to this story, in 1937 Vernon E. Lackey and Salisbury investor John Hanford purchased the building from the Sharpe family. Lackey was the local Southern Express agent. He died in 1969 and Hanford passed in 1978, leaving the property to their families.

John Hanford had married Mary Cathey from Statesville in 1917. Mary's father was local liveryman J. P. Cathey. J. P. was also an early downtown policeman and for a while was in charge of the city scales that stood outside the McRorie/Holmes building. Their union bore a daughter who would become a nationally recognized political leader, Elizabeth Hanford Dole. For 20 years after John Hanford's death in '78, Elizabeth, her brother, Lackey's widow, and Elizabeth's three-time presidential candidate husband Bob Dole owned the Holmes Drug corner.

Elizabeth and Bob, Hanford and Lackey sold the property to a consortium of downtown investors in 1998 made up of LeRoy Plyler, Gloria Hager, David Parker, Elbert Richardson, Bill McMillian, Rick Gregory, John Potts, and others.

Chapter 21
The Southeast Corner

The Southeast Corner
101 South Center
First National Bank/Town Clock

In 1996 county historian W. N. (Red) Watt, released his book *Statesville—My Home Town, 1789-1920.* He had spent years poring over the county's early deeds and land transfers. He incorporated his findings into a map of the 124 approximately half-acre parcels making up the original town of Statesville. The the map below shows Lot Number 5 on the southeast corner of the square outlined.

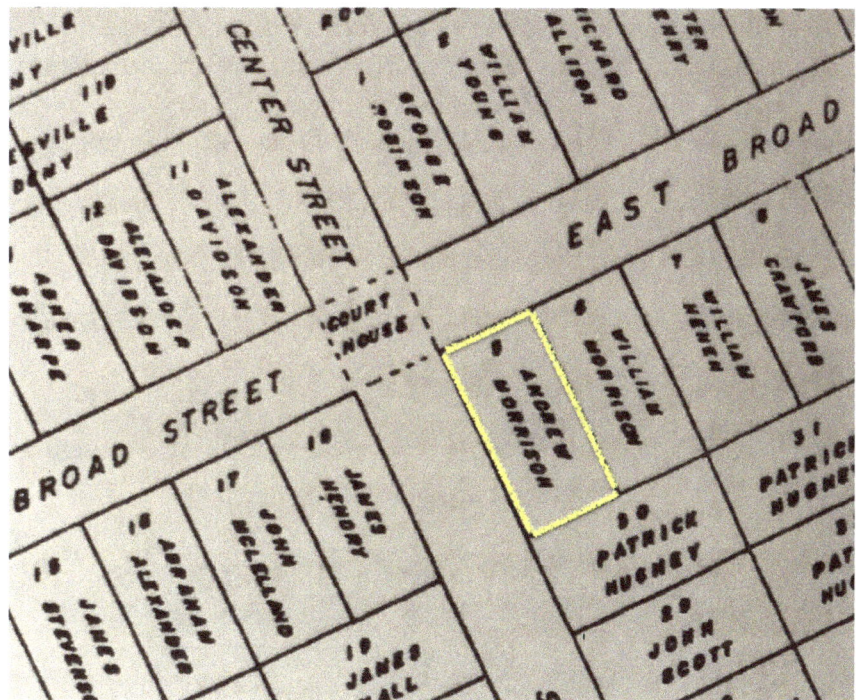

Original lots by W. N. Watt drawn by Grier Surveying showing Lot 5

On August 13, 1790, Andrew Morrison bought Lot 5 for ten pounds, 13 shillings. The property remained undeveloped for the next nine years. In 1799 John Nesbit, who had been operating a store on the Chipley Ford Road near Fort Dobbs, bought the lot and built the town's first store there. His brother, Dr. J. K. Nesbit, assisted him in the business.

The fact that it took years for the settlers of this area to establish a store and that all the early businesses were taverns, is an indication the town was primarily an overnight stopping place for travelers and for rural county residents riding in to conduct court and government business. Afterall, by horseback, residents in the upper and lower regions of the county would spend one day riding in, one day doing their business, and a third returning home. Taverns provided food, drink and lodging for them and livery services for their horses.

Incidently, when the first court session was held at the Iredell County courthouse, John Nesbit was one of the 12 jurors to hear the first case, that embarassing little incident involving the two prostitutes. Nesbit and his fellow jurors found the "ladies," "not guilty."

In 1823 Nesbit's heir, John, Jr., split Lot 5 into smaller tracts. Originally it had a 214-foot frontage on East Broad and 107 on South Center. John N. Hart bought a section facing South Center and a year later he sold it to Newton Crawford who built a store there. Junior sold another section facing East Broad to Joseph Davidson who sold part to Cyrus Simmonds. J. S. Miller bought part of it in 1867. And earlier, Wesley Reynolds had a store just south of Nesbit's about where Wooten's Jewelers is today.

In 1884, A. M. Walker submitted to the *Landmark* a detailed lot by lot description of the town as he remembered it 50 years earlier, in 1834.

Later in the 1960s, local historian Homer Keever detailed the Walker description to artist Edrie Knight who drew this sketch for the *Statesville Record & Landmark*. It shows the one-story house (40) on the southeast corner of the square where J. K. and John Nesbit operated Statesville's first store. The two-story house next to it (41) facing East Broad and owned by Joseph Davidson was empty.

There were three houses on the Center side of the old Lot 5, Lock's shoe shop (39), the Newton Crawford house where John Nesbit lived (38), and the Jacob Rickert house (37).

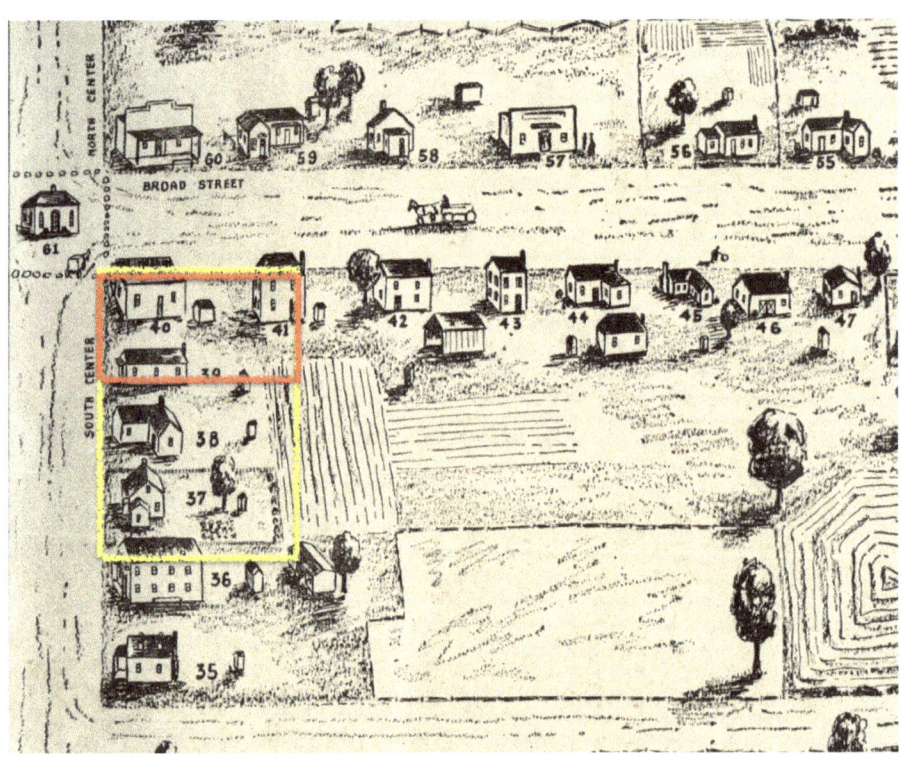

Keever's *Record & Landmark* interpretation of A. M. Walker's 1834 Statesville
Edrie Knight, artist
(Original Lot 5 and First National Bank/clock building outlined)

The Great Fire of 1854 dramatically changed the landscape of downtown Statesville, but somehow missed Nesbit's old store building, by that time Samuel R. Bell's store. Samuel R. Bell retired from the mercantile business in 1858 and put the corner up for sale.

> **VALUABLE TOWN PROPER-TY—FOR SALE.**
>
> The subscriber having retired from the Mercantile Business in the town of Statesville, offers for sale his,
>
> **Store-House & Lot,**
>
> situated on the East corner of the PUBLIC SQUARE, in the centre of Business. This is one of the most valuable stands for business in the Town.
>
> Terms made easy. For further information Apply to S. R. BELL or Dr. DEAN
>
> WILLIAM MURPHY.
>
> Oct. 1st, 1858.   44tf

Iredell Express **ad, 1858**

Although the Nesbit/Bell Store building survived the Fire of 1854, it wasn't so lucky on October 31, 1882 when a Saturday evening fire destroyed it and a couple of neighboring stores. By then, the place was called "the old Bell storehouse" and housed M. J. Phifer's stock of groceries and miscellaneous goods on the street level and M. H. Barringer's beef market in the basement. After Bell closed his store in 1858, a parade of businesses moved in and out over the next quarter century, mostly peddling general merchandise and groceries.

The fire began in a small building behind the Bell building that held carriages and buggies for the Van Pelt & Miller Company. It also spread to the Fielding Watts building on the Broad Street side and a small house next door on the Center Street side.

Remember Fielding Watts? He was Manlius Watts' "master" who sold him to J. S. Miller for $1,500 before the Civil War. Miller owned parts of three of the four corners of the square at one time or another, and as a young man had clerked in the Turner Store on the fourth corner.

The flames drew a large crowd to the square and the town's firefighting apparatus was on the scene quickly as firemen got their hose hooked up and stretched across the street to the cistern on the southwest corner.

Despite the late hour, 10 p.m., a Republican Party meeting was being held down the street at the courthouse featuring several prominent speakers. Upon hearing the alarm, the meeting adjourned and the participants willingly became firefighters. Locks were broken off the burning buildings and stock was carried to the streets to escape the flames.

Fortunately, it was a calm evening with very little breeze, so a repeat of the 1854 catastrophy was avoided, although several surrounding structures suffered damage. The roofs of buildings across Broad even caught fire, but the firemen were able to quickly direct water on them.

The town's newly purchased Lafrance fire truck was a tremendous asset. It had made its first big run to that same location just a few months earlier when the large, outdated tinderbox of a building had caught fire. They saved it that time, but unable to save it a second time. Col. J. S. Miller had a $400 insurance policy on the Bell building. Phifer had $300 in coverage on his stock, and Barringer's policy covered about $25.

Prevailing whispers around town the next day were that the fires were of an incendiary nature since the place had been struck twice in just a few months. It was summized that the land was more valuable without an outdated eyesore standing on it.

The *Landmark* reported: "Too much praise cannot be bestowed on the firemen for their exhibition of nerve and perserverance. They were cool, resolute, and untiring. They have vindicated the wisdom of the town commissioners to buy the (fire) engine. The engine saved many times its value. The citizens, white and colored, worked gallantly and the latter deserve all commendation for their bearing."

From 1882 until 1889, the vacant lot on the corner was referred to as the "burnt corner." From time to time, that same title was assigned to the lot on the southwest corner, and even more rightfully so. Stores there had burned down on three separate occasions over a century.

Entrepreneur William M. Cooper bought part of the old Lot 5 from J. S. Miller in 1884 and the parcel where the bank was to be built was bought from J. S and C. L. Miller in 1889. Cooper's association with Lot 5 and his impact on the city as a whole can't be underestimated. He was one of the town's most prominent capitalist of his day, with fingerprints on all the structures on the east side of South Center, as well as many other aspects of the town. Cooper Street was built along the eastern side of his South Center Street properties and still bears his name.

Cooper, a prominent Wilkes County merchant, distiller, and former state legislator, brought his successful wholesale liquor business to Statesville in 1881. Before coming to Statesville, he had already accumulated substantial land in town. By the time of his death in 1907 at the age of 63, he had acquired over 30 properties, including some of the most valuable downtown real estate. He was one of the town's wealthiest citizens of his day.

Cooper was joined in Statesville by his brother, C.S. Cooper. They specialized in Laurel Valley Corn Whiskey, "made in copper stills in the foothills of the mountains using pure mountain water." Their plant rectified, bottled, and sold the product by the boxcar loads all over the U.S. Eventually Cooper turned the family liquor operation over to his son W. W., and the company relocated to Marion, N. C. where it remained until state prohibition kicked in. The name "Laurel Valley" came from Cooper's store and mill at Laurel Falls near Eagle Mills in northern Iredell.

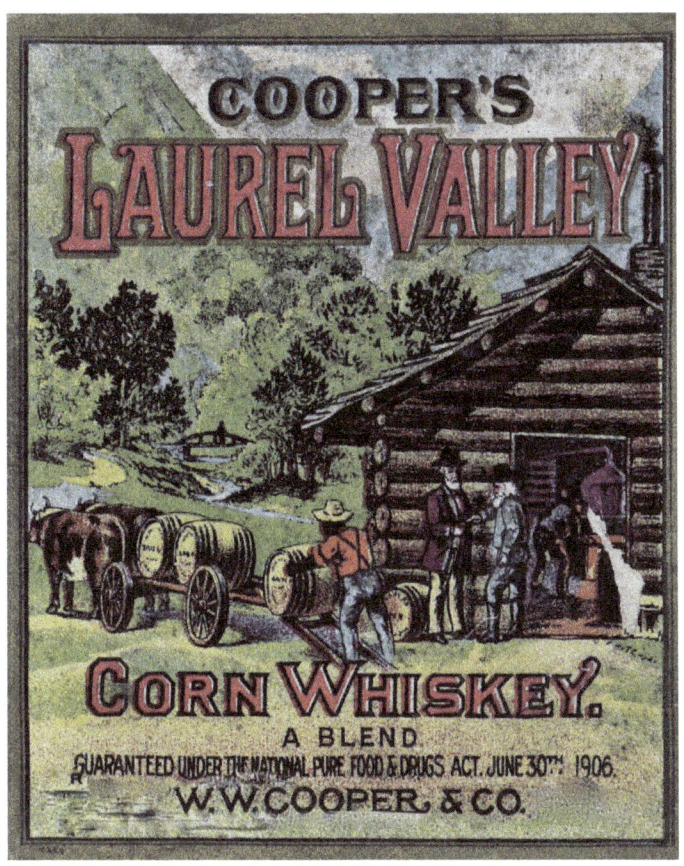

Cooper's Laurel Valley Corn Whiskey, 1880s *SHC*

When Mr. Cooper moved to Statesville, he brought with him quite a bit of investment capital. He used it to open his own bank, the Cooper & Brown Bank, in 1885.

In 1884 Troutman lumberman, J.C. Steele, decided to get out of the timber business and move to Statesville to take charge of the Sword Brick machine which Cooper had bought to build his new hotel. The Cooper House, later renamed the Hotel Iredell, was located directly across from the (old) courthouse where Woolworths and Westmoreland Antiques were later located. Steele then became an agent for the brick machine company and eventually started patenting his own equipment. That move would result in the formation of J. C. Steele & Sons, and a century and a quarter later, Steele's presence can still be found in Statesville.

The May 1884 Landmark reported: "The committee to solicit subscriptions for the new hotel has not yet reported but is about ready to do so. Mr. W.M. Cooper's property seems to be the favorite location and all but about $5,000 has been subscribed."

The hotel was completed in 1885 at a cost of approximately $16,000. Cooper had bought the lot from Dr. J. J. Mott and had hired a Wilmington architect to ensure it was one of the grandest hotels in the state. The paper reported that the community owed a "vote of thanks" to Cooper for his undertaking. The hotel was brick, three stories high, 110' by 100', with its own water works, water closets, and bathrooms on each floor. It had a huge porch that hung over the sidewalk, much to the dissatisfaction of the city fathers in later years.

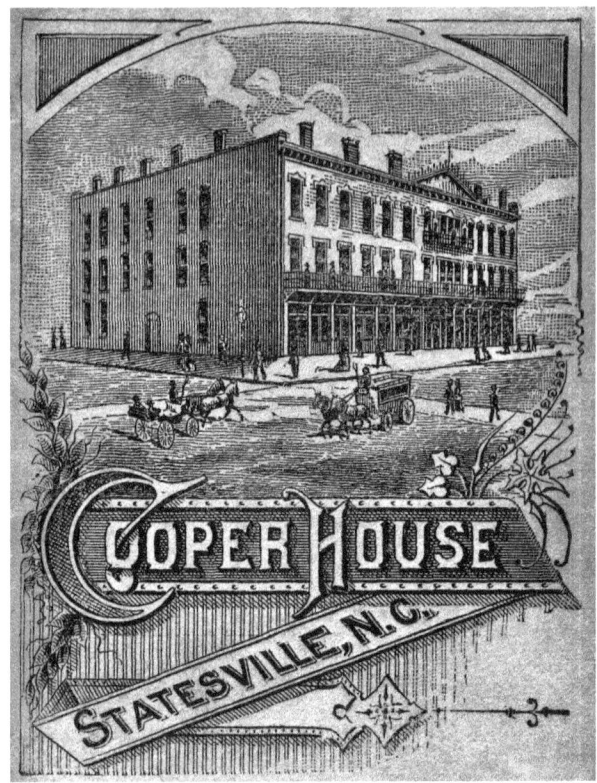

The Cooper House, ca. 1885 SHC

The Cooper House became the Hotel Iredell when C. S. Holland bought it in 1903 SHC

Vice President Adlai Stevenson stayed at the Hotel Iredell and spoke from its balcony to an audience in the street during one of his visits to town in 1907. Governor Zeb Vance also spoke from the perch.

In 1885 the town's Health Committee ordered Cooper to pipe the sewage from his new hotel into the Salisbury Branch instead of a ditch at the edge of the back lot behind the hotel, but he paid them little mind.

Cooper was involved in many other successful ventures around town in the late 1800s, including the development of the Boulevard neighborhood and the Statesville Cotton Mill in south Statesville. His banking house, Cooper & Brown, evolved into the First National Bank in 1887 and he served on the board until his death.

In 1892 his block of wooden buildings between his hotel and the First National Bank burned. Most in town believed that fire, too, was the work of an "incendiary." The Landmark reported that although Cooper had no insurance on the wooden buildings, "he was not losing any sleep over the loss," since, like the building on the square, the property was worth more as an empty lot. He would soon build back the block of storerooms, now called the Center Street Plaza. Behind its current plastic facade is a beautiful red brick beauty with granite accents.

W. M. Cooper Block, ca. 1920s *Stimson*

In 1897 Cooper once again fought the town aldermen over a survey to determine the cost of a new water and sewer system. In 1899 he was elected a director of the Statesville Chamber of Commerce.

An avid outdoor sportsman, three years before his death and Cooper played in a fundraiser baseball game on the "Fats" team against the "Leans."

William Cooper died on August 10, 1907 at his home on Walnut Street. He was married three times and had 15 children. His estate included property in Marion and Asheville and was estimated to be valued at $250,000 to $300,000, quite a sum in those days.

Like most of the prominent businessmen in town, Cooper was a Mason.

SHC W. M. Cooper House, 624 Walnut, 1940s

Oil portrait of W. M. donated to Statesville *SHC*
Historical Collection by Frank Cooper in 2011

The Bank

As early a 1876, several Statesville businessmen had begun calling for a "national bank." But it was 1887 before such an ambitious endeavor would become a reality. Soon a group of wealthy gentlemen were meeting at the banking house of Cooper & Brown in the "bank building" at 130 West Broad. From those meetings the First National Bank of Statesville was born.

The federal National Bank Act of 1863 provided for the federal charter and supervision of banks known as national banks. They were designed to circulate a stable, uniform national currency, secured by federal bonds, and deposited by each national bank with the U. S. Comptroller of the currency. The act also provided for the supervision and examination of banks and for the protection of noteholders.

The process of starting a national bank was pretty straightforward. A capital investment of $50,000 was sold in $100 shares. Shareholders would meet and elect directors and officers. The president was the figurehead or face of the bank, and the cashier was responsible for its day-to-day operation. The capital stock was then invested in U. S. bonds drawing 5% interest per year. The bonds were deposited in the Treasury in Washington and held as a reserve for the bank to issue the currency it then used to conduct business. The feds then printed bank notes in $5, $10 and $20 denominations for the local banks which were one-by-one hand signed by the local officers. These notes were released into general circulation like traditional banknotes.

The $50,000 in stock was quickly raised at the February 8, 1886 meeting, and a few minutes later the stockholders went into their first directors meeting. Nine directors were elected, as well as the offices of president, cashier and teller. Years later, the originial cashier, George Brown, reminesced that 13 days after that first meeting, the bank only had $15,751.35 of the $50,000 in commitments on hand. But it was the community's confidence in those leaders, not necessarily the cold cash, that got the bank off the ground and made it successful.

The First National Bank of Statesville issued their first notes in 1887. They are highly valued by banknote collectors today and bring several thousand dollars if one can be found.

First National's first issue, 1887 *SHC*

The first issue remained in circulation until 1907 when the bank returned $30,000 in currency to Washington to be destroyed and replaced with a new issue of notes featuring President William McKinley and 1860s Treasury Secretary Hugh McColloch.

In 1907 the bank cashed in old 1887 notes for new crisp ones like these *SHC*

Behind the teller windows at First National, ca. 1907 *Stimson*

William Maris Cooper was a savvy businessman and people who knew him trusted him with their money. He was elected as a charter member of the board of directors, and his banking partner George H. Brown was elected to hold the crucial position of cashier. Cooper would eventually be elected president of the bank when his brother, John, died in 1906. During his tenure as president, First National increased their capital from $50,000 to $100,000.

Treasury notice of permission to commence business *Landmark*

In 1922, fifteen years after Cooper's death, the First National survived a major blow when federal examiners came in one morning and discovered a shortage of $84,892. That evening, assistant cashier Cameron Pennington sat on his front porch at 210 North Kelly Street, now the parking lot for Congregation Emmanuel. He had survived a hard day at work. At 9:00 he retired to his upstairs bedroom and shot himself in the left temple with a pistol. He left a note saying that his account books were correct, but implied that those of his boss, J. W. Guy, were not. Guy lived directly across the street at 217 North Kelly and heard the gunshot. Folks wondered what went through his mind.

Guy was arrested the next day. He pled guilty to embezzlement and other banking crimes and died of a heart attack shortly after his trial.

Guy's replacement was Herbert Newbold. Newbold had been employed as a North Carolina state bank examiner in Raleigh when he took the job in Statesville. He served as First National's cashier for 11 years and became a fixture in the community.

Newbold was cashier on January 26, 1933 when the death knell struck the bank. The bank failed to open its doors that morning in order to conserve its assets and it never opened again. It had become the latest victim of the Great Depression … and some poor decisions.

By October, Newbold had defaulted on his North Center Street home and had been indicted by a federal grand jury of misapplication of bank funds related to the bank closure. Also indicted were Harry P. Grier, Jr., president of H. P. Grier engineering company and C. A. Kyles, secretary-treasurer of Moore-Kyles automobile company, the Chevy dealer in town. Newbold was implicated in cashing checks totaling approximately $4,500 knowing that the accounts did not have the funds to cover them.

In the first round of court proceedings in 1934, the case against Kyles was thrown out for lack of evidence. By the time the Newbold and Grier cases were eventually disposed of in 1935, the two had made full restitution to the bank and were given a slap on the wrist and a $500 fine.

But that was not the end of the saga. The federal court ordered for the judgment to be stricken and the case returned to the docket. It finally came back up four years later in 1939 and Newbold was fined an additional $250 but was given a year to pay it off. Each received a two-year probation sentence. The court ruled that, "although banking laws had been violated by the two men, it was all in good faith and that no hidden or deliberate misappropriation of funds was intended."

Newbold moved to Richmond and accepted a position with the Reconstruction Finance Corporation, a federal agency whose role was to provide financial support to state and local governments and make loans to banks, railroads, and other businesses in order to boost the country's confidence and help banks resume daily functions during the Depression. The Newbold family maintained contact with their many Statesville friends and when Herbert died in 1962, he was buried in Oakwood Cemetery.

Incidentally, for you conspiracy theorists, a few months before the bank closed its doors, a suspicious fire was discovered one night in the janitor's closet under the staircase. Firemen were able to extinguish it and save the building. They ruled it a "spontaneous combustion," but years later, people wondered if possibly … well you know the rest of that theory.

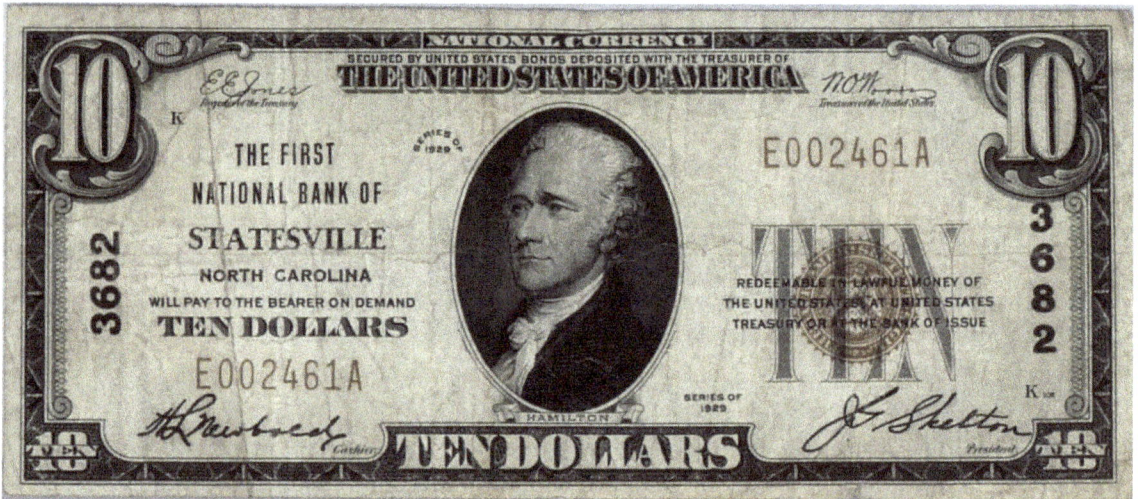

Last issue of currency for First National of Statesville in 1929   SHC

The Bank Building

At the January 1889 First National Bank stockholders meeting, a healthy report was presented. The bank had $67,000 on hand in deposits and farmers had borrowed $8,000 during the year at 8% interest. A motion passed to award stockholders dividend payments totaling 4% of their investments. The semi-annual 4% return continued to be paid out consistently until 1913 when it rose to 5%. Eventually it hit 10% in the 20s.

With dividend money burning a hole in their pockets, the men began talking about the need for a new bank building—a stoic structure that projected the well-deserved sense of confidence in the thriving institution. Since October 1887, the First National Bank headquarters had been located in a storeroom in W. M. Cooper's hotel. Directors soon announced they were purchasing the vacant lot on the square for a new bank building. The directors included most of the town's "movers and shakers," and the First National was the dominant bank in town until its collapse in 1933.

Workers began imediately digging the basement for a modern, three-story structure—the building that stands there today.

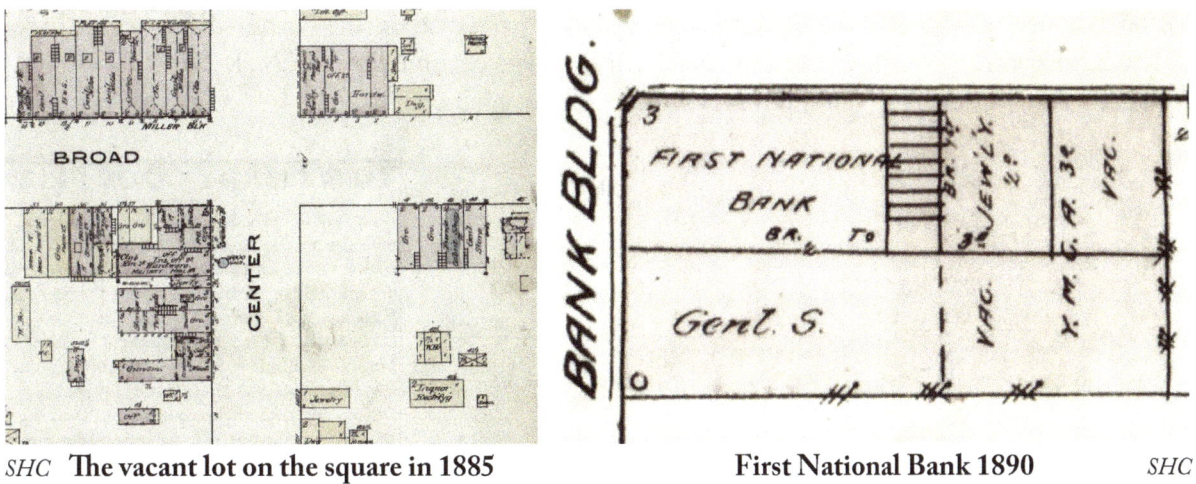

SHC **The vacant lot on the square in 1885** **First National Bank 1890** *SHC*

The contract for the new bank building was awarded to Cecil & Watson of Lexington. The brick was hauled by rail from Charlotte and the lumber came from Kincaid & Brothers of Rock Cut.

The builder boasted that interior rooms would include 28 incandescent lights, the first new construction in town to install electricity. The roof would have a tower and a decorative casement "crown" with the date of construction, 1889.

DSDC   **Ornate "crown" work**   *DSDC*

Engraving in the *Landmark* Trade Edition, 1890

203

The banking house was located on the first floor with the entrance on the corner. There were three store fronts. The large room fronting Center on the south side was occupied by the N. B. Mills Co. The two on Broad housed R. H. Rickert jewelry and N. R. Tunstall's drug store.

Original tenants' *Landmark* ads, 1890

Within a few months of opening, the rooftop of the bank was determined to be the perfect spot for a popular sport of the day, carrier pigeon racing. Express agent, R. K. Murdock visited New York City and brought back 50 homing pigeons belonging to the Empire Flying Club. The next morning, the birds were released from the roof of the bank as 15-20 spectators watched from the street. They circled for 13 minutes then took a northeast course and were out of sight a few minutes later. Then Murdock waited by the telegraph for the report from the Big Apple that they had arrived. Unfortunately, the results were not printed in the next day's newspaper.

The next month a flock of 100 birds was released, this time from the window ledge of the Telegraph Express office. They left Statesville at 5:15 in the morning and at 3:49 that afternoon the Brooklyn club telegraphed that the carriers were starting to arrive. Club members meticulously calculated that the 506.43-mile flight had been covered at 1,403.9 yards per minute. Over the next few years, clubs from New Jersey and Delaware also participated in the fun, but eventually, pigeons became the bane of the bank building. It seems that banks love deposits, but not from pigeons.

SHC Over the years, pigeons have left their mark on the third floor, ca. 2013 SHC

Marshall & Brawley moved into the main storefront in 1892 replacing the N. B. Mills company. They had lost their store in a fire that destroyed the old wooden building between the bank building and the Cooper House Hotel. Like many small enterprises of the day, the company partnership changed every year or so and as it did, so did the company name. Marshall & Brawley became Marshall & Jenkins and eventually J. W. Marshall before moving to West Broad in 1896. Their storeroom was then occupied by Cooper & Gill grocers.

A CARD.

We desire to express our gratitude to all those who in any manner aided in saving our goods at the recent fire.

We are now located in the building in rear of N. Harrison. January 1st we will move to the storeroom in the Bank building now occupied by N. B Mills & Co.

Call and see us.

Damaged goods will be sold cheap.

Respectfully,

MARSHALL & BRAWLEY.

Statesville, N. C., Dec. 22, 1892.

NEW GOODS!

Holmes & Coutts' famous Banquet Wafers, Graham Wafers, Graham Crackers, Brownies, Cream Lunch, Extra Toast, Pretzelettes, Select Sodas, Ginger Snaps, Cheese Wafers, Orange Novelties. Ferris Hams, which are the best that are cured in this country. Kalamazoo Celery, Cape Cod Cranberries, Fresh Grits, Oatmeal, Rice, Cream Cheese and Maccaroni.

Mr. D. J. Kimball is now with our house and cordially invites all of his friends to come and see him.

Cooper & Gill,
One Door South of the Bank,
Sept. 18, 1896.   Center St., Statesville, N. C.

Landmark 1892   1896 *Landmark*

The first occupant of the third-floor space was the Young Men's Christian Association. The Statesville Y.M.C.A. had been in operation since at least 1878.

In 1893 T. D. Miller built a 20x50 foot, one-story building, attaching it to the south side of the bank building on Center. R. H. Rickert moved his jewelry store to the new place and W. W. Foushee moved his musical instrument store to Rickert's old spot. Foushee also made room in his music house for watch/jewelry repairman and optician Robert L. Moore.

Jewelers, watch repairers, and gun dealers were notorious for changing locations at the drop of a hat. Since their inventory required less manpower to pack up and move than, say, a hardware store, they bounced all over town. Most notable was gun and locksmith J. U. Lamprecht. He must have kept his stock on wheels, possibly because every time he got settled in, his shop would burn down.

Lamprecht's shop must have been a fascinating place to visit. He carried guns, scissors, table and pocketknives, pistols, keys, sewing machine needles, and gun cartridges, flasks, caps, belts, pouches, and parts. He also had copper liquor distillery fixtures and supplied the whiskey revenuers with their barrel marking stencils. His set of scales served as the official "keeper of standard weights and measures for Iredell County." The paper said he could build anything from a watch to a locomotive.

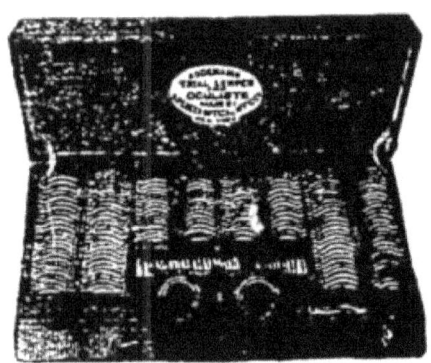

Robert L. Moore's shop at Foushee's Music Store, 1895 *Landmark*

The "Chowder-Chucker" Club (I was afraid to research much further), consisting of 25 or so local young men was meeting in the upstairs hall in 1894. The same year, Dr. Phillip Laugenour opened up a dentist office on the second floor. Laugenour was the town's local historian and wrote many historical sketches for the papers. Also, on the second floor, Miss Addie McElwee opened an art studio and Messrs. Brown & Guy and W. E. Nattress had insurance offices there. A stockbroker and the Long Island Cotton Mill also had offices on the second floor.

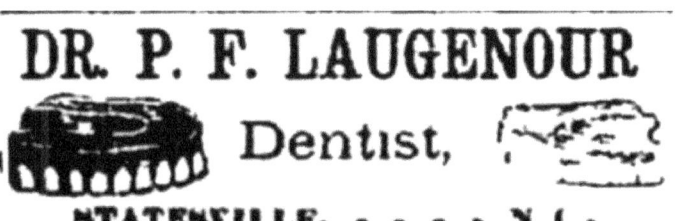

1895 *Landmark*

In those days, amateur telegraph operation had become a popular hobby. Durand Cooper, the bank's bookkeeper, Robert Moore, and Dr. Laugenour set up telegraph wires and instruments in their places and learned how to use them. In 1897 the Western Union Telegraph office moved from Cooper's Hotel to the first floor of the bank building beside Z. E. Turner's store.

In 1895, Methodist minister Rev. James Willson (not Wilson) opened a grocery store in the corner room of the bank building. He ran it for 10 years before selling out to W. H. Powell.

When the town received its first telephone system in 1895, the central office switchboard was located in the First National Bank building. It used the "Mason's System" and hooking up to it cost $12 a year for residential and $24 a year for business service. E. C. Hein moved here from Ridgeway, SC and took charge of the system.

In the teens, N. R. Richardson, the Methodist conference colporteur, was making his headquarters in the bank building and operating a bookstore selling Bibles and religious literature covering several denominations.

Some of the bricks on the front of the building were dinged by gunshots from the infamous Cowles-Gregory duel in 1898. The bricks were conversation starters for years later. Cap. Gregory's bullets missed Col. Cowles. Two months later Gregory, a cotton broker, opened an office beside the telegraph office and received reports on the price of cotton every half hour.

The lodge hall on the third floor was shared by several organizations including the Pythians, Knights of Honor, Royal Arcanum, and Masons, sometimes hosting up to 100 members per meeting. The Chamber of Commerce held their organizational meeting there in 1899 and by late 1900 they had established a permanent office there.

The lodge members installed electric overhead fans in 1898 to encourage attendance during the hot summer months. Water and sewer service were added to the building in 1899.

Will Gaither opened a candy and fruit store next to the telegraph office in 1899. He also sold oysters and ran a lunch counter there. The Bell "long distance" telephone office was located in Gaither's oyster parlor for a short stint. Gaither bought a bakery and moved out in 1900. Eugene Turner took over his place selling "everything from hammers to corsets" at his "One Price Cash Store." But after two months, the revolving door continued when he bought out C. F. Meacham's store and moved.

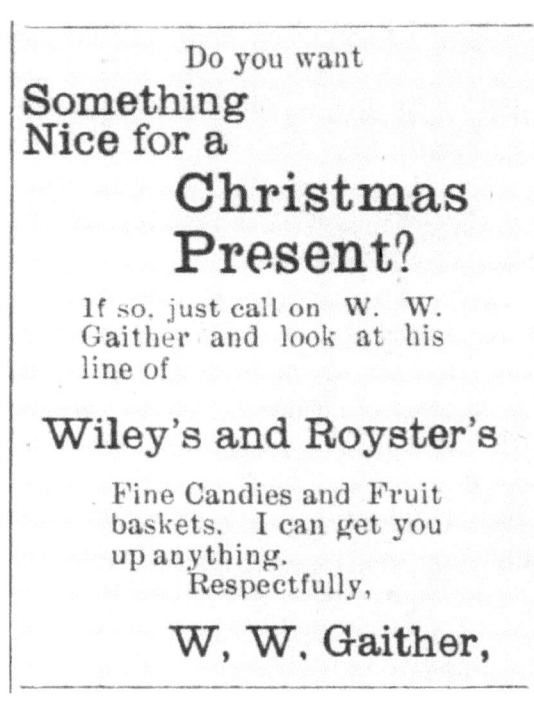

Mascot **Will W. Gaither, 1899**

Telegraph & Cable office on Broad St. Side *SHC*

For some unknown reason, the U. S. government had rented a room on the second floor from the time the place was built in 1889 until 1899, for "document storage." They paid $75 per year for 10 years. When they ended the lease, they sold the entire contents of the mystery room to a local citizen for $10. Of course, there was quite a bit of discussion around town about what the contents were and why the government had wasted so much money—yet another mystery.

When the One Price Cash Store closed on the East Broad side in 1900, H. B. Alexander moved his grocery store and oyster parlor into that room.

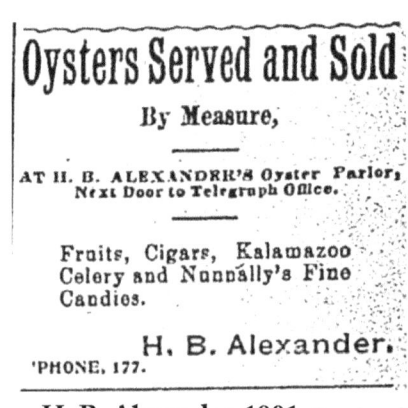

H. B. Alexander, 1901 *Landmark*

Louis Clarke, father of 1924 Olympic Gold Medal winner "Pinky" Clarke who lived on North Race Street, moved his cigar factory to the second floor over Cooper & Gill Grocery on the Center Street side in 1900. He had already moved his whiskey distillery to Salisbury, and he soon moved his residence to Pennsylvania because of North Carolina's liquor prohibition act.

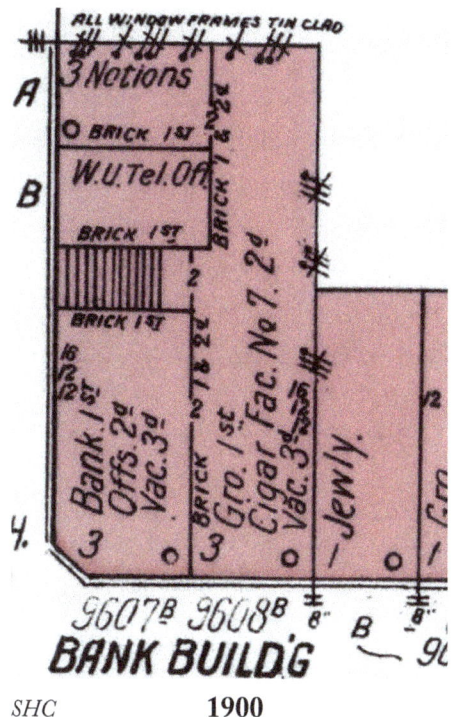

SHC **1900**

View of Brigadier General J.F. Armfield funeral on Broad from second floor of bank in 1916 *Stimson*

The W. E. Nattress law office and the U. S. Army recruiting station were sharing the Chamber of Commerce room in 1901. A men's prayer group was also meeting in the Chamber's room every Sunday afternoon at 3:30. J. D. Cox moved his oyster parlor there in 1904. Fresh oysters were a popular commodity and, when in season, were shipped in weekly.

Landmark **1904**   **1907** *Landmark*

In 1907 W. D. Atwell remodeled the room vacated by the Southern Express office for yet another grocery store. Durand Cooper started Home Electric selling fans in his spot on the second floor as the musical chairs continued. Hartford Insurance was upstairs as well.

The same year, a major plate glass and marble overhaul was done to the building. The interior was outfitted in mahogany and all rooms were refurbished and modernized. A new electric sign was installed on the corner by the Masonic Lodge and was attracting a lot of attention.

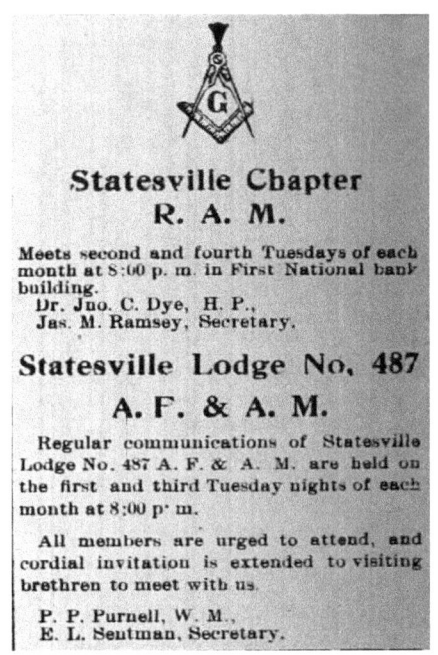

SHC **Lighted Masonic Lodge sign**   **Meeting announcement**   *Landmark*

In 1909 T. W. Frasier was hired to build a new exterior smokestack for the furnace. The original one encased inside an interior wall was beginning to fail. In 1912 the S. M. & H. Shoe Company moved into J. B. Gill's old grocery store.

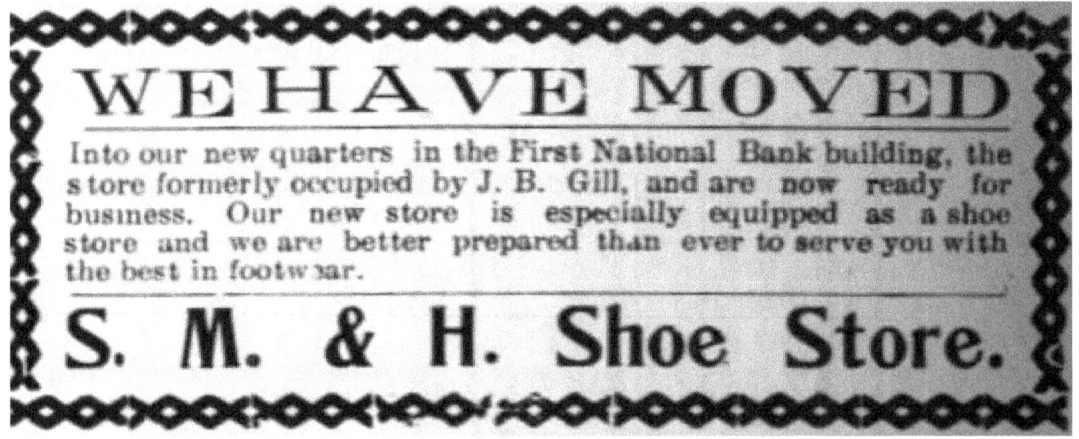

S. M. & H. Shoe Store   *Evening Mascot*

The Knights of Pythias moved their lodge hall from the Patterson building to the third floor of the bank building in 1913, sharing the upstairs with the Masons.

Knights of Pythias sign remained upstairs in 201 *SHC*

Lumberman J. B. Foster and W. L. Gilbert, auditor for the Carolina Hardware Merchants Association opened offices on the second floor in 1914 and H. C. Gaither moved his grocery store in. Also, J. G. Colvert had a grocery store there briefly in 1914.

In 1915 the second-floor tenants included: Room 1, R. V. Brawley, real estate; Rooms 2-4, Isadore Wallace, real estate; Room 3, J. B. Foster & A. L. Lawrence, lumber; Room 5-9, Hasty Vance, dentist; Room 6, City Electrical Dept.; Room 8, vacant; Room 10, Lyric Theater office; and Room 11, Kincaid Brothers, lumber. The Pythias and Masons occupied the third floor.

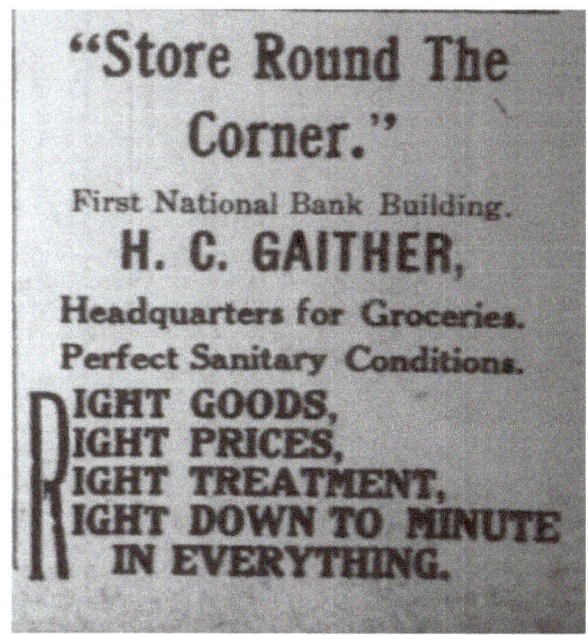
Landmark **H. C. Gaither Grocery, 1914**

R. V. Brawley Real Estate & Auction *Landmark*

The Western Union Telegraph office moved in '17, and S. M. & H. Shoes became Mills Shoe.

In 1921 two new built-in bank vaults were installed at the First National, complete with a manganese steel door with quadruple screw seals making it "excelled by none south of Richmond." The bank made some adjustments to their office layout, too. The cashier's office was moved to the rear of the banking house and the teller window was relocated to the front.

The Iredell Bargain House opened in the former shoe store in 1927, and Gable's, a chain ready-to-wear clothing store took the Center Street spot in 1928. Gable's was a South Carolina based company and the Statesville store was their first in the state.

In 1928 the bank allowed local airplane enthusiasts to paint a sign and arrow on the roof directing pilots to the Statesville Airport. The sign said STATESVILLE in 10 ½ foot letters extending 100 feet. A large "4" indicated that the airport was four miles away. The arrow was 25 feet long pointing toward the airport. Floodlights were installed on the clock to light the roof. A similar sign was to be placed on the roof of Statesville Chair Company.

Dr. John Schafer also moved his optometry office there in 1928.

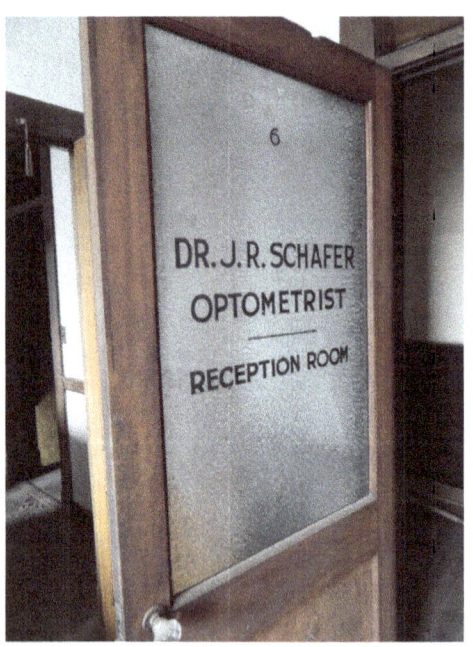 

SHC   **Welcome to Dr. Schafer's office**   *SHC*

In 1929 with the Great Depression quietly lurking on the horizon, stockholders spent $16,000 to upgrade the second and third floor rooms. The Statesville Industrial Bank moved their office to the 106 East Broad room in 1929 resulting in a curious couple—two banks under one roof.

The upstairs walls were finished in Kraftex, hardwood floors were installed, the woodwork was finished in mahogany, and new light fixtures were hung. Drs. James Alexander and James L. Presley moved their offices into two of the newly remodeled rooms.

Both the local Republican and Democrat parties had offices upstairs at differing times.

In the winter of 1930, a nasty rumor started circulating through town that the First National was insolvent. Each time the tale was told, the amount of the shortage had grown larger. Such rumors were pretty common in those days. And after all, the bankruptcy of the Commercial National Bank beside the courthouse on South Center a few months before didn't help matters.

The *Landmark* spoke up in support of the bank writing, "If the originators and spreaders had exercised the same diligence in analyzing the personnel of the First National Bank and its resources, as they have in spreading the libel, they would have found the facts. But as is well known, people who peddle scandal and libel do not want facts. Facts are not as delightful to their taste." I wonder how many readers saw a similarity between that rumor and the editor J. P. Caldwell's tall tales in the 1890s about a wild beast roaming the streets and eating babies.

The article also stated that the bank was offering a $500 reward for the conviction of the person who had started the rumor.

People's Bank, the competition a block down the street, took advantage of First National's misfortune and poked a little fun at the "reward" by placing an ad headed with, "THE REWARD of a Savings Account."

THE REWARD
Of A Savings Account

IS THE SATISFACTION OF KNOWING THAT YOU HAVE THE CASH and can spend your own money whenever you want to spend it.

Spending in advance and paying later mortgages the future.

A new quarterly savings period opens April 1st. Start an account now.

Save and let your savings earn. We pay 4 per cent interest on time and savings deposits.

PEOPLE'S LOAN AND SAVINGS BANK

Landmark   **March 14, 1930**

The competition down the street *SHC*

When the First National Bank shuttered its doors in 1933, the occupants included: 1-3, Grier-Lowrance Construction; 4-6, Grier, Grier & Joyner, attorneys; 5-9, W. C. Current, dentist; 8-14, J. L. Pressly, physician; and 11-13, J. M. Alexander, physician.

The Knights of Pythias and Masonic Halls were still on the third floor.

Gable's clothing was at 103 South Center. The J. C. Alexander Brothers grocery store was at 102 East Broad, and the Statesville Industrial Bank was at 106 East Broad.

Dr. Current's office   **Grier-Lowrance Const** *SHC photos*

Statesville Industrial Bank in the First National Bank Building, strange bedfellows   *Landmark photos*

Auction   Landmark

The bank building remained in limbo while the lawyers and courts determined how to dispose of it. Three years after the bankruptcy, on September 24, 1936, the building and several other pieces of real estate owned by the bank, were auctioned off to the highest bidders.

When the auctioneer's hammer dropped, the Belk's department store chain of Charlotte held the winning bid of $37,125. With new ownership, attention turned to the fate of the town clock. Since 1890 the city had been granted passage to the rooftop to wind and repair the clock. But shortly after buying the building,

Belk asked the city to relinquish that agreement to allow them total flexibility in designing the building to meet their needs. Without much of a choice, the city aldermen voted to relinquish the agreement and allow Belk's to remove the clock if they so desired. As might be imagined, that caused quite a panic among many in town.

Finally in February 1941, an announcement was made that the town clock could continue casting a shadow on the square. A compromise agreement called for the removal of the old bell, however.

It was also announced that the ornamental cornice system overhanging the sidewalks would be removed and replaced with a parapet wall and terra cotta coping. The queen's bedazzled "crown" was being replaced with the non-descript roofline that currently adorns the structure.

DSDC **Before** **After** *DSDC*

In September of 1939, the final remnants of the First National had been cleared out to make way for Statesville Drug who was moving a few doors up the street to the place they would call home for well over half a century. Dr. J. L. Morrison also moved his office to the bank building.

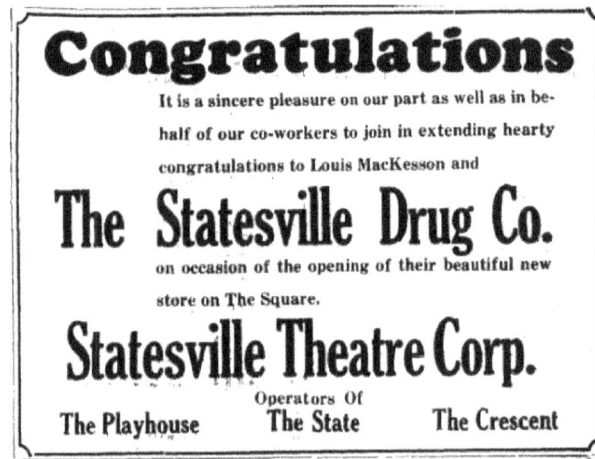 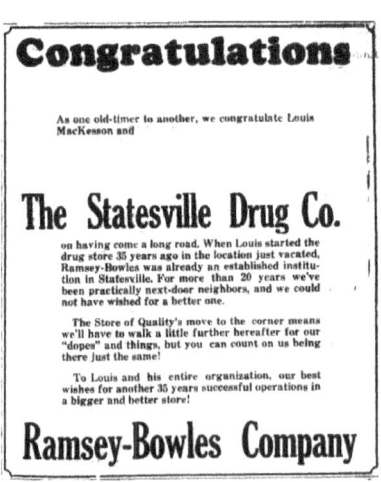

Neighbors congratulate Statesville Drug on their move in 1939 *Landmark photos*

Statesville Drug was founded in 1904 by Dr. T. E. Anderson, A. B. Saunders, O. L. Smith, and Louis W. McKesson. It was originally located in the former Marble Hall Saloon at 115 South Center, now occupied by Mezzaluna II restaurant. Like most drug stores of its day, it had a fancy soda fountain. Theirs was a modern marvel called a "Liquid Iceless" model they bought in 1909.

Optometrist R. M. Rickert moved his office to the second floor in 1941.

Parade float, ca. 1907 *SHC*

Landmark **Dr. R. M. Rickert, Jr. Please be kind to your operator, 1940** *Landmark*

During WW II, military personnel in uniform passing through the Statesville bus station were offered free refreshments at Statesville Drug hoping they would leave here with a warm spot in their hearts for "the best town in North Carolina."

The company was sold by the McKesson family in 1948 to Sam G. Hickman of Lenoir and Doyt S. Cornelius of Mooresville. Hickman became manager and Louis and the rest of the staff stayed on. About that time, the pharmacy, a member of the Rexall brand franchise, started keeping regular Sunday hours from 9-11 a.m. and 2-4 p.m. for the first time. In 1950 the Sunday afternoon hours were extended to 6:00.

1930s *Stimson*

SHC **1940s**

1950s SHC

Dr. Morrison moved to the Stearns building, and Dr. James Little set up his dental office in '48.

As a free service to the community, Statesville Drug, like Holmes Drug, was an unofficial ticket agent for plays, concerts, beauty pageants, ballgames, the circus, etc. If a promoter would drop off a handful of tickets, the staff at the drug store would sell them. On Fridays you could buy your Statesville High football game tickets and avoid the ticket line at the game.

In 1950 L. W. McKesson retired and yielded his head pharmacist role to Bill Howard. McKesson had been with the company since its inception in 1904 and served as its manager until 1948.

In the 40s and 50s the Statesville Band, a group of spirit-minded men and women with an in interest in musical performance, used a room on the third floor next to the Masonic Hall for practice and uniform storage. Remnants of their uniform closet were still there in 2013.

The Statesville Community Band uniform closet on the third floor in 2013 *SHC*

SHC   **Military parade**   **Signage in 1955**   *Record & Landmark*

In July 1959, Sam Jordan, manager of the Statesville Belk's store announced the opening of the company's Toyland store at 103 South Center in the Statesville Drug building.

SHC   **1959**   **Watching the parade from the upstairs windows** *Tharpe*

A sidewalk poetry contest sponsored by the Arts & Science Museum was conducted at the drug store in 1960 where 18 poems from local writers were taped to the East Broad side of the building. Passers-by were to read the poems, vote for their top four favorites, and drop a ballot in a box. The newspaper editor was surprised that a religious vein ran through so many of the poems, with nature and love vying for second place. Mrs. Margaret Woodruff took first place with "Church on the Rock."

Lyle Davis bought half interest in Statesville Drug in 1959 and became an active partner. Davis, who had been associated with the Squibb Co., and B. S. Goode who had been a pharmacist there for six years, directed the prescription department. Davis bought the other half of the company in 1967.

The Statesville Drug building underwent a major facelift in 1962. A modern glass front was installed on both the drug and toy stores along with a new marquee spanning the building. A new entrance was built to the second floor. Efird's Toyland was located in the 103 Broad spot.

STAFF AT STATESVILLE DRUG — Pictured from left are Mrs. Lou Wilson, Mrs. Ruth Emerson, Mrs. Rene Summers, Miss Helen Fulbright, Jim Moore, and A. Lyle Davis, staff members of Statesville Drug Company.

Record & Landmark **It only took eight employees in 1970**

Efird's Toyland next door *SHC*

In 1970 Lyle Davis bought the bank/drugstore building from the Belk Department Stores for $100,000. He added an entrance on the East Broad side, the ceiling was lowered, and new lighting, floors and fixtures were installed.

The company dropped their affiliation with the Rexall Company and joined the eight-year-old Scottie Discount Store chain out of Florida. Scottie's was known for promoting self-service shopping to reduce personnel costs and then passing the savings to customers. The store only had eight employees at the time.

The Scottie Store was a separate company from Davis' prescription drug operation, so it was basically two businesses operating under one roof appearing to be one store. And true to their word, in 1974 the store had reduced its personnel to six.

DSDC

DSDC

Record & Landmark

DSDC   **Scottie Discount, Statesville Drug, and Cato's**   *DSDC*

Pharmacist Lynn Waugh, Jr., a 1967 North Iredell High School and recent UNC-Chapel Hill School of Pharmacy graduate, joined the store in 1972 and bought interest in the company the following year. He was further invested as a partner in 1975 and later purchased the company.

Statesville Drug became Revco drug store in 1999 and then they were acquired by CVS drugs. After CVS moved out, the building stood vacant for the next dozen years.

221

Several tenants were in and out of the 103 South Center side in the 80s and 90s, but much of the time it was vacant. Bob's Discount Shoes was there briefly in 1982, run by, well, Bob, selling ... footwear. Nellie Boan opened the Fashion Nook in 1985, and Bobbie Ruth McLain ran Bobbie Ruth's bridal salon there in 1988. Park's Beauty Supply was there by 2003.

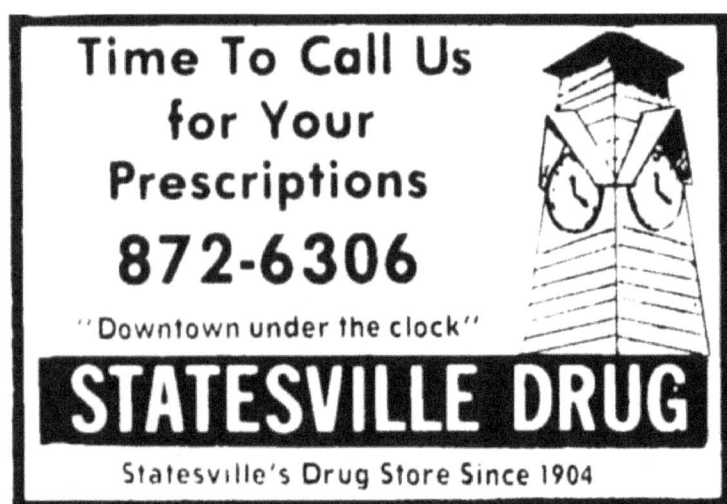

1974 *Record & Landmark* ads

LeRoy C. Plyler purchased the "clock building" from Lyle Davis in 1997 for $234,216.89. Dr. Paul E. Swaney bought the 5,267.90 sq. ft. building in 2003 and is the current owner.

In 2010 the first floor of the former CVS pharmacy became home to the Needle & Thread shop, owned by Teresa Kyles. Kyles had started her quilting shop after being laid off work at the Freightliner plant in Cleveland. The building was remodeled, a handicap ramp was added to the Broad Street side, and the old bank door on the corner was renovated.

The Needle & Thread remained there for a decade and in 2020 "Billy Buck" Blevins moved the WAME Real Country 92.9 and 550 AM radio headquarters 250-feet across the square and into the space. The station offers classic country, live community interest talk programing, and live stage shows from their state-of-the-art Randy Marion Studio.

An unsolved mystery associated with the First National building surrounds a third-floor window. For some reason it is different from the other windows in the building. It doesn't have the decorative "crown" lead encasement all the others have.

Second window from the back corner... *SHC*

Searches of the old newspapers thus far have offered no clue. No one seems to know why or when it disappeared. Did it fall off? Certainly, that would have made the front page of the paper. Was it never installed? And if not, why? Did the builders miscount or run out of money? Even the earliest photographs taken just after construction show the bare oddball window.

One theory is that it is related to the highly secretive organization whose headquarters was just inside—the Masons. The Masonic Lodge had been located in the northeast part of the building since the 1890s. In the early 2000s Statesville lodge member Tom Gregory, who accompanied this writer on a tour of the old hall, speculated that since the window was on the northeast corner, there may have been some masonic symbolism involved. Masons believe the northeast represents "the dark side." But if so, why the second window and not the corner window?

Even today, just inside that window there is a strange lead or galvanized metal box built into the floor. It appears to have possibly held sand and could have been there to contain a fire for some purpose. The building had a centralized heating system so there would have been no reason for a wood stove. Was fire involved in Masonic ceremonies? Hmmm.

Metal box inside the mystery window *SHC*

The following is a true story told in the "Statesville After Dark," Chapter 1 walking history tour. It a story that was told by an elderly lady named Virginia Deitz Malcolm just before she died in 1988. Virginia shared a chilling story about an incident that happened to her as a young lady working at the First National Bank. She was the manager's secretary and she said she loved her job.

> One afternoon Virginia was sitting at her desk, and she heard footsteps coming up the stairs. She watched as a man walked up the hall and into her office. Without speaking, the man reached across her desk, grabbed her by the throat, lifted her up out of her chair, and began choking her. She thrashed around helplessly for what she said seemed like forever.
>
> Eventually she was able to grab a pair of scissors off her desk, swing around, and plunge it into the side of her attacker. Immediately, he turned her loose and dropped her to the floor. She heard him run down the hall, down the steps and back out the front door.
>
> After a few minutes she was able to get up and stumble out of her office. There she saw her boss standing in the doorway of his office smoking a cigarette. She screamed, "Why didn't you stop him?" "Stop who?" said her boss. "The man who just tried to kill me."
>
> When the boss saw that she was serious, he said, "Virginia, I've been standing right here, and you and I've been the only ones up here for the past hour." He half-jokingly told her, "Maybe you've been working too hard, or maybe you saw a ghost." But she wasn't laughing. She believed him. There could be no other explanation.
>
> She returned to her desk, got her purse, left, and never went back to work there. She was convinced that this building was home to some sort of evil monster. Or even worse, maybe the place was causing her to lose her mind (there is a lot of lead paint in those old walls).
>
> Virginia said that a few months passed as she tried to pull her life back together. Then one day she opened the newspaper and read the headline, "*First National Bank Fails to Open its Doors.*" The bank had declared bankruptcy and her boss had been arrested for misappropriating money.
>
> *Instantly*, she realized what had *really* happened that day. She wasn't crazy after all, and she hadn't seen a ghost either. She was convinced that her boss had hired that stranger to kill her, because she was the only person who had access to his records.
>
> Well, theft charges against the boss were eventually dropped, but Virginia went to her grave convinced he'd tried to kill her.
>
> So—was it insanity? She was quite eccentric—she was later known as "the Cat Lady of Walnut Street." Was it a murderer? Or was it a ghost? I guess we'll never know for sure. But one thing I *do* know for sure is that every time I look up at that window, I think of Virginia ... and now ... so will you.

And so, ends, the saga of Virginia, the ill-fated First National Bank, and a plethora of shops and stores that made their homes on Lot number 5 on the square.

SHC

SHC

SHC

Stimson

SHC

SHC

The Clock Building over the Years

Chapter 22
The Southwest Corner

The Southwest Corner
101 West Broad
Stockton Hall/Sloan's/Eagles/Plyler's/GG's

The southwest corner of the square has a storied past that includes some of the town's most beautiful architecture, a community rallying point, and unfortunately an occasional fire. For a while, the post office was located there. Later it housed the town hall, and for many years it was the center of the town's social activity, the opera hall.

The number 18 was assigned to the southwest corner when the new town of Statesville was surveyed and laid out. It was one of 26 approximately one-half-acre lots sold by the Iredell County Commissioners on the first day of the sale, August 13, 1790.

It was purchased that day by James Hendry for 10 pounds, 15 shillings. The original indenture filed in the Iredell County Register of Deeds lists the county commissioners who made the sale as John Nesbit, George Davidson, Jeremiah Wilson, Joseph Sharpe, and Christopher Houston.

Deed for Lot 18, dated 1790   *SHC*

"Red" Watt detailed the early history of Lot 18. The first few years after Hendry bought the parcel were somewhat of a rollercoaster. Hendry sold half of the lot to Charles Conner who sold it to James Nichols, Jr. in 1793. Nichols then sold it to Joseph Forsyth for 55 pounds, and Forsyth sold it to James Irwin in 1801 for 125 pounds.

Although Lot 18 covered the west side of South Center down to about where Court Street is today, for the purpose of this discussion, we will concentrate on the small section of the lot directly on the square.

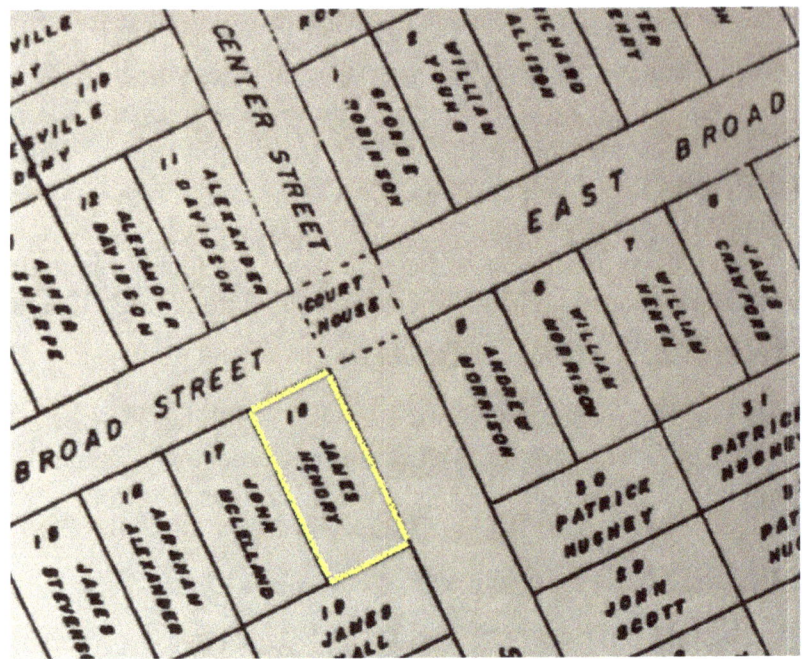

Original lots by W. N. Watt drawn by Grier Surveying showing Lot 18

It would take ten years before James Irwin built a store on the corner around 1801. When Irwin moved to Georgia to become a cotton farmer in 1819, he sold out to Robert Simonton who, like most of the previous owners, was a land speculator; but Irwin retained some sort of partnership in the store, along with 13 town lots and 130 acres. The store was called the Irwin-Simonton Store.

When Irwin died, he was worth $90,000 to $100,000, an incredible accumulation of wealth at that time. His final will and testament seems to indicate he was a bachelor.

Robert Simonton, also a bachelor, died in 1826. After a legal battle, the Irwin-Simonton properties were auctioned off in 1831. Irwin's brothers from Georgia and his brother-in-law, Alexander Huggins, who lived beside the vacant Fort Dobbs site, were the high bidders on the 13 downtown lots, including the part of lot 18 on the square.

According to "Red" Watt's research, the purchase meant that Huggins owned all the property from Meeting to Center Streets on the south side of West Broad. Joseph Stockton married Huggins' daughter Margaret and operated the Stockton Store on the square for years.

Joseph Wilson Stockton was the third wealthiest man in town before the Civil war with property valued at $32,000 and 14 slaves. In the fall of 1859, he began construction on a large, three-story brick building on the square. The first floor contained several storerooms. The top floor was outfitted as a large meeting space. By late winter the building was complete, and businesses began moving in. One of the first occupants was the U. S. Post Office which occupied the second room from the corner. Photographer J. B. Carter also set up an ambrotype photography studio there promising "likenesses in the best style of the art, in cloudy as well as clear weather."

Stockton Corner with Patterson building to the left *SHC*

Professor Andrews' students from the Statesville Male Academy were among the first to use the new meeting hall. As part of their end-of-year examinations, they performed their declamation and composition exercises in front of an audience of 400-500 observers, distinguishing themselves as orators and composers. The students were constantly interrupted by rapturous applause. They were followed by addresses from Rev. W. A. Wood and Rev. Rockwell from Davidson College. Professor Andrews limited the number of young men he accepted into his academy each year to just 25 and claimed his students graduated as both scholars and soldiers, "with as much discipline as found at West Point."

In October 1860 a huge political rally was held in town with speeches from numerous politicians, including Zebulon B. Vance from Asheville. Vance gave an afternoon speech at Stockton Hall despite being hoarse from the three-hour and five-minute stem-winder he gave in the yard of the Presbyterian Church a few hours earlier. The speakers were promoting their allegiance to the federal union.

Their enthusiasm for the Union would soon wither with the outbreak of the Civil War, but the support of Zeb Vance would never waver. Zeb made Statesville his home for a while after War.

The speeches at the church began with 33 rounds of cannon fire, one for each state making up the Union. After Vance's rousing speech, cannons were fired again, and the group paraded to the square. The procession was led by a wagon and team decorated with signs promoting the Union and carrying a ringing bell that represented the 1860 Constitutional Union Party presidential candidate John Bell, who was running against Abe Lincoln.

During the winter of 1860, Joseph W. Stockton's store was the most well-stocked enterprise in town. He carried all sorts of men's and women's clothing, hats, bonnets, boots, and shoes as well as hardware, crockery, paint, groceries, and drugs, basically an early Walmart. But the War would force him to cut his inventory to just the basics.

In 1863 upon receiving a shipment of salt, he made a generous offer in an *Iredell Express* advertisement to provide widows of Confederate soldiers with small amounts of salt until the county shipment came in.

Another example of his public spiritedness was the thoughtful newspaper ad he ran from time to time reminding people to pay the preacher for his services.

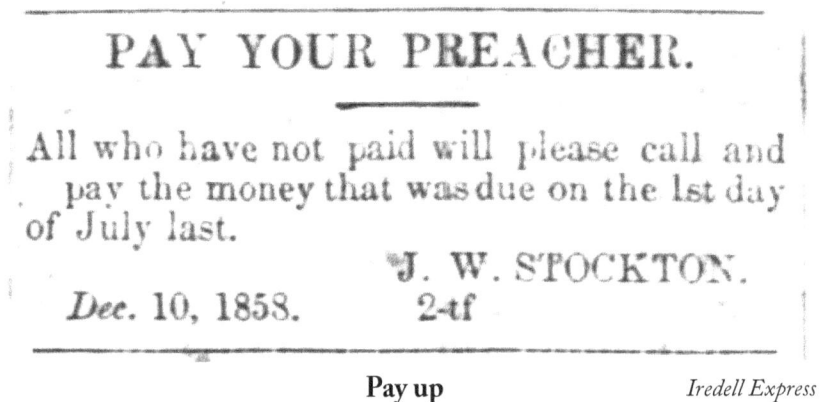

Pay up *Iredell Express*

Near the end of the War, Stockton offered his store as a central collection point for donated food for the 7,000 suffering citizens of Columbia, SC. Columbia had been hit especially hard by the War, and as a result, was occupied by mostly women and children. Central South Carolina had previously been one of the most lucrative markets for the farmers of Iredell County. Stockton collected corn, molasses, bacon, and other food products and shipped them south.

Just before the outbreak of the War, he was also an early scrap metal dealer, advertising to buy 10,000 pounds of castings and scrap iron.

But shortly after the War, Stockton was bankrupt and was forced to sell everything. His beloved Stockton Hall sold at public auction for $3,585. His 450 acres of farmland on the outskirts of town, his extensive railroad stock, and even his house furnishings, horse, wagon, and harness were sold to the highest bidder, a devasting blow to Stockton and the town.

Immediately after his financial collapse, Stockton sold mill stones and industrial bolting cloth. It didn't take an expensive showroom to sell 1,500-pound French burr mill stones. He held a variety of other jobs until his death in 1881. The year before his death, at the age of 75, he was injured while working as a clerk at the express office. Watt's research revealed that Stockton's wife's estate provided for his funeral and tombstone expenses, and he bequeathed his gold watch and any remaining money he had to his daughter. Stockton Street bears his name.

Stockton's building was bought by J. F. VanPelt, Col. S. A. Sharpe and J. S. Miller in 1868, and the upstairs continued to be the town's opera hall. Over the next quarter century, it was home to various doctors, dentists, lawyers, a jewelry store, the Intelligencer newspaper, J. F. Bailey dance studio, and an array of retail stores. A man named Munds ran a drug store there in the 1870s. He had a large thermometer and a bulletin board in front of his place upon which the *Landmark* would post the lowest and highest temperatures of the previous day. One morning Munds' gauge registered ten below zero at 6 a.m.

In later years the building continued to occasionally be referred to as Stockton Hall, but the upstairs was usually called either the "opera house" or "opera hall." The hall had all the luxuries of a concert room in a larger city. There was, however, in 1878 a complaint that the competence of the ushers working there was lacking. It seems that in order to claim a reserved seat, the purchaser had to plant himself in it well before showtime, or else "become disagreeable and put on a side show." At least that's how some ticket buyers saw it.

Dozens of national traveling shows included the Statesville Opera Hall on their southeastern U.S. itinerary. The Hall hosted plays, concerts, minstrels of all types, and of course, operas. In 1870 a traveling ventriloquist called Professor Hughes performed there. The Carolina Comedians were there in 1874. Vocalist and actress Clara Wildman provided nightly performances for a week in 1875. The Berger family with 13, mostly female, musicians performed to a full house. The Iredell Blues military unit held their dances there and Mrs. Morrow's Home School students were regular performers at Stockton Hall. Traveling preachers and rabbis delivered sermons in between, many of them promoting the prohibition of alcoholic beverages.

Clara Wildman *Landmark*

The Berger Family Concert Troupe *New York City Public Library*

The New York Minstrels posted handbills around town promoting their Thursday night performance at Stockton's in 1875. On the night of the show, an orchestra of three musicians played until starting time. Then the promoter, a Mr. Anderson, addressed the small crowd and said that because an insufficient amount of money had been collected at the door, the show would have to be postponed until the next night. He promised that the show would go on Friday night even if only three people showed up.

The next day it was discovered that Mr. Anderson had skipped town early in the morning without paying his bill at the St. Charles Hotel. The hotel manager quickly grabbed the baggage belonging to the three musicians who had not been quite as quick to slip out. With their luggage held hostage, they were forced to remain in town for a few days until arrangements could be made to pay their bills.

The town hall was moved to the Stockton building in the 1870s.

In November 1878 Mr. A. S. Caldwell from Charlotte exhibited for the first time in Statesville one of Thomas Edison's most famous inventions, the phonograph. Caldwell advertised that the machine could talk, sing, whistle and play music. And he was only charging 35 cents for "grownups" and 15 cents for children. In today's money that would amount to about $10 and $4. Little did those ticket buyers know that, 40 years later in 1918, Edison would spend a few hours walking the streets of Statesville while vacationing with Henry Ford and Harvey Firestone.

Another interesting sidenote, LeRoy Plyler who owned that corner of the square for many years was an avid antique phonograph collector and dealer and would occasionally display his talking machines in his clothing store.

In 1881 the opera hall was renovated and a fire exit plan was put into place. With the improvements, even more renowned traveling shows added stops in Statesville. In 1882 a letter to the mayor addressed a growing problem for performers at the hall. The writer said, "When entertainment of any kind is given at the opera hall, it has become the custom of some roughs to annoy the audience and if possible embarrass the performers by hooting and blowing trumpets in the streets in the vicinity of the hall. Can't something be done about this nuisance? This thing is a disgrace to the town and should be looked after at once. There should be no leniency shown on account of race, color, or previous standing in society."

An earlier writer had complained about boys in the audience snickering and making obscene noises during the most intimate scenes. I suppose some would just say, "that's show business."

One of the most popular opera hall shows was the piano performance of the world famous "Blind Tom" Wiggins, a former slave who became one of the most influential pianist of his time. A NC soldier who had seen him perform up north earlier said about Wiggins, "One of his most remarkable feats was the performance of three pieces of music at once. He played 'Fisher's Hornpipe' with one hand and 'Yankee Doodle' with the other and sang 'Dixie' all at once. He also played a piece with his back to the piano and his hands inverted."

unc.music.edu   **"Blind Tom"**   *Univ. of Kentucky, hdi.uky.edu*

In 1880 the postoffice was moved to the storeroom vacated by J. C. Anderson, the town tax collector. This would allow patrons access to their lock boxes day and night. The Iredell Blues armory was located on the second floor of the Patterson Building beside the opera house.

In 1881 D. A. Baker and James B. Woods moved their hardware store from Salisbury to the corner storeroom. Two years later, Baker & Woods moved down the street and T. M. Mills hauled his book, stationary, sheet music and picture store inventory into the corner spot.

For a while W. J. Coite ran his banking business in the back of Mills' store with an entrance on West Broad Street. Coite agreed to provide a corner of his office rent-free to the Western Union Telegraph Co. Up until that time the telegraph had been inconveniently located several blocks from the business district, at the depot. The telegraph company approved a "loop" to be run from the depot to the square.

In 1890 former mayor J. F. VanPelt unsuccessfully petitioned the town to reimburse him for half the cost of replacing the plank flooring in front of the Opera Hall. And in 1892 C. E. Propest moved his bakery, candy and fruit stand back to its former location next door to W. S. Phifer who was selling ice, soda water, gingerale, sarsasparilla, and milkshakes.

On Wednesday morning, December 28, 1892 Statesville's third major downtown fire in a month wiped out the Stockton corner as well as the adjoining Patterson building. The opera hall was gone, along with the two storerooms in the basement, and the offices on the ground floor.

It would be five years before the town would have another opera hall, this one in the new Wilhelm-Mills building on the southeast corner of West Broad and South Meeting. Later a third opera hall was located at 125 North Center Street. Ironically all three of Statesville's opera halls were eventually destroyed by fire.

From 1892 until 1900 that corner of the square was, for the first but not last time, tagged, "the burnt corner."

Without a doubt, the most elegant building to grace the streets of Statesville was the N. B. Mills building on the square. As soon as Nobel Bloomfield Mills had completed Statesville's first skyscraper, the Wilhelm-Mills building on the corner of Broad and Meeting, he began a new project on the square.

In the spring of 1900, Mills announced plans for a two story building to replace the old Stockton Hall. At the same time, Captain J. M. Patterson released his plan to build a two-story building with basement adjoining the Mills building to the south. The front of the second story would be cut off for offices and the rear of the second story and the first floor and basement would be used as retail store rooms.

SHC **Nobel Bloomfield "N. B." Mills**   **"N. B. M." lightening rod on roof** *SHC*

Both buildings were designed by Charlotte architect Louis Schwend. The Wheeler & Schwend firm had designed the courthouse and the old A. R. P. Church on Broad a few months before. Mr. Mills' building was designed to have three storerooms on the 1st floor, one on the corner, one fronting Broad Street, and a smaller one on Center. There was to be a stairway between the two buildings leading to the second stories of each. Both men boasted that their pressed brick and stone buildings would be beautiful enough to be a credit to the town. And they were.

Templeton & Morrison brick company furnished the brick and C. H. Lester was the contractor. The first brick order was for 40,000. Construction was quick but not without incident. The brick-laying foreman got two fingers severely crushed by a load of brick. An observer, L. B. Patterson had his nose broken when a board fell off a scaffold and struck him. And, approximately 10,000 square feet of flooring and ceiling being readied for the project was destroyed when the Carter Brothers saw mill caught fire. The materials were uninsured.

When the building opened in January 1891, it was said there was not a more handsome building in the state. That of course was an exageration, but the place was ornate. To make sure everyone remembered who the the owner was, Mills put a weather vane type lightening rod atop the building's crown using his initials, N. B. M. (Would that make it a vain vane?)

N. B. Mills building, circa 1910 *Stimson*

The nine offices on the second floor were quickly snapped up. Office room Nos. 1 & 2 were rented to Captain J. B. Burwell, agent for the Equitable Life Insurance Co., Nos. 3 & 4, the corner rooms, went to Mr. Lester the construction superintendent. On the Broad Street side, No. 5 became J. B. Connley's law office; No. 6 was E. G. Gaither, insurance; No. 7 was N. B. Mills' private office; No. 8 was rented to David J. Craig and some other men as a "bachelor's quarters" or "sleeping room;" and No. 9 was Dr. Thomas E. Anderson's medical office.

It was in one of those offices that a group of prominent businessmen gathered in 1906 to form a new club, the Commercial Club. The purpose of the Commercial Club was to, "provide a comfortable and pleasant place for social intercourse, pleasure and entertainment for members; to provide a suitable and convenient place where members may resort with their friends visiting in the city for business or pleasure; and to encourage any and all business enterprises promoting the material development and upbuilding of the city of Statesville."

The Commercial Club had a nine-member Board of Governors and any male town resident 21 years old of good moral character was eligible for membership. No "habitual drunkard was eligible for membership." Apparently occasional drunkards were okay. Among the house rules were the following: club rooms open at 8:00 a.m., members will not be admitted after midnight; no gambling or playing for prizes will be permitted; no dogs allowed in the rooms; no books magazines and newspapers or other articles shall be removed from the rooms; coarse, boisterous, profane or vulgar conversations or conduct tending to disturb the peace will not be tolerated; no liquors or other intoxicants allowed in the rooms; and only sacred and classical music shall be rendered in the rooms on Sunday.

A different sort of social club was also making changes to the downtown in the early 1900s. That club was the Hoe-downers club, made up of young men with too much free time on their hands. They claimed to promote "the social and spirituous welfare of the town." Today they might be called pranksters, vandals, or even gangsters. There is no evidence that anyone got physically hurt by their mischief, but some of their activities were evil nonetheless.

The Hoe-downers only came out at night and were especially active around Christmas time for some reason. Occasionally they would pry the signs off stores, then nail them back up on different stores. Then, according to the paper, the next day, out-of-town shoppers who were looking for millinery goods would show up at the hardware store. One night the guys swiped all the display carts that had been left overnight in front of businesses, rolled them into the middle of the square and chained them together.

The paper also mentioned that one year the Hoe-downers released wild and exotic animals into town. Was this a veiled hint that they were somehow involved in the sightings of the "Santer," the elusive wildcat-like creature that roamed the downtown alleys and backlots in the 1890s? That might explain why one of the club members was reportedly caught scaring the public with eerie screeching sounds one night during the Santer days.

The Hoe-downer's most infamous escapade, however, came in 1900 when the Mills building was under construction. One of the members caused a rukus up at the depot in order to lure the cop on the downtown graveyard shift, a man they called "Grandpa" Morgan, away from his post. As soon as "Grandpa" was out of sight, the men began their shenanigans. Using the lumber that was stacked on the sidewalk for the Mills building, they built a fence entirely across West Broad at the square. What statement they were trying to make is anybody's guess.

But, while the Hoe-downers were admiring their handiwork, "Grandpa" circled around and slipped up on the surprised builders. He made them tear down their wall and return the lumber to its proper place.

The lumber fence story didn't make the paper until 23 years later when one of the culprits confessed to it and named his accomplices. The letter in the *Landmark* from the club's former president, M. L. Gunn, offered some background on the devilment of the Hoe-downers. Gunn said that he and his men "shouldered the work that belonged to the vigilantes in the early days of the old west, but combined business with pleasure." Gunn bragged that their efforts "discouraged some of our colored brethren from paying any visits at all after dusk and thus fanned the fire of religion." Coincidentally, sightings of the Santer had served that same purpose of intimidating black townspeople.

In March 1907, Dr. A. S. Orne and wife passed through Statesville in route from Mississippi to the northeast. The Orne's had spent a few days in Statesville two years before and had attracted considerable attention. Dr. Orne had planned to spend a week or two in Statesville but was forced to leave early when he received a letter from what he termed as the "Hoe-Down Club." The letter warned that if he did not leave town, he would be with tarred and feathered.

Dr. Orne was a self-described holiness missionary from New York City and an expert on the reformation of juvenile criminals. He traveled across the U. S. in his "gospel wagon" with the inscription "STOP SINNING" emblazoned on the side. He was a crusader for the implementation of youth curfew regulations, compulsory school laws, and separate juvenile court systems in which youthful offenders are kept separate from older and more hardened criminals. His argument was that 99 percent of the criminal class comes from the ranks of neglected children. While in Statesville, he inspected the jail and county home causing a stir.

The Hoe-downers apparently saw Orne as a northern outsider who had no business sticking his nose into the affairs of their town. But the doctor wasn't much more popular up north. In New Hampshire he was bombarded with rotten eggs. At another stop he was run out of town as his image was hanged in effigy. And still other towns joined in on the Statesville tar and feather threat.

On a hot summer night in 1895, policeman Morgan was investigating a suspicious woman who was attempting to elude him. When finally apprehended, the female was found to be a male in a woman's dress who had been put up to the prank by some of the townspeople for the purpose of entertainment on an otherwise quiet night—most likely another example of the Hoe-downer Club.

The first merchants in the three street-level rooms of the new N. B. Mills building were Sloan's Men's Clothing, in the prime corner room, "Rickert the Jeweler & Optician," on Center, and Stimson & Anderson drug store on the Broad Street side. In preparation for their move, the drug store offered a reduced price on their Nyal's Hair Restorer, only 50 cents a bottle.

Stimson   **January 1901**   *Landmark*

TWENTY-FIVE YEARS AGO

I began the Jewelry business here. In that time I have moved six times, each time into a larger store. The generous support given me by the trading public has enabled me to do this. I now want to express my sincere and most hearty thanks for your patronage and to extend you a cordial invitation to visit me in my bran-new store in the Mills Building. In the past, I have ever tried to deal honestly with every one and will pledge you the same treatment in the future. If you will buy your Jewelry, Silverware and all goods in my line of me instead of ordering from Northern houses, and will pay me the CASH as you have to when you order of them, I will guarantee you as good goods and as cheap prices as they give. Try me.

RICKERT, ~ ~ The Jeweler

MOVED!   MOVED!!

We have moved into our new store in the Mills Building (one door above our old stand) where we can be found with a full line of DRUGS. We have trial packages of

Medicines and Toilet Articles Free of Cost.

Our friends will please call and get samples of each, which will prove their merits.

Jan. 29, 1901.

STIMSON & ANDERSON,

Landmark — **Rickert the Jeweler and Stimson & Anderson in the Mills Building** — *Landmark*

The Patterson building attached to the south side of the Mills building was completed at the same time and the complimenting architecture of the two gave them the appearance of being a single structure. Ramsey, Tomlin & Bowles was the first tenant there. Eventually they would become Ramsey, Bowles & Morrison.

Ramsey, Tomlin & Bowles

Have Moved Into Their

New Store, Patterson Building

CENTRE STREET.

LOOK OUT FOR

White Goods and Embroideries

Ramsey, Tomlin & Bowles..............

Jan. 29, 1901.

Stimson — **Ramsey Tomlin & Bowles** — *Landmark*

In 1907 the Commercial Club moved next door on Broad Street where there were "baths and other club conveniences making it among the best club rooms in the state. Tobe W. Ellis and R. H. Maynard leased one of the vacated rooms for their photography studio specializing in postcards, penny pictures and home portraits.

In 1909 a new ladies' ready-to-wear clothing store was organized by a large group of men and opened in the Broad Street room of the Mills building. Dr. A. G. Phifer opened a dental office and Dr. John C. Dye moved his medical practice upstairs.

Sharpe Gray had a barbershop in the Mills building in 1914 and E. H. Crouch had a shoe repair shop there. Like many small businessmen, they picked up and moved their shops on a regular basis. Marvin Joyner was fixing shoes in Crouch's room in 1916 and continued into the 1920s.

Sentinel   J. M. Joyner shoe repairs shop, 1917   Crowell's hat sale   *Landmark*

In 1917 G. L. Crowell from Louisburg, NC bought the Sloan Clothing, Co. Robert Sloan stayed on and worked for Crowell after cleaning out his stock with a "Daddy Rabbit Sale," which was what he called his "Going out of Business Sale." Crowell then re-stocked the place with a fresh inventory of boy's and men's clothing and furnishings. Crowell Clothing maintained their prominent location on the square until 1926 when the Forester Prevette Co. took over and continued the boy's and men's clothing tradition in the space.

In the mid to late '20s Dr. W. C. Weatherman had a dentist office upstairs next to Dr. J. F. McLaughlin's medical office, and W. J. Matheson had a real estate office on the Broad Street side prior to moving across the street to the Miller Block.

By 1928 the Forester Prevette clothing store had been replaced by Ray & Gilliam's boy's and men's clothing and they lasted for the next 10 years. In 1934 R. H. Rickert moved his jewelry inventory out of his long-time prime spot and Dexter H. Lazenby moved his jewelry inventory in.

For a couple of years in the late 1930s, the Piedmont Barber Shop operated from the vacated drug store stand.

Herbert Morrison opened the College Club, aka the Boy's Club, on the second floor in 1940, but it didn't last long. The Iredell Democratic Party office also made a short stop there in 1940.

In 1941 owner Lonnie Mills announced that the Eagle Five & Ten Cent Department Store chain would be opening a store in the Mills building. To get ready for the new tenant, D. H. Lazenby would be forced to relocate his jewelry store and the entire structure would be remodeled and upgraded to the tune of $20,000.

Part of the upfit process would involve removal of the beautiful roof top architectural features as well as the stately rounded corner tower that made the ediface unique. The removal of the tower caused considerable grumbling among the townspeople. The result was a much simplier look, and the Patterson place next door, home to Efird's department store, was butchered as well. The Mills and Patterson block was no longer the majestic crown on the square.

Stimson **Before 1941 renovation** **After 1941 nenovation** *SHC*

The 42x80 foot retail space was the Delaware based Eagle's Stores largest store in its three state operation. The renovation project included removing the street level staircase between Eagle's and Efird's. Access to the upstairs offices was a staircase located on the Broad Street side. Sad evidence of the destruction of the original rock arched staircase doorway can still be seen between the current buildings,

By the time Eagle's Five & Ten Cent store opened in February 1942, the company had changed its name to Eagle's Five Cent to One Dollar store. But shoppers continued calling it "the five and dime." A few years or so later the company converted back to the 5 & 10 cent concept and later complicated matters by changing to 5, 10 and 25 cents. To keep it simple, most local shoppers just called it "the dime store."

Eagle's brought Grover Huntley from Lenoir in as the manager and his formidable sales force included Mrs. John Shaw, Sarah Hines, Elizabeth Miller, Katy Crouch, Helen Herrin, Willie Caldwell, Chester Stewart, Freddie Gantt, Blance Hatchette, Dorothy Moore, Nora Yates, Betty White, Mary Walker, Mrs. D. M. Knox, Mrs. Sam Kennedy, William Knox and Henry Deal. Six other sales ladies were brought in from other Eagle's stores to help out the first few weeks.

Well, they called the southwest corner of the square "the burnt corner" for a reason. A few days before Eagle's would celebrate its one year anniversary, disaster struck. In the middle of the night on February 22, 1943 fire broke out in the basement. Fire companies from as far away as Mooresville fought the fire for over seven hours, but in the end, all that was left of the Mills building was the brick shell. It was the third time the corner had been wiped out in 90 years.

Some immediately speculated that the flames had started in the second floor office of the War Rationing Board office to hide the manager's sloppy bookkeeping. The office issued permits for new autobile tires, innertubes, gasoline, sugar, etc. During the war, when a man needed a new tire for his A-Model he had to apply to the ration office for a a coupon to buy it. Even if a citizen needed a bicycle, the board would meet on Friday afternoon and vote whether or not to approve the request. Because of the adversarial nature of his job, the Rationing Board manager wasn't a very popular man in town. It's not surprising that the conspiracy theorists lit in on him the morning after the fire.

Although the fire destroyed Iredell County Book Number 1 of the year's supply of blank ration coupons, Book Number 2 had been safely stored in a fireproof vault at the postoffice. So when the office opened back up the next day in the courtroom of the courthouse, service was not interupted.

But, fire chief L. M. "Red" Gaither announced that the fire had started in the basement of the building where Eagle's inventory was stored. The call came in to the fire station at 5 a.m. from alarm box number 5. By that time, flames had already spread to the second floor. When fire fighters arrived, a strong wind was blowing to the south preventing them from getting close to the building. They directed their efforts next door to the Efird's store in the Patterson building to keep the flames from spreading. Fortunately, by 6:00 the wind had shifted and firemen were able to direct water from the roof of Efird's onto Eagle's.

Lyons   **West Broad side**

South Center side   *Lyons*

Aftermath of Eagles Department Store fire   *Lyons*

The Eagle's merchandise in the basement continued to smolder and flare up for the next two days. All hoped the brick walls of the building could be saved, but the damage was too severe. When bricks began falling onto the sidewalk, the lot was roped off and workers built scaffolding to delicately remove the walls.

Owner Lonnie Mills announced a few days after the fire that the Eagle's store owners had agreed to set up shop again as soon as he could replace the building. The cost of the fire was estimated at over $100,000 and the replacement cost of the building was projected at $50,000. The problem was, federal construction regulations were strict because of the war and permission would have to be granted by the federal government. Also, there was a similar snag with purchasing scarce building materials during the war.

Mills applied to the War Production Board for permission to rebuild, but since it didn't directly contribute to the war effort, his request was denied. As a result, it would be five years before a replacement would be built.

Over the next few years there were occasional suggestions on what useful purpose the "burnt corner" could serve. One person suggested a wall of honor for the military men and women who had served during the war. In 1945 when it was announced that President Harry Truman would be visiting the city, plans began for the corner to be transformed into a public restroom area with 35-40 toilets to meet the needs of the thousands of visitors who would be coming in to see the president. Banners and flags were strung from buildings and power poles throughout the downtown. But before the restroom project was complete, President Truman cancelled his visit and the lot remained vacant.

Later Walter Holshouser took advantage of the bad situation and opened a snack and Coca-Cola stand in a make-shift shack on the vacant lot. The corner also offered a good vantage point to watch a parade.

Holshouser's snack stand SHC

In May 1948 Eagle's Five & 10 received a permit from the city to build a new store on the square, and just before Thanksgiving W. P. Delk Construction of High Point put the finishing touches on the project.

The new place sported a "see through" glass front entrance on South Center and another on West Broad. Also, an interior 80-foot archway connecting the Efird's Department Store next door offered a third entrance. A second floor mezzanine served as the ladies ready-to-wear, lingerie, and millinery departments for nextdoor neighbor Efird's. The cost was $40,000.

The new store had 500 linear feet of counter space comprising 13 counters with roomy aisles between them. The store hired a sales force of 60-65 to meet the Christmas rush. They left their Toyland and Christmas decoration shop two doors down where they had been temporarily located since the fire.

Eagle's "dime store" specialized in cut-rate household goods, toys, etc. They remained in operation on the square until the mid 1980s. By then, their name had changed to Eagle Stores.

Other businesses on the second floor of the southwest corner of the square included Dr. James M. Holland's dental office, Jay Little's Studio of Dancing in the late '50s; Leslie Howard's Institute of Music in the 1960s; and Karen Sherrill's Academy of Dance Arts and United Financial Services in the '80s.

After Efird's closed in 1972, the company's manager, Rex Henderson, immediately took over that storefront with his own place in January 1973. Rex's Department Store remained one door from the square for the next five years.

After Eagle's closed in 1985, the corner was once again vacant for a few years. In 1987 Marion's Fashions moved their women's clothing store from the Landmark Building to the square.

Tharpe   **Efirds became Rex's in 1973**   *Tharpe*

Tharpe   **Eagle's front and rear entrances**   *DSDC*

Tharpe   **Candy and peanuts at the rear entrance and popcorn outside the front door**   *Tharpe*

Chapter 23
The Northwest Corner

The Northwest Corner
102-106 West Broad
Miller Block/Hines/Sherrill White

The beautiful iconic building on the northwest corner of Statesville's square is known as the Miller Block. It was built in 1881 by William Clark Miller a local merchant and entrepreneur.

The Miller Block is located on Statesville's Lot 11, which was originally sold to Alexander Davidson by the Iredell County Commissioners August 30, 1790 when the new town was taking shape. Ten years later John Latta owned the lot.

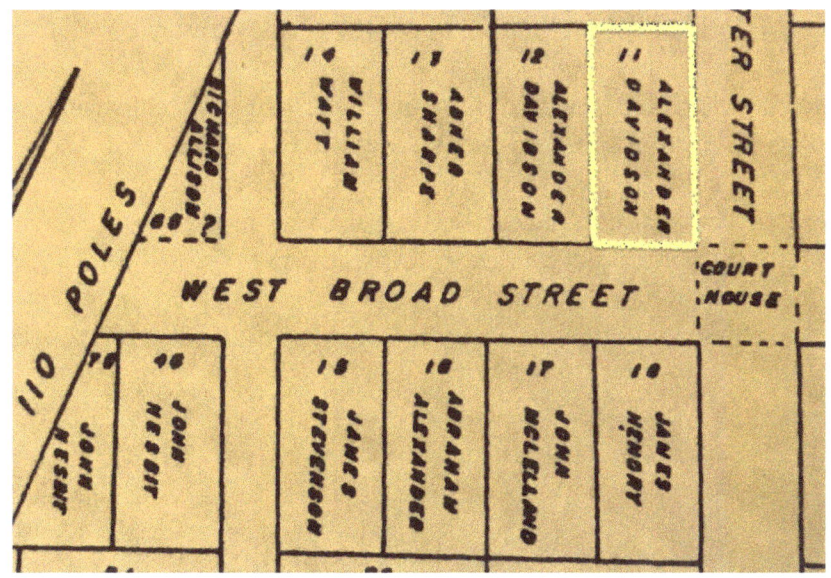

Original lots on West Broad Street
Compiled by W. N. Watt. Drawn by Grier Surveying

Foard & Garner's general merchandise store was the earliest known structure on the northwest corner of the square. William Simonton had a store there in the 1810s. The Village Hotel, the town's main hotel in the mid-1800s, was often advertised as being on the square, but it was located to the west side of Lot 11, just beyond a building containing six small offices.

The Village Hotel was one of the largest full-service hotels in Western North Carolina. It offered travelers a place to rest and get a hot meal. And in the alley around back, there was a livery stable that fed and sheltered guests' horses. It's possible the Village had started out as George Robinson's tavern.

Mary Worke bought lots 11 and 12 at an auction for Robert Simonton's heirs in 1830. In 1833 she sold the lots to Samuel Welch. The hotel would have been included in the sale. In 1836 Whitfield Kerr bought the Village Hotel, but died soon thereafter. William Harbin was operating it in 1840. Early drawings place it on Lot 11, but it may have been just slightly over the line.

The weekly ads for the Village Hotel disappeared from the Salisbury newspapers after 1854. The hotel was destroyed in a fire that year. Lot 11 lost its wooden buildings and was a vacant eyesore for the next 27 years after the infamous "Fire of 1854."

Noted N. C. Agricultural & Mechanical College botany and entomology professor, Charles W. Hyams, reminisced in a 1932 *Landmark* letter about catching tadpoles as a boy in the small frog pond where the Miller Block now stands. That would have been shortly after the Civil War.

In the spring of 1881, W. C. Miller began hauling 300,000 locally made brick to town for his new building on the square. At the time, the lot was called the "burnt corner." Interestingly, the southwest and southeast corners would be called the "burnt corner" in later years. Fires haven't been kind to downtown Statesville, especially before organized firefighting came about.

By October, contractor Bill Munday and crew were putting the finishing touches on the town's newest shopping destination. Early on it was called "the new block," but it soon became "The Miller Block." A young carpenter named Jack Blankenship built many of the window frames.

There were three storefronts in the Miller Block. The first merchants to occupy them were L. Pinkus & Co. on the square; J. C. Irvin & Co. in the center; and M. Stein & Co. on the west side.

Construction took exactly seven months from the time the first brick was delivered in March until the doors were open in October. Quite a feat even with today's equipment.

The Sanborn Insurance map drawings below show the layout of the Miller Block over the years.

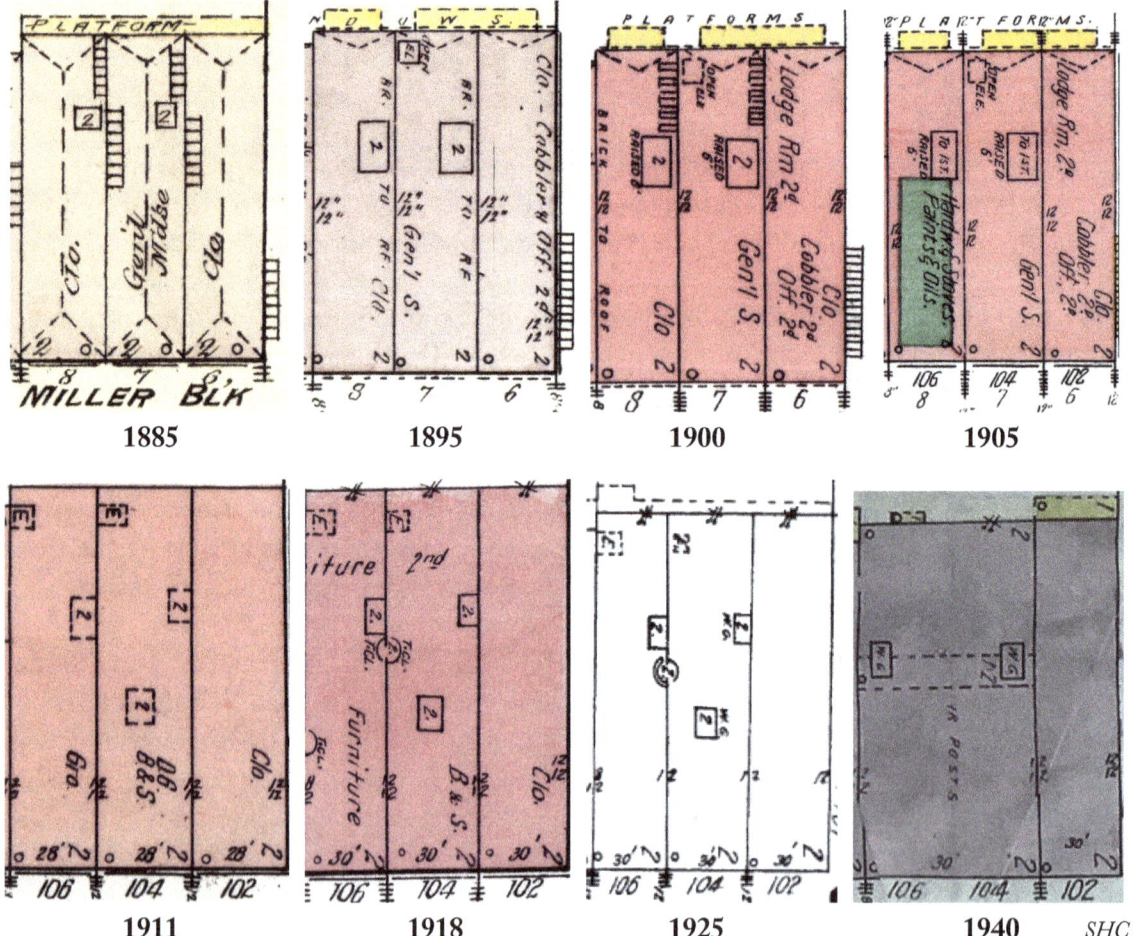

Engraving of the Miller Block printed in the 1890 *Landmark* Trade Edition

The 102 Storefront

The original address of the storefront closest to the square was No. 6 West Broad. It's address then changed to the 100 West Broad, but around 1907 it officially became 102 West Broad. Louis Pinkus ran the first business there, a general merchandise store called L. Pinkus and Company. Pinkus had come to town in 1872 and was initially in partnership with W. A. Eliason.

After a short tenure, Pinkus returned to his previous location down Broad Street and entered the thriving root and herb business. In 1882, Nathan Harrison, a New York merchant, moved to town and opened a men's store at L. Pinkus' former location. Probably in the spirit of one-ups-manship against his neighbor and competitor Simon M. Stein who ran the Baltimore Clothing House, Harrison called his place the New York & London Clothing Co. He eventually ditched the large city references and the N. Harrison Co. operated from the Miller Block for 35 years.

In December 1892, fire struck the Miller Block for the first time, but it survived. Bystanders were able to carry armloads of stock from the three stores. Stores to the west weren't as fortunate. About the same time, the W. C. Miller estate sold the building to other members of the family.

In 1894 the Iredell County Board of Education moved their office to one of the upstairs rooms over Harrison's. There they administered tests to potential teachers and held board meetings. A meat market was located in the basement with access from the back alley.

Also in 1894, John Sherrill, a 29-year-old salesclerk, was found dead in his room on the second floor of the Miller Block. He had just bought a bicycle, and it was surmised he had overexerted himself learning to ride it. There was living space for at least five male boarders at a time over Harrison's as well as a doctor's office and dentist office.

In 1899, General Andrew D. Cowles died in his room there. He had made his living as an attorney and was appointed Statesville postmaster for a four-year term during the President W. H. Harrison administration. Three years before he died, Cowles was appointed adjutant general of the entire North Carolina National Guard, organizing the state's volunteer units in the Spanish American War. An illness had confined him to his upstairs room for six weeks prior to his death.

A Good Place to Marry From.

It would seem that the rooms over Harrison's clothing store are not conducive to celibacy. A few years ago five unmarried men had rooms there. Three of these dropped out at different times and got married and the fourth, Mr. R. L. Poston, will be out by this time next week. Mr J. T. Sherrill is the only one left and he is getting shaky. It is not likely he will stay there long. It is rumored that two gentlemen of the town who should have been married long ago, will endeavor to rent rooms there in the hope that it will help them off.

Landmark **1894**

Mr. Harrison Tells How It Was.

To the Editor of The Landmark:

Knowing you always wish to publish the truth, allow me to correct an error in your last issue which seemingly does me a great injustice. You stated that Henry Marsh and myself had a "scrap in the back lot." I beg to state that I was attending to private business in the rear lot of my store when Marsh came upon me unbeknown and assaulted me in the most cowardly manner. I was in such a condition that it was impossible to defend myself. I have been a citizen of this town for 15 years and have never got into a scrap.

Yours very truly,
N. HARRISON.

1897 *Landmark*

Throughout much of the 1900s, the Patriotic Order Sons of America (P.O.S of A.,) the Odd Fellows, the Heptasophs, and the Loyal Order of Moose fraternal lodges used the upstairs as their lodge hall. The Hurst Turner American Legion Post and various civic groups met there too.

E. H. Crouch and J. S. Fry maintained shoe repair shops on the second floor in the late 1890s and early 1900s. In 1917 the Statesville Gas Co. was there.

In 1900, the Statesville Police Department moved its headquarters into an upstairs room. An external staircase on the Center Street side of the building provided quick access and egress. The town board of aldermen held their meetings there in the early 1900s as well. In 1907 the owners refused to make necessary safety improvements to the exterior staircase, so the aldermen voted to require them to replace it with a metal one. The owners quickly changed their tune, and the requirement was rescinded. The repairs were made, but by 1905 the stairs had been permanently removed.

In 1902 the court ordered the property to be sold on the courthouse steps to the highest bidder in order to settle an estate dispute, but members of the Miller family retained ownership.

The Crowell Clothing Co. bought out the stock of N. Harrison Clothing in 1918 and operated briefly under the name Statesville Clothing Co. Then Kelly Clothing Company opened in 1920.

Kelly's became known as the place in town to purchase Boy Scout apparel and supplies in the 20s. Holcomb Plumbing company occupied the basement. The Statesville Library was moved to the second floor over Kelly Clothing in 1923 and remained there for a while.

Also, E. S. Johnson, "the wallpaper hanger" had an upstairs shop there in the 1920s, as did H. A. Wilson the sign painter. W. J. Matheson managed his real estate enterprise on the second floor beginning in 1913. He was still there in the mid-50s at the age of 80. As a young man, he had sold menswear downstairs in the Harrison Clothing store.

Tharpe **"Uncle Jake" Matheson had a Real Estate Office on 2nd floor**

View from Window *Tharpe*

In 1929 J. S. Moore and J. G. Shelton bought the Miller Block for $8,750. In 1930, Kelly Clothing filed for bankruptcy and Mills Clothing moved in. After two years, Sherrill-White shoe store moved from 104, next door, to the corner room.

Ladies hung out at Mildred Parker's Cut & Curl beauty salon in the basement of the Sherrill-White Shoe store for many years. The entrance was on the Center Street side of the building.

A variety of tailor and sewing shops moved in and out of the upstairs over the years, as did real estate and insurance offices. Echerd's Sewing Shop was there in the '20s and the Moose Sewing Shop operated there from 1936 until 1956. The Becker Tailor Shop was there during the same period. Annie Frick had a seamstress shop upstairs from 1958 until 1968.

Wilson & Rhyne real estate, Joe Wilson surveying, and Plyler Insurance had upstairs offices in the 1960s and 70s.

But the business with the longest run in the Miller Block was the Sherrill-White Shoe Co. The Sherrill name was included in a number of business iterations there over the years, beginning in 1886 and lasting into the 1990s. They started out in the 104 storefront and moved to 102 in 1932.

The law offices of J. Pressly Mattox and James B. Mallory opened on the square in 1993.

The 104 Storefront

Number 7 West Broad Street was the original address for what is now 104 West Broad. J. C. Irvin was the first merchant there in 1881, selling general merchandise of all kinds. He remained there for five years before getting out of the retail business in 1886 and entering the booming tobacco trade in town. He was also vice president of the First National Bank.

Landmark **Irvin & Co. sold a little bit of everything**

Mills & Sherrill took over in 1887 *Landmark*

In 1886, N. B. Mills and F. A. Sherrill, former clerks with J. C. Irvin Co., opened up Mills & Sherrill Co., selling general merchandise and staple groceries.

The name changed to Harris & Sherrill Co. in 1887 and then to F. A. Sherrill Co. in 1889. Their wholesale division was on the second floor along with Mrs. A. V. Bennett's dress shop.

In 1901, F.A. Sherrill decided to retire from retailing and spend more time with his flour milling business, Statesville Flour Mill. Foy White bought into the company, and it became Sherrill-White Co., remaining at the same location. J. H. White, who had been with the F. A. Sherrill operation, also joined the corporation.

A tailor shop operated by J. H. Wilson opened on the second floor in 1901.

In 1913 the Sherrill-White Co. bought out the inventory of the S. B. Miller Shoe Co. That year the entrance to the store was improved by removing the step(s) to add a gradual slope. Before the streets and sidewalks were paved, many store entrances were one to two feet above street level.

For nearly half a century, a variation of the Sherrill family business remained in the middle storefront of the Miller Block. In 1932 the Sherrill-White Shoe Co. moved next door to the former Mills Clothing Co. spot on the square and remained there another half century.

That year, hardwood floors were installed, and a new modern front was built for the J. C. Penny store. Penny's had restored the 106 side after a fire in April 1932. It was at that time that the wall between 104 and 106 was removed and the two storefronts became one large storeroom.

West Broad street paving in the 1930s *Stimson*

J. C. Penny's remained at 104-106 West Broad until they moved to a new facility on South Center in 1960. The Hines Shop remodeled the store in 1960 and quickly settled in, specializing in women's and children's clothing and shoes. Nita's Hat shop was also located inside the Hines store for a while, and the Statesville Jaycees had a meeting room on the second floor.

Stimson **The Miller Block "crown" was added in the early 1900s and removed in the early 1950s** *Stimson*

The 106 Storefront

M. Stein & Co. was the other original business in the Miller Block. The Stein company was an extension of a Maryland venture called the Baltimore Clothing House. John Stephany was manager and part owner. They offered a large inventory of first-class gentleman's clothing.

Stein proudly displayed his Jewish roots in his advertising, calling his place "The Great Fashion Temple of Western North Carolina."

Stephany became sole owner of the company in 1887 and changed the name to J. Stephany Co. They were located in the most westward of the three store fronts, at the time No. 8 West Broad. The address was 106 from 1907 until 1932. Then it was merged with the 104 side for the Penney's expansion. The mailman kept it all straight.

John Stephany was born in London and had a twin brother who served as the head of the Jewish Charities of London for 50 years. John was president of the local Jewish congregation and served as a town alderman. About a third of the downtown merchants then were of the Jewish faith.

In 1885 Jules Lowenstein opened a saloon in the cellar of the Baltimore Clothing House pouring corn and rye whiskey, peach and apple brandy, blackberry wine, and beer "by the measure." Lowenstein, a dentist from New York, had discovered after moving to Statesville that he could make more money selling whiskey than pulling teeth. He is best remembered for his prominent wholesale contribution to the trade.

Landmark **1885**   **1893**   *SHC*

256

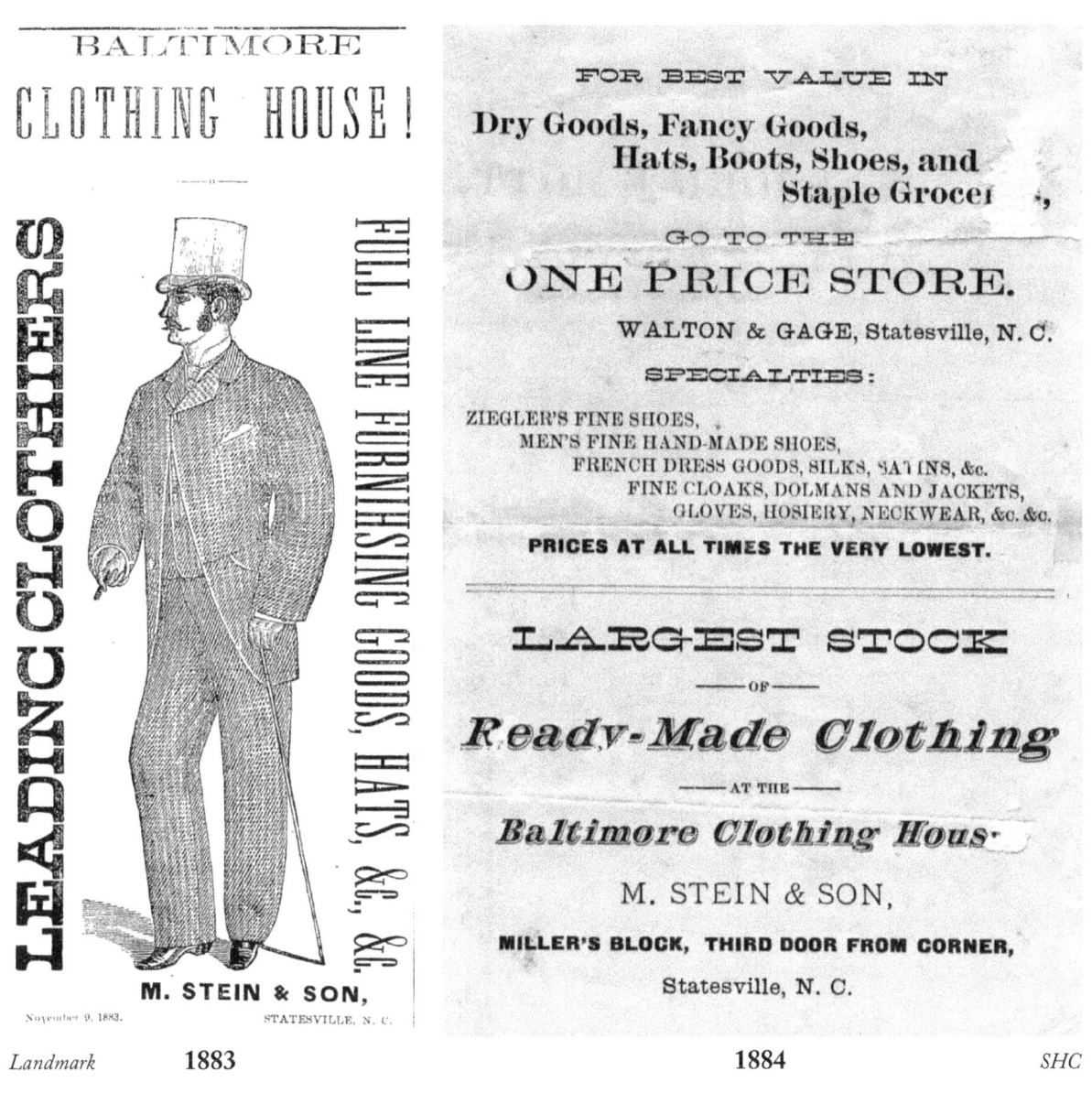

Landmark 1883 1884 SHC

R. V. Brawley and J. L. Sloan moved their men's clothing store to the Stephany stand in 1894 calling it Brawley & Sloan, and also doing business as "The Statesville Clothing House." In 1897 Brawley sold out his half to J. G. Shelton and the firm became Sloan & Shelton.

Shelton began focusing on other interests in 1900 and the company became the Sloan Clothing Co. A few months later, the store was moved across the street to the new N. B. Mills building on the southwest corner of the square, and a Mr. Porter tried for a few months to get his shoe store off the ground at the 106 location. Soon, the Evans Hardware Company had set up shop there.

In 1898, parapet walls were built between the roofs of the three storefronts to improve fire safety.

The Evans Hardware store lasted there for a few years until they built a new store on East Broad in 1908. Colvert Grocery moved in for a short stay. In 1911 Colvert moved out and the Crawford-Bunch Furniture Company moved in.

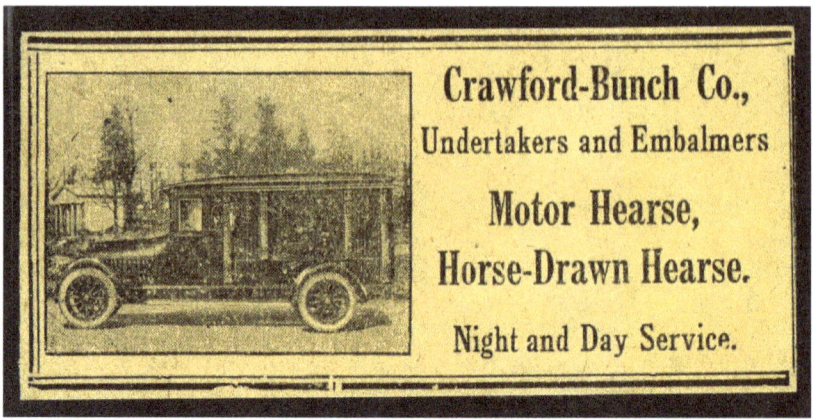

Landmark   **1911**   **1922**   *SHC*

Messieurs Crawford and Bunch were also undertakers and embalmers and opened an "up to date" undertaking business in the rear of the building. Bunch bought out Crawford in 1923 and moved to 129 West Broad a few months later. Eventually they became Bunch-Johnson.

In 1924 when the Bunch enterprise moved out, major improvements were made, and the J. C. Penny Company opened a store there. Penny's thrived at 106 for eight years, then disaster hit.

SHC   **Crawford-Bunch Furniture, 1914**   **J. C. Penny, 1924**   *Landmark*

On April 4, 1932, a fire gutted all three floors of the J. C. Penny store. The alarm sounded at 11:15 p.m. Both the white and "colored" fire departments responded and fought the fire for four hours. An undetermined source in the basement, most likely bad wiring, started the blaze that resulted in $75,000 in damage to the inventory and structure.

The Sherrill-White Shoe store next door at 104 sustained serious water damage, and merchandise in J. B. Reece's store to the west at 108 received smoke damage as well.

J. C. Penny's quickly moved into the vacant Montgomery Ward Building on North Center and for four months conducted a "fire sale" while repairs were being made. When Penny's reopened, they had expanded their store 100% by also renting the middle storefront of the building, the 104 address, where Sherrill-White Shoes had been. The shoe store shuffled next door to the square where Mills Clothing had just moved out.

Penney's fire sale in the Montgomery Building *Landmark*

The 1932 store improvements included skylights that lit both the first floor and mezzanine. Large "Airplane fans" moved air through the sales areas. Drinking fountains were placed around the store serving cold water pumped through large ice boxes in the basement. A bright yellow and black J. C. Penny's sign and a new plate glass window system were added across the complete 50-foot frontage of the store. A modern heating plant was installed that could be converted into a cooling system in the summer.

The improvements increased the tax value of the building from $720 to $800 per linear frontage foot in 1933.

An unusual "who-dun-it" crime took place at Penny's in 1930. It involved a robbery, a shooting, and hidden loot.

JOYCE FREED FOR LACK OF EVIDENCE

J. C. Penney Company Declines to Prosecute Former Local Manager Charged With Robbing His Own Store—All the Money Recovered by the Company.

Mr. Theo. G. Joyce, former manager of the J. C. Penney department store here, had a preliminary hearing before Mayor J. B. Roach in the municipal court room Monday afternoon at 4 o'clock, on a charge of robbing his own store on the early morning of Sunday, August 24, and was released for lack of evidence. All the missing cash, approximately $700, was accounted for and the J. C. Penney Company declined to prosecute the young man who had previously been rated a successful store manager and had a clear record up to this time.

The only witness on the stand at the hearing Monday afternoon in the local municipal court was Mr. P. G. Sherbondy, of Concord, who appeared as an official representative of the J. C. Penney Company. Mr. Sherbondy testified that every penny of the money reported missing had been accounted for; that $592 had been found hidden in the basement of the store and $100 was in Mr. Joyce's pockets at the time of the alleged robbery. The store official testified that young Joyce, as manager of the local store, had a perfect right to hide the company's money anywhere in the store or keep it on his person, since the local manager is held accountable for the proceeds of the day's business. Mr. Sherbondy stated in open court that the J. C. Penney Company would not prosecute Mr. Joyce and then the mayor announced the young man's release.

At 12:30 o'clock Sunday morning, August 24, Mr. Joyce telephoned police headquarters from his store on West Broad street, notifying the officers that he had been shot in the leg and his store robbed by an unknown night prowler. Three local police officers rushed to the scene, broke through the glass in the front door, found Mr. Joyce lying on the floor, with a pistol wound in his left thigh, the bullet, fired at close range, passing downward without touching bone. The officers transferred the injured man to a local hospital and made investigation, finding no evidence from the blood stains and the pistol buried in the ashes of the stove that the shooting was done by an outsider. The money being missing, except $100 found in Mr. Joyce's pockets, the officers charged Joyce with the whole transaction and apprehended him, the young store manager being released later in the day under a $1,000 bond signed by a representative of the J. C. Penney Company. Officials from the store headquarters came to make investigation, located all the money and the company was released from endorsement of the bond, a new bond for $500 being made and signed by local friends of the defendant for his appearance in the Mayor's court Monday, September 8. Numerous friends of the young man, including counsel, worked energetically and without remuneration, to clear up the case.

1930 *Landmark*

In August of 1934, fire struck the J. C. Penny store again. Several thousand dollars in merchandise was lost and the building suffered damage from the basement to the roof. The smoke was so thick that it was sucked into the ventilation system at the Playhouse Theater a block away causing panicked moviegoers to rush from the building.

There was a minor rehab job in 1950, and then in 1954 a major renovation squared off the display windows to provide a wider entrance. The entrance was also moved closer to the sidewalk. An office on the mezzanine was moved and green and gray tile was added to the façade. The result was 14,000 square feet of floor space. Owners in the late 50s were E. M. Shelton and Harry Moore.

Penney's models, 1950s *Tharpe*

J. C. Penny's remained at 104-106 West Broad until 1960 when they moved to a new building on South Center. When they left, still another renovation took place that brought new boxed in display windows, air conditioning, and walnut and cypress paneled fixtures. The downstairs ceiling was lowered three feet and acoustical tiling was installed.

The Hines Shop, carrying women's, children's and infant's clothing and shoes, moved in immediately after the renovation. Nita's Hat Shop was located there as well for a few years.

Lucille's gift and book shop took over the building for a few years in the 1984. Lucille Outlaw was the owner and Richard Kimball was the master goldsmith. Lucille's inventory included a large assortment of Christian books.

SHC   **1940s**   *SHC*

261

SHC   **1940s**   **In between tenants in the '90s**   *DSDC*

DSDC   **1980s**   *DSDC*

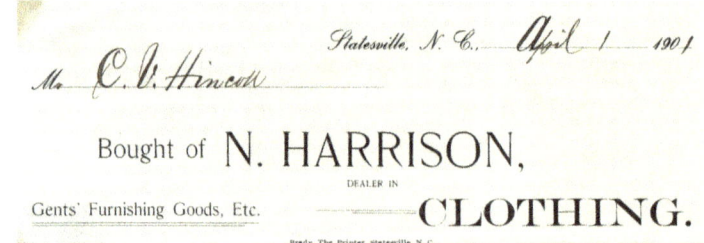

Billheads from a few Miller Block tenants   *SHC*

Chapter 24

Conclusion

Conclusion

If we wanted to be technically accurate, the square would not have been called "the square" from the late 1850s through the early 2000s. It would have been called "the quadrilateral." Whether due to human error or human greed, the angles of the four corners of the Broad and Center Street intersection were far from equal. But, although our square has been geometrically imperfect, it has been nearly flawless in its role as "the place where it all comes together."

Early historian E. F. Rockwell described Statesville this way: "The site of the town is high, dry and healthy. It is in view of the Brushy mountains and receives fresh summer breezes from them and from the Blue Ridge beyond." That certainly remains true today.

Local horse and mule salesman Fred H. Conger eloquently summed up the qualities of Statesville's downtown and square. In 1915, while spending a few nights in a larger, more cosmopolitan city to the east, he opined about his splendidly attractive hometown. He boasted about the beauty of Broad and Center Streets, "Our square is the center of a real city; there is no mud or dirt; the light at night is perfectly brilliant." "The view in all directions is one of beautiful lights and fine streets and sidewalks; and you can walk clear out into the country on our main streets and not get in the mud."

Back then, the amount of mud, or lack thereof, separated the sophisticated cities from the backwoods villages. Mud was the bane of cities, and although Statesvillians waded through their share of muck and mire in the town's infancy, by 1915, paved streets and sidewalks gave it that big city feel. Mud was not just an inconvenience, it deterred trade and growth. Today we take our smooth, broad, clean sidewalks and streets for granted.

Conger reminisced about how forward-thinking town aldermen had wisely increased property taxes enough to transform the place from a "Mudtown" into a fine "Hometown." "When I travel to our neighboring towns and then come back home, I tell you, I am proud I live in Statesville."

Mr. Conger, so am I. And since that time, there are countless other examples of how selfless, determined mayors and aldermen have fought to keep the "Best Town in NC" *the best*.

And, so, ends this chronicle of the town square in downtown Statesville, North Carolina. As of this day in January 2021, there is a cloud of uncertainty hovering over Statesville and the world in general. I would like to say the future of our town is a bright one. But the Covid-19 pandemic is a daily reminder that the prospect of a rosy future is far from certain. Old geezers like me are sequestered at home trying to avoid the worst while hoping for the best.

And so, for better or worse, this tome is a byproduct of those dark, unsettling pandemic days. It was almost entirely researched from my recliner with my dog, Bosco, by my side and my wife, Penny, in the kitchen trying to keep Bosco and me fed. Here's hoping that in another 130 years, and under more pleasant circumstances, someone will come along and write the sequel to "The Square," and that it, too, will be full of stories of success, prosperity, and good times.

Photo Gallery

Tharpe   **Typical day on the square**

Marching in the streets   *Tharpe*

Tharpe   **Lassie or an imposter?**

Showing off the new equipment   *Stimson*

Stimson   **Iredell Blues ready for inspection**   *Stimson*

SHC **Early 1900s**

Make-shift fish market *Stimson*

Stimson **The "Polk on the Square"**

Looking west *Tharpe*

View from the center of the universe—In the shadow of the clock *SHC*

Appendix
Footprint Views

Footprint Views from the Sanborn Insurance Maps, 1885-1965

The footprint of the square has changed over the years as a result of fires and new construction. Off and on there has been a vacant lot on the square, but the last time was in 1946.

In 1885 the vacant lot was on the southeast corner. The bank building was there in 1890. Five years later, fire had leveled the southwest corner. The Mills Building was there by the 1905 listing. It burned down in 1943 and the Eagles department store was built in 1946. It shows up on the 1965 map.

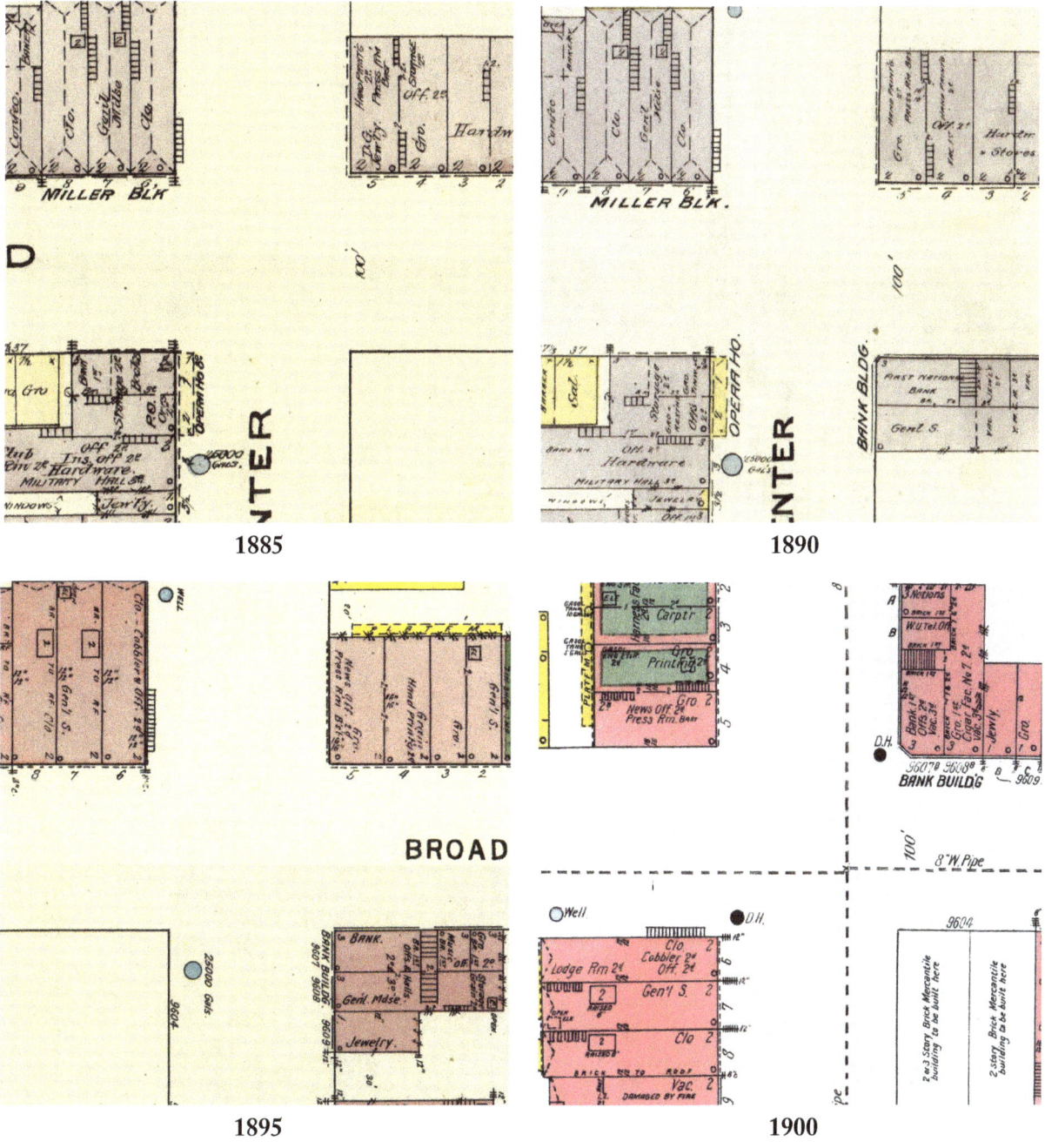

1885

1890

1895

1900

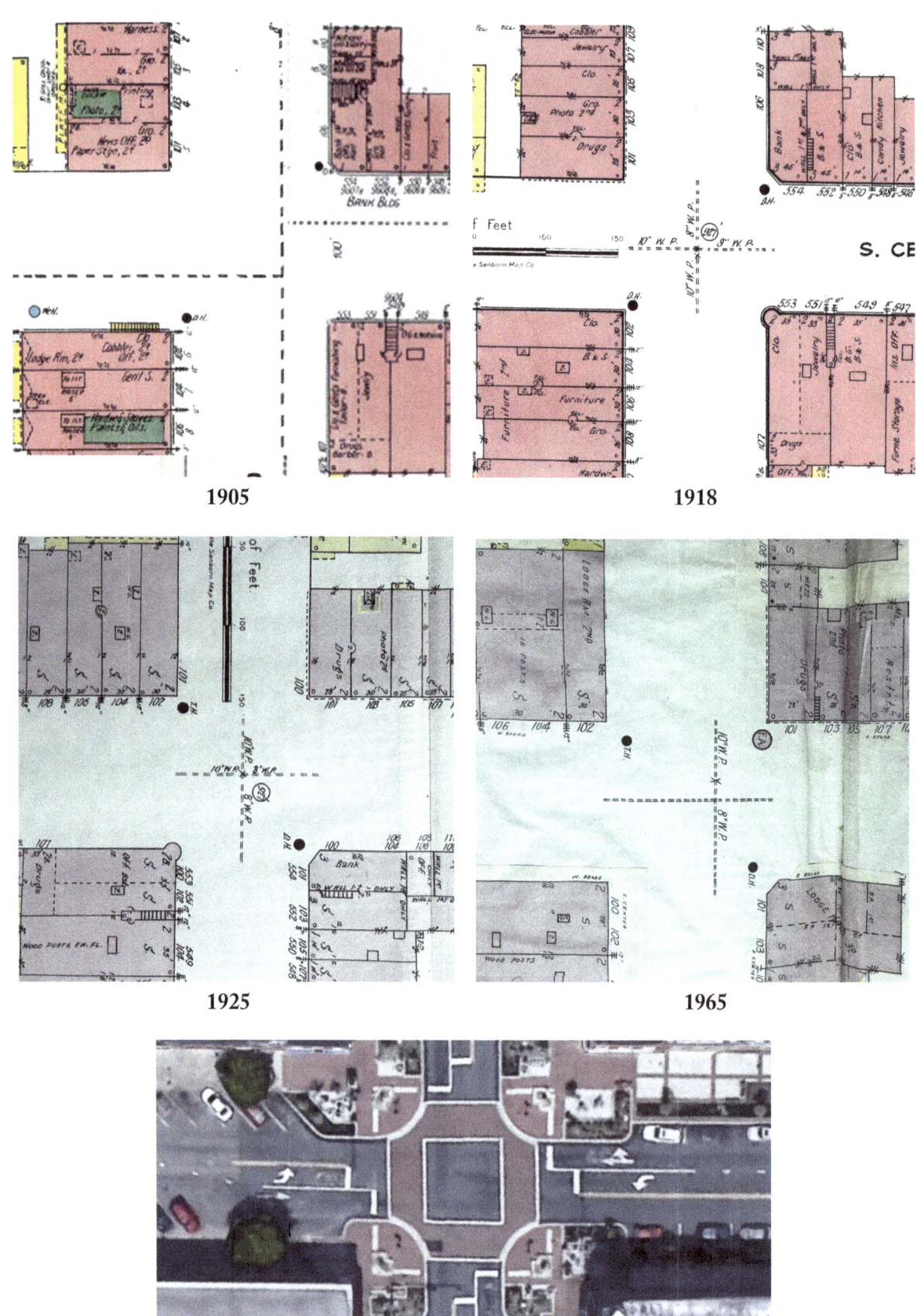

About the author

Steve Hill is a retired high school teacher and administrator. He is the proprietor of the Statesville Historical Collection, the world's largest emporium of photographic images, archaic documents, ephemeral antiquities, natural oddities, supernatural legends, and trivial trinkets related to Statesville, NC.

www.ingramcontent.com/pod-product-compliance
Lightning Source LLC
Chambersburg PA
CBHW080730300426
44114CB00019B/2541